# From anecdote to experiment in psychical research

**Robert H. Thouless**

# From anecdote to experiment
# in psychical research

Routledge & Kegan Paul

London

*First published in 1972*
*by Routledge & Kegan Paul Ltd*
*Broadway House, 68–74 Carter Lane,*
*London EC4V 5EL*
*Printed in Great Britain by*
*W & J Mackay Limited, Chatham*

*ISBN 0 7100 7285 6*

# Contents

# Illustrations

## Figures

## Tables

# Introduction

When my Pelican *Experimental Psychical Research* went out of print in 1968, I had the intention of preparing it for republication with minimal revision. I thought that all that would be necessary would be to bring it up to date by including the outstanding recent work, and to improve its continuity by correcting certain dislocations that had been made in its text. It has not happened like this. When I got down to the work of revision, I found myself very dissatisfied with the original text. So I was led to make a more drastic revision than I had intended. This has turned it into a new book, about twice as long and following a different plan.

The audience that I have had particularly in mind is composed of those who are already acquainted with other fields of scientific research. My main purpose is to convince them that something of importance and interest is developing on the experimental side of psychical research. My experience in this field has led me to a strong conviction of the reality of such things as extra-sensory perception, psycho-kinesis, etc., but it is not my main purpose to communicate this conviction to others. My intention is rather to correct the common impression (even amongst those accepting the reality of the psi-phenomena) that nothing much is happening in the field of experimental psychical research.

In truth much is happening and a pattern is beginning to emerge. Anyone who knows the vast volume of published experimental work in the technical journals of parapsychology will understand that the main task of the author of a book on this subject is to decide what he shall leave out. This decision is a highly individual one; no two authors are likely to make the same choice. What is selected is determined by the purpose of the book. My own purpose was not to make a summary of the whole field, a task for which I am not well suited. My own more limited purpose was to demonstrate experimental psychical research as a living field achieving some interesting results and holding the promise of achieving far more in the future. This book is not a map of the whole field, it is rather a series of sketches of points of interest within the field. The result of this is that I have left out much important research and failed to mention many important research workers whose work does not happen to illustrate any of the particular points I have been concerned with. I regret the apparent neglect of many whose work I esteem.

It is hoped that this book will also be found of some interest to a wider audience than those whose primary concern is scientific research. It is realised that some of this wider audience will find repellent all mention of the mathematical techniques which are used by experimental parapsychologists as they are by workers in other branches of experimental science. For the sake of those readers who dislike arithmetic, I have relegated, so far as I could, all treatment of quantitative matters to certain of the appendices which can remain unread without serious loss of understanding of the rest of the book.

No one can write on this subject without owing a considerable debt to that distinguished pioneer J. B. Rhine. My own debt is a more personal one since he read my typescript, and I have profited both by his encouragement and his criticisms. To Mrs Rhine too I am indebted for her criticisms of the chapter on psycho-kinesis. I wish to take this opportunity of expressing my gratitude to them both, and my admiration for their work.

R. H. THOULESS

# I

# The beginnings of psychical research

'Psychical Research' was the name at first given to the attempt to make a scientific study of certain odd events of a kind not easy to explain since currently accepted scientific principles of explanation would lead one to expect that such events would not occur. An example is the claim made by some people that they know what is in someone else's mind although there has been no communication between the two persons by the ordinary sensory channels of hearing or sight.

The term 'psychical research' to cover the study of such events has often been replaced by other terms. The most widely used of these is 'parapsychology'. Although this has sometimes been used in a more limited sense to cover the experimental approach to the phenomena studied in psychical research, it is now very commonly used to stand for the whole field of what was once called 'psychical research'. Either term may be used: 'parapsychology' is more generally used in the United States but 'psychical research' remains the more generally understood term in Great Britain.

The apparent fact of communication between one mind and another without use of the ordinary sensory channels was at one time called 'thought-transference' and later came to be known as 'telepathy'. Even more oddly, knowledge may be reported of some outside event which is not known to anyone else, such as the presence of a letter in a concealed drawer, or a fire in an empty house. This has been called 'clairvoyance'. The more general term 'extra-sensory perception' (generally shortened to ESP) is now very generally adopted to cover both telepathy and clairvoyance. Some people also claim to be able to foretell the future: this alleged power may be called 'precognition'. There are also reported cases of people being able to cause movements or to affect the direction of movements of material objects without contact with them. This used to be called 'telekinesis' (distant-movement), perhaps a better name than the more generally used modern name 'psycho-kinesis' (mind-movement), which is commonly shortened to PK.

Another term that will sometimes be met with is one originally suggested by Dr Wiesner and myself. We were inclined to think that there might be no real difference between what were called telepathy, clairvoyance, and precognition, that they might be the same capacity working under different circumstances. We suggested that this capacity might be indicated by the Greek letter $\psi$ (psi) which would also have the advantage over such terms as ESP that it implied no theory about the psychological nature of the process but could be used merely as a label. This suggestion has been widely taken up and the term 'psi-phenomena' is as well understood (at least in the United States) as the term 'paranormal phenomena'. We also suggested that this Greek symbolism might be extended to cover the difference between ESP and PK, the former being called $\psi_\gamma$ (psi-gamma) and the latter $\psi_\kappa$ (psi-kappa). This suggestion has not, however, been generally accepted.

Other events of an odd and unexpected kind which may be regarded as belonging to the field studied by psychical research are the alleged seeing of ghosts or of apparitions of people not physically there who may be living or dead, the alleged appearance on unexposed photographic film of representations of people or of distant scenes (an alleged occurrence now often called 'thoughtography'), the healing of illness or bodily injury without the use of normal medical means, the receiving of messages by automatic writing or other means which purport to come from the spirits of dead persons, and so on. It is difficult to find any common feature of all these events except that they are the sort of thing one would not expect to happen. Their occurrence would seem to contradict the expectations based on our common-sense thinking and on our knowledge of science. A useful adjective that has been coined for this class of unexpected events is 'paranormal'. Giving them a name does not, of course, imply that such events exist; we need a name either to affirm them or to deny them. The word 'paranormal' should not be equated either with 'supernatural' or 'magical'; both of these words imply something about the origin of such events. 'Paranormal' implies no theory about the events except that we should not expect them to happen.

The natural thing to do with stories of alleged paranormal phenomena is to pass them by with the assurance that they can't be true because they conflict with 'common sense'. It is not surprising that many people do reject the paranormal on this ground and that they are inclined to regard a research interest in it as somewhat eccentric. Yet there is at least strong enough evidence for some of the alleged paranormal phenomena to create a case for further enquiry, and there are good grounds for distrusting common sense as a guide to what is possible and what is not possible. 'Common sense' may be the name we give to nothing more authoritative than the thought habits that we happen to have derived from our ordinary experience. These thought habits certainly do not lead us to expect that our actions can be influenced by the thought of another person unless he expresses his thought in speech or in some other way. Nor do our thought habits lead us to expect that light will bend round corners. Our common sense proves to be an unreliable guide to what we have not experienced, whether this is the diffraction of light or the properties of sub-atomic particles; it cannot be allowed to have a decisive voice in determining our attitude towards the paranormal.

Accepting stories of the paranormal as a reasonable research interest does not, of course, imply that the psychical researcher accepts them all as true. Many are mistaken records of natural events; some are lies told with the intention to deceive. One of his first tasks is to make as good a discrimination as he can between the true and the false. Very often stories of the paranormal must be judged doubtful; they can still be used as guides to further investigation, preferably by the method of experiment; no great harm is done if the psychical researcher allows a false lead to guide him to experiments that do not come off. His system of enquiry is a self-correcting one; such experiments will lead to no results, but that is a situation that every research worker must get used to.

It is not that the psychical researcher believes everything he hears about the paranormal, but that he is willing to consider as possibilities many things that the man guided by common sense would unhesitatingly reject. To be a psychical researcher, or to have an even intelligent interest in psychical research, requires a certain open-mindedness as to the boundaries of the possible that comes hard to the man of common sense.

The truth is that the field of the paranormal is one in which people are inclined to have too high a conviction of certainty one way or the other. One still finds, even at the present day, a situation commented on by Sir William Crookes in 1874 of a too easy credulity on the part of some people and an equally irrational incredulity on the part of others. The quality of mind required of a psychical researcher is not an inclination to believe in stories of the marvellous or an inclination to reject them, but a willingness to allow the degree of his belief or unbelief to be determined by the evidence and not by his prejudices or by his wishes, or by current fashions of thought.

In order to be able to free ourselves from the tendency to be too certain one way or the other on the complex and difficult problems raised by a study of the paranormal, it is necessary to accustom ourselves to a language using references to many degrees of certainty and doubtfulness as well as the simple division into the categories of 'true' and 'false'. We must be prepared to make such judgments on statements about the paranormal as, for example: 'I am not certain about this matter, but what I know makes me strongly inclined to think so-and-so', or 'On the whole, I am inclined to believe that . . .', or 'I know so little about this that I do not feel justified in holding an opinion, one way or the other'. These are ways of using language employed in everyday life to indicate different degrees of doubt or conviction which may result from different amounts of information or from different judgments of the reliability of the information available. We shall need these and many more ways of indicating degrees of conviction if we are to talk adequately about what we can believe in the region of the paranormal.

There is a natural tendency of our minds to prefer to be certain one way or the other rather than to accept the relatively uncomfortable mental attitude of uncertainty or suspension of belief. If willingness to suspend belief is a necessary attribute of the psychical researcher, he should not go to the opposite extreme of always suspending belief indefinitely, however strong may be the evidence. The point of adopting an attitude of uncertainty is that one may then adopt means of enquiry that will reduce that uncertainty by increasing the amount or the reliability of the evidence. There have been psychical researchers who have taken a pride in refusing to have a definite opinion on any subject connected with the paranormal. They seem to have avoided the rash certainties of the simple man who uses only the categories of 'true' and 'false' and to have adopted a more sophisticated way of avoiding the making of judgments by employing only the single category of 'doubtful'. They may describe themselves by the contradictory title of 'convinced sceptic' and claim that their attitude is peculiarly 'scientific'.

This, however, is to misunderstand the nature of scientific enquiry. It is characteristic of scientific investigation that it may begin with a readiness to treat as doubtful many things that the man in the street regards as certain. Its aim, however, is to devise means to remove more and more of this uncertainty. The situation is not different in the scientific investigation of the paranormal. It is ninety years since the Society for Psychical Research was founded for the purpose of making such a study. If now we could make no more definite statements about what is true or false in the field of the paranormal than could our grandfathers (or great-grandfathers) when the investigation started, we could properly condemn the whole enquiry as a great waste of time. No doubt the answers to various problems in this field have not become as clear as the founders of the Society might have hoped; the enquiry has proved much more difficult than it appeared at first sight. But it remains true that knowledge has advanced and much of the field can be seen more clearly now than it could ninety years ago.

The first recognition in modern times of the fact that paranormal events might be of sufficient interest to deserve scientific study was during the last half of the nineteenth century when a number of individuals interested founded in London the Society for Psychical Research in 1882. The first president of the new society was Henry Sidgwick, a former Fellow of Trinity College, Cambridge, who became Professor of Moral Philosophy. Other founder members were: F. W. H. Myers, an inspector of schools who was also a Fellow of Trinity, William Crookes the famous chemist, and Edmund Gurney, a man of many parts who became the Society's secretary. The story of the early days of this intellectual adventure has been well told by Dr A. Gauld in a recent book (Gauld, 1968). The founders of the Society knew that they were venturing into a field where passions are strong and they expected criticism and misrepresentation. This expectation was fulfilled. Even now it is sometimes imagined that they were credulous people easily taken in by fraudulent marvels. A study of the early records should dispel this idea. Certainly they made their mistakes, sometimes in the direction of too ready belief, sometimes in the direction of over-stiff rejection of evidence. On the whole, however, it would seem that the marvellous was as unacceptable to Sidgwick, Myers, Crookes, and Gurney as it would be to any other men of their education and intelligence. They differed from other men, not in expecting the marvellous, but in being unusually ready to discard their common-sense expectations if these were contradicted by experience.

The example set by the English Society for Psychical Research was quickly followed in other countries. A few years later, an American Society for Psychical Research was founded. Similar societies have also now been started in many other countries. The universities were more slow to accept Psychical Research as an appropriate subject for study. In 1927, however, William McDougall, Professor of Psychology at Duke University in North Carolina, started a laboratory for the study of paranormal phenomena under J. B. Rhine. This has now been detached from the university as the Foundation for Research into the Nature of Man. Other universities have accepted such studies as an academic research activity; Utrecht and Freiburg have departments for the study of the paranormal headed by professors, so also has the University of Virginia. No doubt the number will increase; at the moment there is some shortage of trained investigators in the subject who could fill university posts, but this shortage would be overcome if there were sufficient demand.

Although the modern investigation of the paranormal by scientific methods may be considered to have started with the foundation of the Society for Psychical Research in 1882, or perhaps in the work of Crookes shortly before that date, it has been pointed out that the idea was put forward two and a half centuries earlier by Francis Bacon (Bell, 1956). His ideas on the subject are to be found in a little-known book *Sylva Sylvarum* (a collection of collections) published in 1627, the year after his death. The last part of this book is concerned with experiments on the paranormal, or, in the author's own words: 'Experiments in consort, monitory, touching transmission of spirits and forces of imagination'. His suggestion was that from much that was commonly regarded as superstitious and magical one might be able to separate out something that is 'clean and pure natural'.

The somewhat obscure reference to the field of the paranormal quoted above becomes more clear when Bacon begins to describe the particular things he wants to see investigated. These include telepathic dreams and the cure of warts by means of charms; both of these had been experienced by himself. He also wanted to have experimental investigation into healing 'by the force of the imagination', the problem that is now called that of 'paranormal healing' which includes miraculous cures and the activities of psychic healers. He also considered as proper subjects for investigation how the force of imagination might affect the behaviour of birds and the growth of plants. The first of these has not, in fact been investigated by modern parapsychologists but the influence of human thought on protozoa has been investigated experimentally by Richmond (1952), and there have also been experimental studies of the influence of human thought on the growth of plants. Bacon suggested the experimental rule that imagination 'hath most force upon things that have the lightest and easiest motions'. He illustrates the meaning of 'light motions' by reference to 'casting of dice'. This was, of course, the method actually used in Rhine's Parapsychology Laboratory at Duke University for the study of PK; apparently Bacon did not carry out any experiments with dice because he thought it unlikely that imagination would have any effect on dead matter.

Bacon also discussed what we should now call experiments in ESP under the name 'binding of thoughts'. He said: 'The experiment of binding of thoughts should be diversified and tried to the full; and you are to note whether it hit for the most part though not alway.' 'For the most part though not alway' is, of course, a good anticipation of what has been found in ESP experimentation. Bacon also made the ingenious experimental suggestion that an experiment of 'binding of thoughts' would be more likely to succeed 'if you tell one that such an one shall name one of twenty men, than if it were one of twenty cards'. That one might get better success in ESP experiments by using targets of human interest instead of cards is a suggestion that has often been made in more recent times. In fact, experimenters still mostly use cards because the arithmetical treatment of their results is simple, but the use of other kinds of target may prove to be more fruitful for some percipients.

This is the sort of practical suggestion that might be made by someone who has done something but not very much in the way of experimenting on such matters himself. Perhaps Bacon had tried some experiments on ESP. If this is the case it makes more startling the fact that it was more than two centuries before such experiments were tried again. Why, after so long a pause, was there a revival of interest in the scientific study of the paranormal about the end of the last century? There are really two questions to be asked on this matter: Why not earlier? and Why then?

Why not earlier? Probably because in Bacon's day and for a century afterwards witchcraft was a legal offence punishable by death, and the practices of witchcraft were often the kind of thing that is studied in psychical research, for example, foretelling the future, influencing other people's actions by mental means, and influencing physical events (such as wind or rain) by mental means. The experiments in Rhine's laboratory on the influencing of falls of dice by mental means or on the precognition of the future order of a pack of cards might have led to the experimenters being burned at the stake if they had been carried out some two hundred years earlier.

The situation in Great Britain was changed in 1735 by the passing of the Witchcraft Act. The laws against witchcraft were repealed and the offence that remained was not the practice of witchcraft (which was regarded as a mere superstition) but the claim to exercise magical arts which was punishable as fraud. This may not have created an atmosphere more favourable to psychical research. It is true that there would probably have been little risk that an experimenter who claimed to have obtained successful results in a PK or a precognitive experiment would have been imprisoned under the Witchcraft Act. But such experimentation would have been more heavily discouraged by the condemnation of public opinion, which would have regarded beliefs in the influence of mind on material objects and in the power of foretelling the future as mere superstitions which could not reasonably be made the subjects of a serious enquiry. In the years after 1735 the belief in witchcraft was too recent for any impartial enquiry into matters that would be popularly regarded as connected with it. A longer time had to elapse before a President of the Society for Psychical Research could say: 'It is a scandal that the dispute as to the reality of these [paranormal] phenomena should still be going on . . . that the educated, as a body, should still be simply in the attitude of incredulity' (H. Sidgwick). Earlier, no doubt, the attitude as to these phenomena would not have been one of doubt but of positive rejection as superstitious nonsense belonging to the days of witchcraft. This attitude of rejection had not, of course, disappeared at the time of the foundation of the Society for Psychical Research; it had however sufficiently weakened for it to be possible to propose the paranormal as a possible subject for scientific study.

These considerations suggest that part of the answer to the question of why psychical research started in the last half of the nineteenth century was that witchcraft as a social force was sufficiently far behind to be no longer a decisive factor in determining what questions would be considered suitable for enquiry. There were, however other factors which made this a likely subject of interest at that time. One factor that must be considered is the rise of spiritualism in the middle of the nineteenth century. It was rather more than thirty years before the founding of the S.P.R., in the year 1848, that a farmer of the name of Fox was living in a small village called Hydesville in New York State with his wife and two daughters at home. The daughters were Margaret (14) and Kate (11). Noises of raps were reported in the house and it was said that the children were too frightened to sleep. Then on 31 March of that year, Kate was supposed to have established contact with the source of raps. Saying 'Mr. Splitfoot, do

7

as I do', she clapped her hands several times and the same number of raps followed.

Her parents then took part, using a code for communication (two raps for 'Yes'), and started asking questions. It appeared that the ostensible communicator claimed to be the spirit of a pedlar who had been murdered in that house and whose body had been buried in the cellar.

This could obviously be a fabrication (probably subconscious) created by the members of the Fox family but there was some confirmation for the story. The cellar was examined in the following summer and some traces of human remains were found but no body. Not until fifty-six years later (in 1904) was a body discovered under the house.

Whether this was a genuine outbreak of occult forces in Hydesville or (as Podmore believed) a case of a naughty little girl deceiving her parents by cracking her joints and pretending that the noises came from outside her (Podmore, 1902), these events had far-reaching consequences. The practice of communicating with spirits by means of raps became widespread. A number of people, including the two Fox sisters, became professional mediums. Other methods of communicating were developed, such as speaking in trance and automatic writing. Amateurs also used the movements of tables round which they sat with their fingers resting on its surface while the table spelled out messages by its movements. This 'table-turning' as a popular amusement reached its climax about 1853. A more serious development from these ostensible communications with spirits was the growth of Spiritualism as a new religion.

There were reports of stranger things than communication with spirits by raps or automatic writing to arouse the interest of the curious in the new phenomena of spiritualism. There were also accounts of 'physical phenomena', movements of objects without contact and the appearance of physical forms, even of complete human bodies. These took place generally in restricted light or in darkness and they had already attracted the attention of William Crookes some years before the Society was founded (Crookes, 1874).

There were thus a number of questions raised by the spiritualist phenomena which invited dispassionate and impartial enquiry, particularly since they were subjects of impassioned controversy both by their convinced upholders and also by their equally convinced critics. There were a number of questions to be answered, as to which, if any, of the reported phenomena were genuine, and, if any of them proved to be genuine, as to what was their explanation. It was perhaps hoped that the methods of scientific enquiry adopted by the Society would enable them to answer these questions within a short time. If so this hope was disappointed. There is still controversy as to which phenomena are genuine, and we are still far from completely understanding their explanation.

Although the emergence of the problems of spiritualism during the last

half of the nineteenth century may have been an important factor in causing the foundation of the S.P.R., the problem of spiritualism was one only
of several subjects of investigation that it undertook. It was also concerned
with thought-transference, mesmerism, and certain apparently paranormal phenomena that had been reported by the chemist Reichenbach.
But the impartial study of the phenomena of spiritualism was part of its
aim, and the original intention was that the study would be carried out by
the combined efforts of convinced spiritualists and of others not committed
to the spiritualist view. A few years after the foundation of the Society,
however, there was dissension between the spiritualists and the non-
spiritualists, the former finding the attitude of the Society too sceptical.
Many spiritualists then resigned from the Society. This source of tension
still exists although many prominent spiritualists (as Sir Oliver Lodge)
have remained active members of the Society. The Society has been
accused of being over-credulous and of being over-sceptical. It has, in
reality, adopted no official attitude on the questions it investigates. Some
of its members are ready to believe in the marvellous, others are very unwilling to believe. Both attitudes are consistent with a devotion to enquiry
into the paranormal.

## References

BELL, MAY (1956), 'A Pioneer in Parapsychology', *Journal of Parapsychology*,
 xx, 257–62.
CROOKES, W. (1874), *Researches in the Phenomena of Spiritualism*, London
 (reissued 1953).
GAULD, A. (1968), *The Founders of Psychical Research*, London.
PODMORE, F. (1902), *Modern Spiritualism*, London. (Reissued as *Mediums of the
 19th Century*, New York, 1963.)
RICHMOND, N. (1952), 'Two Series of PK Tests on Paramecia', *Journal of the
 Society for Psychical Research*, xxxvi, 577–88.
THOULESS, R. H. (1942), 'The Present Position of Experimental Research into
 Telepathy and Related Phenomena', *Proceedings of the Society for Psychical
 Research*, xlvii, 1–19.

# II

# Anecdote and experiment

The basic materials from which psychical research starts are stories which people tell of extraordinary and unexpected things having happened to them: of dreams that have afterwards been fulfilled, of convictions that they know who has rung them up on the telephone before they have lifted it up, of having seen people, either living or dead, at places where they could not have been, and so on. Such stories do not form a very good basis for a scientific study of the paranormal since their value as evidence depends on the reliability of the people telling them and on the circumstances in which they are told, whether, for example, soon after or long after the event.

The weakness of such stories as evidence may be illustrated by one reported in the early days of psychical research. The following story, for example, is to be found in the first volume of the *Proceedings of the Society for Psychical Research* (Barrett et al., 1882–3):

> On September 9th, 1848, at the siege of Mooltan, Major-General R——, C.B., then adjutant of his regiment, was most severely and dangerously wounded, and supposing himself dying, asked one of the officers with him to take the ring off his finger and send it to his wife, who, at the time, was fully 150 miles distant, at Ferozepore.
>
> On the night of September 9th, 1848, I was lying on my bed, between sleeping and waking, when I distinctly saw my husband being carried off the field, seriously wounded, and heard his voice saying, 'Take this ring off my finger, and send it to my wife.' All the next day I could not get the sight or the voice out of my mind. In due time I heard of General R—— having been severely wounded in the assault on Mooltan. He survived, however, and is still living. It was not for some time after the siege that I heard from Colonel L——, the officer who helped to carry General R—— off the field, that the request as to the ring was actually made to him, just as I had heard it at Ferozepore at that very time.—M.A.R.

Certainly the incident described may have happened exactly as recorded, and it may have been a genuine case of thought-transference or some other mode of extra-sensory perception. To one convinced of the reality of ESP on other grounds, this seems not unlikely, particularly since the incident was one involving emotional stress which would seem to be favourable to the occurrence of ESP. As evidence of the reality of ESP, however, the story is without value.

The narrator of the story was the wife to whom it happened, so the story is at first-hand. If we ask when the account was recorded, the answer does not seem to be so satisfactory. It appears that, from being an adjutant, R—— had been promoted to Major-General, which implies the lapse of many years. To be of value as evidence, it would be necessary that the incident should have been recorded before the confirming evidence was known to the percipient, otherwise memory may distort the incident to make it more striking and more evidential than it really was. Moreover, it is to be supposed that the officer's wife was often anxious about him when he was in action, and we do not know how often the anxiety led to semi-hallucinatory experiences of seeing him wounded; semi-hallucinatory experiences are not uncommon in the condition between sleeping and waking. Knowledge of how often Mrs R—— had such experiences is necessary for a judgment as to how likely is the chance coincidence of the experience with the occurrence. That both the wounding and the experience took place on the same day seems striking, but it is unfortunate that the time of the experience was not independently recorded. In recollection of events in the past there is a tendency to remember them in a form which makes them fit into whatever theory one has formed to account for them, whether this theory is of the guilt of an accused person or of the para-normality of an event. This fact makes coincidence in time a somewhat doubtful piece of evidence unless it is corroborated by independent record-ing of the time of the event and that of the ostensibly paranormal experi-ence. Mrs R——'s narrative uses the term 'at that very time' which suggests a close coincidence of time but it seems unlikely that the attack took place during the night when Mrs R—— was trying to go to sleep; this phrase may be merely an effect of the tendency to systematise a memory of the past.

The most striking piece of evidence is certainly the giving of the ring which is hardly likely to be an element fabricated by the uncertainties of memory. The sceptic might, however, ask whether it was a matter under-stood between husband and wife that the ring would be sent if he were seriously wounded. The sceptic might also ask whether the wife's experi-ence of the ring having been sent had been recorded before she heard by normal means that it had been sent.

To ask such questions as these is not necessarily to adopt an attitude of disbelief to the story; this seems not unlikely to be true. They do, how-ever, imply doubt as to the evidential value of the story. The conscientious psychical researcher must be very unwilling to admit this or similar stories as evidence.

It is easy to say what one would require of a spontaneous observation of an apparent case of thought-transference before accepting it as watertight evidence. The person who experienced it should have recorded it with a note of the time of the occurrence and delivered it to some reliable person before he had the opportunity of discovering whether it corresponded to any actual event. The person to whom the event occurred should also have made a record of it together with its time and delivered the account to some other person before hearing of the experience of thought-transference. The evidence would then be derived by a comparison of the two records.

It is also easy to see why few, if any, spontaneous cases fulfil these conditions. Those who claim to have experiences of thought-transference in their daily lives do not generally know which experiences are of this nature until they later learn of the event of which they appear to have had paranormal knowledge. None of us can be expected to record all the hunches we have and to give these records to someone else to take care of on the chance that they may turn out to be examples of some kind of paranormal knowledge. So the observational evidence we have is generally vitiated by the fact that the records were not made until after the verification of the supposed paranormal experience, with all the possibilities of distortion of memory which result from thinking and talking about the event afterwards.

How much the passage of time may distort the memory of an event supposed to be paranormal is shown in extreme form in a case published in the early years of the Society for Psychical Research.* This was an account of an apparition seen by Sir Edmund Hornby, a judge of the consular court in China (*Proc. S.P.R.*, 1884). Judge Hornby reported that on an occasion eight years earlier, he had seen a journalist in his bedroom in the early hours of the morning, that he had told the journalist the judgments he had decided to give next day, and that he had heard next morning that the journalist had died in his own house at about the time that Hornby had the experience of seeing him. This seemed to be a case of an apparition seen at about the time of death, but subsequent enquiry showed that nothing of the sort could have happened since the date of the journalist's death was months before Hornby reported having seen him and that no judgments had been given by Hornby on the actual day of the death. Judge Hornby agreed that, if these facts turned out to be true, his memory must have played him the most extraordinary trick. So apparently it had.

No doubt this is an extreme example of falsification in memory, but the fact that so much falsification can take place reinforces the case against supposing that knowledge about the paranormal can be much advanced

---

* This story is only to be found in the first printing of vol. ii of *Proc. S.P.R.* On reprinting it was replaced by another case. This is unfortunate. One learns also by one's errors, and such learning is not helped by obliterating errors.

by the mere collection of anecdotes about alleged paranormal events. This will not even provide convincing evidence of the reality of the paranormal, still less will it by itself give theoretical understanding of the nature of the paranormal.

From realisation of the fact that one cannot advance towards scientific understanding of the paranormal by the mere collection of anecdotes, there are two possible directions of advance. One is to look at the problems raised by the anecdotes in order that one may devise experiments in order to solve them. The other is to improve the conditions in which the anecdotes are obtained in the hope that they may become reliable sources of information. One can find out, for example, when the alleged incidents were recorded, what independent corroboration there is for them, improve conditions of recording by inviting people to send in records of what, for example, they imagine to be precognitive dreams, so that records are out of the sender's hands before their fulfilment, etc.

The first of these two methods of advance is the one the present book is about; it is the way that would be most likely to commend itself to anyone with a scientific training. It is a method which has been widely used in the sciences, and which has been conspicuously successful in providing understanding of how things happen. Thus people had seen thunderstorms for many years without understanding their nature; then physicists did experiments in which they produced sparks between electrically charged objects and laid bare the theoretical explanation of thunderstorms. It is true that the spark produced in the laboratory is a trivial event compared with a thunderstorm, but it is an event of the same kind, and, because its conditions can be observed and measured, it can be the source of a scientific understanding which can never be gained merely by looking at thunderstorms. In the same way, the experimenter in psychical research may try to replace such sporadic events as an officer being wounded in an attack by some trivial event not known to the percipient and then see whether it can be correctly reported by the percipient.

Critics of the use of the experimental method in psychical research often say that the trivial activities we ask experimental subjects to perform, such as guessing cards or reproducing hidden drawings, may not reveal paranormal capacities since these may only work in conditions of emotional stress between people united by a bond of affection. This is a criticism which seems less important to the practical research worker than to the arm-chair critic. If it were wholly true that ESP only takes place in situations of emotional stress, this would certainly be a grave difficulty in the way of devising a fruitful experiment in psychical research. If, as seems to be the case, it is only partly true, it creates a difficulty in successful experimenting which challenges us to find better and more fruitful ways of experimenting. It is a surprising fact that experiments in which people are asked to do trivial and uninteresting things like guessing cards do succeed much better than the above criticism would lead one to expect. It may well be that more people would show ESP capacities if they were tested by means of tasks in which real emotional forces were involved; such tasks are not easily adapted to experimental conditions. Meanwhile experimental tasks of the trivial type have given us a lot of information about the paranormal which will be discussed in later chapters.

Both refinement of observations and the use of experiments were methods explored in the early days of psychical research. For many reasons, however, the main weight of the activity of the early psychical researchers was in the direction of accumulating more and better records of spontaneous cases. One of the earliest S.P.R. publications was *Phantasms of the Living* which was mainly the work of Gurney (Gurney et al., 1886). This contains accounts of some experiments on telepathy but it is mainly a collection of anecdotes which had been tested as far as possible by personal interviewing of those reporting the experiences. It is implied that further progress in psychical research should be by accumulation of more stories with better attestation of the adequacy of the conditions of their reporting. Gurney's idea seemed to be that experiments were of value as proving the reality of telepathy, but that this was only a preliminary step towards the task of elucidating its nature by the examination of reports supplied by those who claim to have had paranormal experiences of various kinds. The later book on survival by F. W. H. Myers followed the same pattern (Myers, 1903).

Both of these books were magnificent collections of stories of the paranormal. The idea behind *Phantasms of the Living* of classifying and ordering the stories that people tell of the marvellous was a bold and original one for the execution of which later psychical researchers are heavily in debt to the authors. Yet to one trained in the methods of experimental science, it may seem that this work set psychical research on an unprofitable course, particularly in its grave underestimate of the importance of experiment as a method of advancing theoretical understanding.

In the experimental sciences, experiment is not merely a method of confirming what takes place; it is above all the method of testing and guiding theoretical advance. If a theoretical possibility is suggested by observation or by a preliminary experiment, the experimentalist asks: 'How can I devise an experiment to find out whether this is true or false?' This was not how most of the early psychical researchers thought, they accumulated anecdotes and based theories on them but did not take the further step of devising experiments to see whether the theories were true or false. They do not seem generally to have realised that the essential requirement of a fruitful scientific theory is that it should lead to observable consequences that can in principle be tested by experiment.

I do not think it is unfair to say of the early psychical researchers that they were not experimentally minded. This is hardly surprising when it is noticed that, intellectually distinguished as many of them were, few had had any training in scientific research while many of them had had no scientific training at all. It is true that Crookes was an experimental scientist of considerable distinction, and he showed a wholly experimental attitude towards the paranormal phenomena of Home (Crookes, 1874). But, by the time the S.P.R. started its work, his research interests were no longer in this field and he seems to have played no part in the early S.P.R. experimenting. Barrett was a Professor of Physics, but in Dublin, so he could not play any considerable part in the early experimenting. In the early days there was no one with research knowledge of the biological sciences, which would have been more closely relevant to the experimental problems of psychical research than was that of the physical sciences. It was, of course, too early for an experimental psychologist to have been available; the first laboratory of experimental psychology was opened in Leipzig in 1879, only three years before the founding of the S.P.R. It is unfortunate, however, that no experimental physiologist was in a leading position in the Society; perhaps they were unduly influenced by the unfavourable opinion of psychical research that had been expressed by the most influential physiologist of that time, Helmholtz.

It would, of course, be absurd to blame the early psychical researchers for their lack of experience of scientific experimentation. Rather one must admire the boldness and determination with which people whose training lay in classics or philosophy tackled this unfamiliar field. It does, however, suggest an explanation for some of the defects of these early experiments, both for their restricted aims and for the inflexibility of their design. The general tendency was to make large numbers of observations under identical conditions. This might be the best way of accumulating evidence of the reality of some paranormal phenomenon provided that the conditions were adequate to ensure that the paranormal process in question was the only possible explanation of the results obtained.

To discover something about the nature of the paranormal process concerned requires a different kind of experimental design with systematic variation of the experimental conditions. This the early experimenters neglected to do, so the experimental results were generally somewhat uninformative. It is, for example, surprising to discover that in the early experiments on thought-transference, there was little systematic attempt to interfere with various possible sensory channels of communication in order to see whether one of these was being unwittingly used. Also there was no attempt to test experimentally the hypothesis, that was taken for granted in all the early 'thought-transference' experiments, that the condition for a successful response by the experimental subject was the fact that someone else was thinking of what he had to do. Thus the authors of *Phantasms of the Living*, discussing some of Richet's experiments on guessing cards, remarked that the guiding condition which makes the percipient guess right 'could be nothing else than the fact that, prior to the guess being made, a person in the neighbourhood of the guesser had concentrated his attention on the card drawn' (Gurney et al., 1886). This, however, is by no means a necessary conclusion from the success of the experiments. It is a hypothesis to explain that success which may be right or wrong, and its rightness or wrongness could only be tested by comparing results when someone is concentrating his attention on the card to be drawn with those obtained when no one knows what card is drawn. It is a mark of the inflexibility of the early experiments that no test of this hypothesis was then made, and the question was not answered until it was experimentally tested by J. B. Rhine half a century later. Then it was found that the success of the percipient in guessing the right card did not depend on anyone else concentrating on it or even knowing it; he could succeed just as well if no one knew which was the right card (Rhine, 1934).

Although the early investigators had carried out experiments, psychical research was not at that time primarily an experimental science. The tendency was to regard the accumulation and validation of large numbers of reports of ostensibly paranormal events as the right way of finding out about psi, while experiments served the subordinate purpose of providing convincing evidence of the occurrence of telepathy or other psi-phenomena. A more completely experiment-oriented approach was set into motion in 1927 when the first university laboratory for the experimental study of the subject was started at Duke University in North Carolina under J. B. Rhine. From that time, parapsychology, like other branches of scientific research, used experiment as a means not merely of verifying the fact of psi but of finding out about its nature and properties.

One of the results of the emergence of experiment as a means of parapsychological investigation was a tendency to neglect such collections of reports of spontaneous cases as are to be found in *Phantasms of the Living*. In 1948, however, J. B. Rhine pointed out that such collections still had a useful role even for the experimentalist (Rhine, 1948). If they were no longer to be appealed to as proofs of the reality of the paranormal or as means of settling theoretical questions about its nature, they remain important as means of suggesting hypotheses which may afterwards be tested by suitably designed experiments. It is indeed important that the experimental psychical researcher should be well aware of what people report of their ostensibly paranormal experiences in order that his experimental researches may be in close touch with the problems of psi as they appear in the outside world and should not be a mere laboratory game. There are numerous examples of questions posed by reports of spontaneous psi experiences which a mere study of these reports cannot solve. Some of them, it must be admitted, cannot yet be solved by experimental methods either; they remain problems for future experimental solution. One may ask, for example, whether, in telepathic communication between two individuals, the active role is played by the sender or the receiver of the communicated information, whether it is a case of one of the individuals sending a message, or of the other individual getting hold of a piece of information in someone else's mind. Stories of spontaneous telepathic experiences raise this question; a study of a large collection of spontaneous cases may suggest an answer to it. But whether the answer is right or wrong can only be settled when someone devises and carries out an experiment which will give one result if one of these alternatives is right and another result if the other alternative is right. So far as I know, such an experiment has not yet been done. It is one of many challenges to the ingenuity and skill of future experimenters.

If this is accepted as the proper role of reports of spontaneous cases of ostensibly paranormal events, we need no longer attach to the question of rigid verification the importance that was properly attached to it by the earlier psychical researchers. If we are to draw theoretical conclusions from our collection of spontaneous cases, we must be very sure that none of them are distorted by failure of memory or by lying. If we are only going to use them to indicate possible conclusions that are to be tested afterwards by experiment, there is no reason for being so particular. If the stories are sometimes erroneous, the worst that will result from this will be that experimenters may be misled into trying an experiment that does not yield the expected result. This is a fairly common occurrence in experimental work anyway and it is not a serious one.

There is a further point to be considered about the question of rigid verification of records of spontaneous cases. If records of spontaneous cases are scrutinised carefully and all those are rejected which do not satisfy rigid criteria of adequate recording, that is, rejecting all those that were not recorded on the spot, or of reported apparitions that were not seen by at least two persons, etc., we shall, probably, cut out eighty per cent or more of the material reported. We shall then no longer have a complete sample of what is reported, and the very restricted sample we have may be distorted by the process of selection we have adopted. Apparitions seen by only one person may have different properties from those seen by more than one person; there may be differences in kind between the sort of paranormal event that is immediately recorded and the sort that is not. For the experimental psychical researcher who wants records of spontaneous cases to suggest possibilities and not to prove conclusions, it may be more important to have a representative sample than to have one that is free from errors. It is probably impossible, in any case, to ensure complete freedom from errors, and the effort to attain this unattainable ideal may result in a large number of genuine but poorly attested cases being rejected, with great loss to the experimentalist who wants the records to suggest as many problems as possible for experimental testing.

The first person to carry out the project of using records of stories of the paranormal in this way was Dr Louisa Rhine (1961). She started making a large collection of case records in the Duke University Parapsychology Laboratory with the idea that this material was to be used to provide suggestions for research but not as proof of anything. Supplementary validation was not required so long as material seemed to have been communicated in good faith by apparently sane individuals. They were intended as collections of what people report, not of what is known to happen.

In a series of articles in the *Journal of Parapsychology* Mrs Rhine has used her collection of cases in order to see what indications it gives for experimental testing. The first of these was in 1951, when she considered the proportion of cases in which the person having the paranormal experience was convinced of its paranormality, having a dream for example of some future event and being convinced by it that the event was going to take place (Rhine, 1951). Such conviction is common in spontaneous cases; it has been rarely checked so far in the laboratory. Mrs Rhine also finds that there are certain conditions in spontaneous cases under which conviction of paranormality is greater. These may suggest types of experiment in which such conviction can more easily be found. Here, as elsewhere, the supporting experimental study has not yet been made, but Mrs Rhine's work provides a rich field from which future experimentalists can extract problems for laboratory investigation.

## References

BARRETT, W. F., GURNEY, E., and MYERS, F. W. H. (1882–3), 'First Report on Thought-reading', *Proceedings of the Society for Psychical Research*, i, 13–34 (30–31 for paragraphs quoted).

CROOKES, W. (1874), *Researches in Spiritualism*, London.

GURNEY, E., MYERS, F. W. H., and PODMORE, F. (1886), *Phantasms of the Living*, London (republished abridged, New York, 1962).

MYERS, F. W. H. (1903), *Human Personality and its Survival of Bodily Death*, London (republished abridged, New York, 1961).

RHINE, J. B. (1934), *Extra-Sensory Perception*, Boston.

RHINE, J. B. (1948), 'The Value of Reports of Spontaneous Psi Experiences', *Journal of Parapsychology*, xii, 231–5.

RHINE, LOUISA E. (1951), 'Conviction and Associated Conditions in Spontaneous Cases', *J. Parapsych.*, xv, 164–91.

RHINE, LOUISA E. (1961), *Hidden Channels of the Mind*, New York.

*Proc. S.P.R.* (1884), 'Fourth Report of the Literary Committee', ii, 180.

# III

# Experimental precautions

For whatever purpose experiments in psychical research are carried out, whether to provide new evidence for the reality of some psi-phenomenon (such as ESP), or to find out something about the nature of such a psi-phenomenon, or to test the psi-abilities of a particular individual, or to make an exploratory study of some problem in the field of psychical research, some precautions must be taken to ensure that what is studied is really the paranormal phenomenon it is supposed to be and not some natural event that might be mistaken for a paranormal one. The kind of precaution that must be taken depends on the problem with which the investigator is concerned but, whatever the problem, he wants to be able to discriminate between genuine psi-phenomena and spurious ones. Anyone who starts experimenting without knowledge of the questions that have been raised about experiments in the past is in danger of falling into some error of method which may make his results inconclusive.

Obviously the experimenter must guard against the possibility that the experimental subject is deceiving him either by himself or in collusion with someone else who is giving him information. The most inexperienced ESP experimenter is likely to think of this possibility; he may be less on his guard against the possibility that the subject is receiving information by some unnoticed sensory cue, of sight or hearing. For a soundly conducted experiment, it is also necessary that there should be no possibility of spurious evidence of ESP being given by mistakes in recording the results of the experiment. There must also be no process of selection by means of which successful results are more likely to be included in experimental results than unsuccessful ones.

To avoid these sources of error is part of the standard procedure of all properly conducted parapsychological experiments. In the early days of psychical research experiments were often carried out without some of the safeguards that would now be considered to be essential. These days are, however, past and it is only the enthusiastic new investigator, unfamiliar with the recognised canons of sound research, who might carry out experiments of which the results could be vitiated by neglect of some of the necessary precautions.

We can, for example, imagine such an inexperienced investigator carrying out an experiment in which the object is to see whether an experimental subject can correctly name a card looked at by the experimenter but invisible to the subject himself. This experiment might be carried out in some such way as the following. The experimenter might be seated at a table with the experimental subject (the 'percipient') facing him on the opposite side. The experimenter might then look at each card in turn, keeping its face carefully turned away from the percipient. While he is waiting for the percipient's response the experimenter may write the target symbol with a ball-point pen on a pad on the table in front of him, afterwards writing down in the same way the percipient's guess. He may want to encourage the percipient by telling him when he is right, or he may prefer to indicate this by making a tick at the side of a correct response; he may even tell the percipient what the card was irrespective of whether the guess was right or wrong. There may be a small audience, including perhaps friends or relatives of the percipient, who sit behind the experimenter and can see the target card when it is turned up. After the guesses are completed, the experimenter may go through the pack with the percipient, showing him what were the target cards for each guess. The pack will, of course, be thoroughly shuffled and cut before it is used for the next run of guesses. If, towards the end of a run, the percipient complains of feeling tired and unable to do himself justice, the experimenter may perhaps agree to stop at that stage and not to count the final run, not because it showed a low score but because that low score is presumed to be the result of the irrelevant factor of the percipient's tiredness.

There is, no doubt, an element of caricature in the above description. An experiment so neglectful of elementary precautions against error would not, of course, be tolerated in any psychical research laboratory and has perhaps been rarely carried out anywhere. I think, however, that all of the errors of method here suggested could be found in some non-professional experimental investigations in ESP, and it may be of value to consider what these errors are and how they may be eliminated.

We notice first that, by allowing the subject to see the backs of cards and by writing down the symbol of the target card before the guess is made, the experimenter has made it possible for the percipient to be guided by sensory cues. By telling the percipient when he is right, the experimenter has made it possible for him to use a process of rational inference to increase his chance of being right. This could be the case if the experimenter merely ticked the right answer without comment, since the percipient might see or hear the ticking. By himself writing down both target and guess, the experimenter has made it easy to get spurious results by recording errors. If to avoid giving sensory cues, the experimenter refrains from writing down the target symbol till after the percipient has guessed, he very much increases the likelihood of recording errors. The decision not to count runs made when the percipient says he is too tired to score well is quite improper since it introduces selection in a direction favouring high scores; the eliminated series will be low-scoring ones. Re-using of the same pack after shuffling is also a feature of the experiment which would be better eliminated since it makes possible the intrusion of rational inference on the next series of guesses if (as will pretty certainly be the case) the shuffle has been an imperfect one.

The experimenter has probably been aware of the possibility that his subject might try to deceive him by seeming to have a greater power of ESP than he really has, so he will have taken the precaution of providing his own cards and seeing that these are never handled or closely examined by the percipient. He has, however, left the door wide open for cheating by collusion since he has allowed an audience to be present who might be signalling information to the percipient. It is not sufficient that the experimenter may be satisfied that no signals have passed; he must eliminate the possibility that there could have been signals he did not detect. The safest way of ensuring this is the rigid application of a rule that no one be present in the experimental room except the percipient and members of the experimental team.

There is obviously one experimental situation in which this rule cannot be enforced; the situation in which the object of the experiment is to see whether relatives, friends, or perhaps identical twins show unusual power of telepathic communication. An example of such an experiment is that of the two Welsh boys investigated by Dr Soal (Soal and Bowden, 1959). The experiment was carried out with cards carrying five kinds of picture target and the scores obtained were remarkably high. The experimenter was on the look-out for the possibility of signals passing between the boys and was satisfied that there were none. It remains possible that signals were passed by some means not detected by the experimenter; it has been suggested that this could be done by a Galton whistle which gives notes too high to be heard by an elderly experimenter but which might be clearly audible to the young percipient. There is no reason for supposing that the Welsh boys were signalling to one another and the evidence is against it (Thouless, 1961). Particularly, it is hard to reconcile this explanation with the fact that the boys continued to give high scores when an unannounced change was made in the pictures used as targets. Arguments against signalling are, however, less satisfactory than experimental precautions that preclude the use of signals. These experiments fall short of providing completely convincing evidence that the Welsh boys were communicating by ESP. This is plainly no fault of the experimenter but is a limitation of any experiment designed to test ESP between friends or relatives unless such an experiment can be carried out with the agent and percipient in complete sensory isolation from one another.

If the possibility of cheating by the percipient is excluded, there still remains the possibility that he may be guided (perhaps unconsciously) by some sensory indication of the target. The probability of getting right may be increased by visual indications received from the backs of the target cards; some of these have detectable indentations on the back from the figure printed on the face. So, at least, the percipient must have his back to the agent so that he cannot see the backs of the cards used, and it is necessary for the experimenter to make sure that there are no mirrors or other reflecting surfaces by means of which the cards could be seen.

One must also consider the possibility that the percipient might be unconsciously guided by auditory cues. This suggestion was made early in the history of experimental psychical research by the Danish psychologist Lehman, who thought that the percipient might be guided in choice of response by involuntary whispering of the name of the symbol by the agent looking at it. This is obviously not a possibility in those forms of experiment (such as 'down-through' guessing or precognition) in which the agent does not know the target card. In the telepathic type of experiment, in which the agent does know the target, it is a possibility although I do not know of any evidence that it is a real cause of success in any condition of guessing. The experimental psychologists have obtained evidence which suggests that subjects' responses can be determined by sensory cues of which they are not consciously aware. Such experiments are obviously themselves open to the objection that their results might, in part or altogether, be due to ESP. Parapsychologists have, however, been aware of the possibility that their subjects might have a normal capacity for sensory discrimination without awareness of the sensory criteria by which this discrimination takes place. They have, therefore, made it an essential requirement of an experiment in ESP that it should have been carried out under conditions such that the results could not have resulted from unnoticed sensory cues. They have also considered the possibility that if the experimenter, knowing the target card, uses the word 'now' or other verbal signal to show when the next card is to be guessed, he might be unwittingly using a different intonation for different card faces, which might guide the percipient, equally unwittingly, to make a correct guess.

With these possibilities in mind, it may be felt desirable, in experiments in which the agent knows the target card, to have the percipient in another room and to risk the possibility that this physical isolation may interfere with his ESP processes. Even in another room, it will be necessary that any signal as to when the next guess is to be given, should be made mechanically or by some third person who does not know the target card. Alternatively the signal may be from the percipient to the agent to tell him when to start looking at the next card. Most simply, of course, such precautions may be made superfluous by adopting some form of experiment in which there is no agent who knows the right card. For many years most (though not all) ESP experiments have been of this non-telepathic type.

There is a more elementary possibility of giving guidance by sound which would only be left open by a very incompetent experimenter. This is the guidance given by the sound of the experimenter writing down the target symbol. This noise may be easily detected and discriminated if symbols are written with a ball-point pen or a pencil on a hard surface; we cannot be sure they will not be heard if written by any other means. If the percipient is in the same room, and the experiment is one in which the experimenter turns up each card in turn, it is obviously necessary that he should not write down the symbol of the target card as he turns it up. He can just as well put the target cards into a pile and record their order after the guesses are completed. That method will also have the advantage of minimising recording errors.

There is also the possibility that the percipient may be guided by some process of rational inference. This is fully excluded if he is guessing through an unknown pack of cards without any information as to success or failure. The situation is different, however, if the percipient is told of his success or failure during the course of his guessing. If, for example, he guesses 'circle' for the first guess and is told that this is right, and he avoids 'circle' for the remainder of his guesses, it is obvious that if there are equal numbers of each target in the pack, his mean chance expectation of success for the remaining twenty-four guesses will be five, bringing the total mean chance expectation from five to six.

If he gets further information about what cards have been turned up, the expected success rate will be higher than this. If, for example, he is told every card that is turned up in the standard ESP pack, and he performs the considerable memory feat of remembering all of this information and allowing it to guide his future guesses, his mean expectation of success will be eight or nine instead of five. Yet it may be necessary for some experimental purposes that the subject should be given some information as to his success during his guessing; it may even prove to be the best way of encouraging the subject to score well.

Such information cannot properly be given if one is using the ordinary type of 'closed' pack with five target cards of each kind in the pack, since any information given during the guessing will alter the expectation of subsequent successes. To allow for this change in expectation would not be practicable since it would violate one of the canons of good experimenting: that of keeping the arithmetic as simple as possible. It would also be open to the objection that it would leave a considerable margin of uncertainty as to the expected score since we should not know how much of the relevant information the percipient could remember well enough to be effectively guided by it. The best way of dealing with this difficulty, if it is desired to give information to the subject during his guesses, is to use 'open' packs such as were used in the Soal-Goldney experiments with Shackleton (Goldney and Soal, 1943). In these packs, cards have been prearranged with the help of a list of random numbers and without restriction as to the number of each target that appears in a pack of twenty-five. With such a pack, there is obviously no objection to the percipient being told either when he has succeeded or what the target really was after each guess; the likelihood of the next target is not affected by what cards have gone before it. The preparation of such packs does, however, take up a good deal of the experimenter's time, and it does not seem worth while unless it is for the purpose of performing an experiment whose design requires that information should be given to the percipient during the experiment. Otherwise, it seems better to use the simpler closed pack and to avoid giving the subject any information while he is guessing.

One possibility of rational inference that was not taken sufficiently seriously by the early psychical researchers was that of the likelihood of an intelligent guess as to what the experimenter was going to think next if one knew what he thought last. When it was said, in early drawing experiments, that objects were drawn 'at random', what was often meant was that the experimenter drew the first thing he thought of. This, however, is obviously non-random being largely determined by what he thought of last. If an experimenter has drawn a jug as his first object and a tree as his second, a percipient can at least guess that the third drawing will not be a jug or a tree. How well he can guess what will come next depends partly on how well he knows the experimenter; without such knowledge, it would be a reasonable guess that the third drawing would be of some kind of animal. It would be difficult to find out how much this possibility might affect the percipient's expectation of making hits. The only safe thing is to eliminate it altogether as Whately Carington did (and as any modern experimenter would do) by making a random selection of what is to be drawn by a process such as determining a page in a dictionary by some chance method and drawing the first drawable object named on that page. This possibility does not arise in card-guessing experiments, although it would arise if, in a pure telepathy experiment, the experimenter chose the first card that came into his head. Such an experiment would be very imperfect; the target must always be selected by some means more random than human choice.

One must also consider how far the percipient might be guided by rational inference if the experimenter follows the procedure of showing the percipient the order of the pack after the first series of guesses, then shuffles and cuts it and uses it for a second series of guesses. It may easily be confirmed, by stacking a pack in prearranged order and then asking someone to shuffle it thoroughly, that this behaviour does not break up the prearranged sequences fully; generally it will, in fact, be found that they are very little broken up. The instruction to cut also leads to a division of the pack in a position somewhere near the middle. There is, therefore, a situation in which a process of rational inference might influence the percipient's score, although I know no experiment which shows how much it could influence it.

This difficulty can be completely got over by introducing a cut at a randomly determined point after the shuffle. This must be a cut at a point not arbitrarily chosen by the experimenter, but one at a point determined by some mechanical method which will ensure that every point of cut (including the zero point of no cut at all) is equally likely. This may be done, for example, by throwing dice to determine the entry point in a table of random numbers, and making the cut at the point indicated by the remainder left after the two-figure number so obtained is divided by twenty-five. When this is done, it would not matter if the subject had complete knowledge of the order of the pack before the cut; this could not produce better than average scoring unless he also knew the point of cut. This is evident if we consider that elementary arithmetic shows that for a 'closed' pack (with equal numbers of all targets), the average of the scores obtained from all twenty-five positions of cut must be exactly five whatever system of guesses may have been made. For an open deck (with possibly unequal numbers of the targets), the matter is not quite so simple, but the average score will not differ from five by more than the amount attributed to chance in the ordinary tests of significance. For either closed or open pack, this method of a random cut ensures that there cannot be a spurious indication of ESP produced by the percipient's normal knowledge of the order of the pack before shuffling.

While this is a precaution which ought to be taken by the experimenter if he is giving the subject successive runs through the same pack of cards, and although it is a useful precaution in certain other experimental situations, it is not a necessary precaution in all ESP experiments. A simpler way of dealing with this difficulty is not to go on using a single ESP pack, but to have a number of ESP packs for every experimental session and not to use any of them twice over during any single session.

Another possible source of error that the inexperienced experimental researcher may be tempted not to take sufficiently seriously is that of his results being vitiated by errors in recording. It is true, that with reasonable care, these are not likely to be so frequent as to make any appreciable difference to the results of a high-scoring subject. Many ESP findings are, however, drawn from the cumulative evidence provided by large numbers of guesses at relatively low rates of score. Such results are very sensitive to errors in recording; if these are in the direction of increasing the apparent number of hits, they may even produce spurious evidence of ESP from scores that are really at chance level.

One cannot eliminate altogether the possibility that occasional mistakes will be made in recording a succession of guesses or of targets, but one can, without difficulty, ensure that any mistakes that are made will not produce spurious evidence of ESP. This may most simply be done by arranging that the subject's guesses are recorded by himself or by some other person who does not know what is the target card, while the targets are recorded by someone who does not know what guess is made. In some forms of card-guessing experiment, where the subject guesses 'down through' a pack of cards which is not examined till the guesses are complete, or when he guesses the future order of a pack, the guesses are necessarily written down by someone who does not know which guesses are right; the same end can also be arranged in any other card-guessing experiment. The condition that the person recording the target order should not know the guesses is less important. The end of avoiding errors in the target recording can also be achieved by checking the record of target order from the pack itself after the guesses have been completed; additional safety will, of course be given by an additional check by some other person than the experimenter. The most unreliable recording method is one in which both target and guess are recorded by the experimenter at the time the guess is made. Such a method would not be tolerated in any serious ESP experimentation, yet it seems a natural one for the in-experienced experimentalist to adopt unless the objections to it are pointed out to him.

The danger of falsification of results by unwitting selection is also one that the inexperienced experimenter may be insufficiently aware of. It may take place in various ways. The percipient may, for example, say after an unsuccessful experiment that he could not succeed this time because he had a headache or because he was distracted by the noise of road-works outside. A rash experimenter may imagine that he can safely leave out these results from his record since they will have been discarded, not because they were unsuccessful, but for an outside reason. Leaving them out will, however, produce a distorted picture of the percipient's ESP ability since the headache or noise would most likely not have been reported if the session had been a successful one. In all psychological experimentation, one must rigidly observe the rule that any results obtained must be counted if this was the intention before they were carried out. This does not mean that one can never make a decision not to use the results of certain experiments in one's final result, but that such a decision must be made *before* the experiments are carried out. This decision may be made, for example, because one wants to do some preliminary experiments to get the percipient used to the experimental conditions before the first measurement of his ESP is made, or to determine whether he seems on a particular day to be in a suitable mental state for ESP scoring. The rule against selection remains rigid; a decision that an experiment is or is not to be included in the record must be made before the experiment is started. It is safest to write the decision down at the time it is made.

Another way in which selection might affect experimental results is illustrated in an experiment reported in *Phantasms of the Living* where people were asked to guess the suits of cards drawn from a pack of playing cards at their own homes and to send results to the experimenters. The experimenters were aware of the danger of selection since they said: 'there has been here no selection of results; all who undertook the trials were requested to send in their report, whatever the degree of success or unsuccess.' It seems naïve to suppose that the fact that this request was made ensured that it was complied with. The most natural expectation would be that successful results were more likely to be sent in than unsuccessful ones, and that the most likely to be sent in were those that were most successful. It is impossible to guess how far the successes in this experiment (two per cent over mean chance expectation) may have been due to the factor of selection of the more successful sets of responses. The method of experimenting, in which results are obtained at home and the results are known to those taking part before they are sent back to the experimenter, has been uncommon in psychical research. All such experiments are rendered very dubious by the possibility of selection of results having taken place. Such selection is likely, of course, to have been without any intention to deceive and without even any realisation of the fact that not sending in unsuccessful results would produce a misleading result.

These are the main primary precautions which must be considered in any parapsychological experiment. The emphasis on them must depend on the purpose of the experiment; there is no special merit in rigorous precautions if these are not appropriate to the object of the experiment. An experiment may be a 'pilot experiment' from which it is not intended to draw any conclusion but is intended only as a guide to future experimentation. Before starting a new design of experiment, an experimenter may want to see how the new design works and to see whether any modifications should be made in his plan. For this purpose, it is obvious that experimental precautions may be relaxed. They will not be abandoned altogether since the experimenter does not want to be misled into trying out an experimental design that a more carefully carried-out pilot experiment might have shown to be unworkable, but for this purpose something less than a full system of precautions may be needed.

Having done any necessary pilot experiments, the experimenter will embark on an experiment which is likely to have some such purpose as that of finding out something about the nature of ESP. He does not want to modify the design of his experiment till it is completed, and when it is completed, he hopes to publish the results in order to communicate what he has found out to other experimentalists in his subject. For this purpose, he will need the full range of primary precautions that have already been described (and also some precautions against being misled by chance coincidences which will be discussed in Chapter VIII). If his precautions were inadequate, he would be in danger of misleading other experimentalists into thinking that some fact of ESP had been demonstrated when it had not been demonstrated. It is true that the fact that he is wrong is likely to be found out sometime by the failure of other people to reproduce his results, but there will have been a waste of experimental time which could have been avoided by the taking of proper precautions from the beginning.

In order to avoid this waste of time, it is important that, in his research report, the experimenter should have described the experimental precautions he has taken. These will be scrutinised by other experimenters to see whether they are adequate for their purpose. A further safeguard to this end may be provided by having a second experimenter on the experiment. This is not to be understood as a means of ensuring that the first experimenter does not cheat, but to provide additional assurance that all necessary precautions are taken and are fully reported.

Although adequate experimental precautions are important, they must not be allowed so to engross the experimentalist's attention that they interfere with other desirable features of ESP experimentation, particularly with the requirement that experiments should take place under conditions likely to be fruitful in ESP results. A scrupulous experimenter, too openly preoccupied with precautions, can produce in his experimental room a condition of stress and suspicion likely to be unfavourable to psi-functioning. Such stress and suspicion are not necessary to adequate precautions; the ideal should be 'adequate precautions without fuss'. The percipient should not be made to feel that he is a criminal under suspicion but a co-operating member of a team engaged in a scientific enquiry, that is, in a puzzle-solving activity. His co-operation will not, it is true, extend to determining the precautions to be taken, but it will extend to a right to have these precautions explained to him and the reasons for which they are taken. It is part of the skill of a good psychical research experimenter to produce a happy and relaxed atmosphere in his experimental sessions; it is also a part of his skill to combine that atmosphere with unobtrusive but adequate experimental precautions.

So far we have been discussing the common type of ESP experiment in which the object is to find out whether a particular percipient shows ESP ability, whether a particular experimental set-up shows ESP differences, or to investigate some characteristic of the ESP response. There is a very different kind of experiment in psychical research which was of considerable importance in the past although it is of less importance at the present day.

This is the type of experiment whose purpose is to produce new evidence of the reality of ESP. This differs from the type of experiment last described both in its design and in the range of precautions necessary. In its design, it tends to use a very large number of repetitions of an experiment of a single type; in the kind of experiment intended to elucidate the nature of ESP, an essential element is that of varying the experiment so that the results of one kind of experiment can be compared with those of another. The experiment intended to create or reinforce conviction of the reality of ESP must also use a different range of precautions, since it must guard against the possibility that the experimenter is himself guilty of fraud by such devices as the presence of independent witnesses. Such precautions are superfluous in the ordinary run of experiments in psychical research as they would be in any other field of experimental research. The experimenter knows he is not cheating and other experimenters who are doubtful of his results must try out similar experiments for themselves. However honestly they may have been obtained, his results will be of little interest unless they can be repeated.

Researches intended for the special purpose of providing evidence of the reality of ESP or of any other psi-phenomenon are in a different category. For such experiments it is reasonable to demand that precautions shall be taken against the possibility of the experimenter falsifying his results, however remote this possibility may appear to those who know the experimenter. The special problems of researches of this type will be discussed in Chapter X.

## References

GOLDNEY, K. M., and SOAL, S. G. (1943), 'Experiments in Precognitive Telepathy', *Proceedings of the Society for Psychical Research*, xlvii, 21–150.

SOAL, S. G., and BOWDEN, H. T. (1959), *The Mind Readers*, London.

THOULESS, R. H. (1961), 'Were the Jones Boys Signalling by Morse Code ?', *Journal of the American Society for Psychical Research*, lv, 24–8.

# IV

# Card-guessing experiments

When psychical researchers began to turn from the collection of spontaneous cases to see what paranormal phenomena they could test under experimental conditions, one of the first tasks they experimented with was that of requiring the supposed percipient to guess what card it was that the experimenter was looking at. The first type of paranormal event they were concerned to test was thought-transference (or telepathy) and the commonest material for these early experiments was a pack of ordinary playing cards.

Although now a much larger range of cognitive psi-phenomena is studied and other material than playing cards is commonly used, some form of card-guessing experiment has remained in common use, and, although often found fault with, it has proved an extraordinarily fruitful form of experiment.

The essential point of any experiment in psychical research is to find some task in which an experimental subject will only succeed if he has the psi-capacity in question. Obviously a large range of tasks could be chosen but card-guessing has the advantage of using simple material, of being indefinitely repeatable, and of yielding a result that can easily be expressed as a number. The ease with which a degree of success can be expressed as a number is important to the experimenter when he begins to concern himself with such questions as whether ESP scores are better in one condition than another or whether one group of people scores better than another.

It is also important to the experimenter when he concerns himself (as he must) with the question of whether he is dealing with a real case of ESP or whether it is possible that he is being misled by chance coincidences. In card-guessing he has a task in which he knows the number of successes that would be expected on an average by chance (the 'mean chance expectation'), and also it is not difficult to calculate how much a score ought to be better than this before it can be regarded as evidence of some cause being present which enables the subject to succeed in the task. Whether it can also be inferred that this cause is ESP depends, of course, on the adequacy of the precautions by means of which other possible causes of success have been eliminated.

Card-guessing experiments are not only useful as a means of finding out whether or not ESP really occurs. This was an important question in the early days of psychical research but the amount of evidence that has been accumulated in favour of its real occurrence has made this a problem of diminishing importance. The main research problem at the present time in connection with ESP is not that of proving again that ESP does really occur, but that of finding out all we can about it. For this purpose, experiments are still of service, although the design of such experiments will be somewhat different from those intended to test its reality. Instead of frequent repetitions of an unchanging task, the experimenter will more likely want to vary the conditions under which the task is performed in order to see whether these variations of condition cause changes in the experimental subject's performance. We may, for example, arrange that, for some of the subject's guesses, someone else (the 'agent') knows what the card is, while for some of his guesses no one knows what the card is. Or we might arrange that some of his guesses are of cards carrying geometrical diagrams while others are pictures of objects that may be supposed to have emotional significance, of a coffin or of a member of the opposite sex. The problem would then be to determine whether he succeeded better in the one kind of task than in the other and whether any difference that appeared between the two sets of results was greater than the difference that might be expected by chance.

In judging an experiment in parapsychology, it is very necessary to be clear as to what is its purpose. There is a somewhat simple type of criticism which ignores the variety of purposes which experiments in psychical research may have and which seems to treat all experiments as attempts to prove the occurrence of ESP or whatever other psi-phenomenon they are concerned with. So it may be pointed out that a certain experiment does not provide convincing evidence for the real occurrence of a psi-phenomenon when its purpose was perhaps that of a pilot experiment to see whether subjects could succeed better in morning tests than in afternoon ones.

Whatever may be the purpose of the experiment, the card-guessing form of it has many advantages for the experimenter. It is not surprising to find it used early in the history of psychical research. The early members of the Society for Psychical Research were preoccupied with the problem of using experiments as a means of providing conclusive evidence as to the real occurrence of telepathy. The ordinary pack of playing cards provided easily obtainable material, about which many of the subjects of the experiments would be accustomed to making guesses in card games. It is easy to see that the odds against a single chance hit would be fifty-one to one, and it is not difficult to calculate the chance likelihood of any specified number of right guesses.

One early example of the use of this type of experiment was the series of experiments carried out with the Creery sisters (Barrett et al., 1883). These were two young girls who had been reported by their father to show unusual gifts of thought-reading. They were tested experimentally in various tasks which included that of guessing which card was drawn at random from a pack of ordinary playing cards. They succeeded in these various tasks far more often than could reasonably be explained as a chance effect. It was proved, as was pointed out by the experimenters, that the sisters were succeeding either by thought-transference or through some defect of the experiment which allowed the experimental subject to have normal knowledge of which card was selected.

One of the ways in which such normal knowledge could be obtained would, of course, be by signals passing between the sisters when both were present and one had normal knowledge of the cards. Although it had been earlier pointed out by the experimenters that experiments in which both sisters were present were of no evidential value, the discovery that signals did pass between the sisters under these conditions made the experimenters regard the whole series of experiments as suspect and they were not afterwards treated as evidence of telepathy (Gurney, 1889). The evidential value of this series of experiments has, of course, no present-day importance, yet there are principles involved in this decision which have implications for later experimentalists.

The Creery sisters themselves said that they had not used signals in their most successful experiments and only resorted to them in order to avoid disappointing visitors when they could not get right otherwise. This may have been the case, but obviously what the sisters said was not evidence, and the experimenters rightly rejected this explanation as giving any validity to the experiments in which both sisters were present. A more serious point was that some very successful experiments took place when only the experimenters were present with the sister who was guessing, so the signalling explanation of success was in these cases ruled out. The evidence reported under these conditions is impressive. For example, in one of the experiments in which no other member of the Creery family was present, one of the Creery sisters made 14 guesses of a pack of 25 playing cards and was right 9 times. This was a level of success strongly indicating genuine ESP ability. Does the evidential value of such experiments disappear when we know that the Creery sisters sometimes cheated when they were given the chance to do so?

This question raises an important principle in experimenting. The idea that one must only draw conclusions from experiments carried out on trustworthy experimental subjects is not a sound one. If an experiment has been correctly carried out, it is irrelevant whether or not the subject is trustworthy, since the experimental precautions should have made it impossible for him to cheat. If they have not succeeded in doing this, the experiments are of no evidential value. The experiments in which another of the Creery family knew what was the target card being guessed by one of the sisters did not become valueless because of the later discovery that the sisters sometimes signalled to one another; they were worthless as evidence anyway, as was correctly pointed out by the authors of *Phantasms of the Living* before it had been discovered that the sisters sometimes communicated by signals.

If an experiment has been properly designed, nothing should depend on the honesty of the subject. This does not mean that the experimenter should give the subject the impression that he is mistrusted. This is an impression that it is important to avoid since an expressed attitude of distrust might well create a psychological atmosphere unfavourable to successful scoring. The precautions that must be taken can be explained to the subject as necessities in order that the results may carry conviction to other people.

Much has happened in card-guessing experiments since these early days. Experimenters have increasingly used experiments as a means of finding out what sort of thing ESP is rather than as a means of demonstrating that ESP is a reality. There have also been changes in the technique of experimenting. The use of playing cards as experimental material has largely been given up and replaced by the pack of twenty-five ESP cards introduced by J. B. Rhine when in 1927 he started the first laboratory of parapsychology at Duke University in North Carolina. These cards were of five kinds marked with geometrical diagrams: a square (or rectangle), a circle, a star, a cross, and waves.

*Figure 1*    ESP cards

It is a question of some practical interest whether there is any advantage in having five different target cards instead of the fifty-two of the pack of playing cards. There might be some disadvantage since obviously if a subject guessed, let us say, three more than the chance expected number in fifty guesses, this would be a more impressive result if the chance expectation of any guess being right were 1 in 52 than if it were 1 in 5. We can express this by saying that there is some loss of 'sensitivity' by reducing the number of targets.

This loss of sensitivity will not, however, matter if the successful percipient is likely to score much higher on the pack with the smaller number of targets. There is some experimental evidence that this is the case and that the higher success rate with the five targets more than compensates for the loss of sensitivity. It is easy to see that this might be the case. If the condition for successful paranormal cognition is that a number of responses should be about equally likely to occur, this condition is likely to be better fulfilled with a small number of targets than with a arge one. The choice of five targets in Rhine's pack was probably originally a lucky guess; it looks as if it was a good choice for trying to demonstrate paranormal cognition.

The use of five alternative targets has been very usual among experimenters even when they have given up the geometrical diagrams introduced by Rhine. When, for example, Soal and Mrs Goldney started their experiments with Basil Shackleton, they used cards with coloured pictures of five animals: elephant, giraffe, lion, pelican, and zebra (Soal and Bateman, 1954). Their experiments were highly successful but there is no evidence to show that the pictures were more successful than diagrams would have been; it may be that they had found an unusually gifted subject. More recently Rýzl has used only two alternatives; cards that might be green or white side uppermost (Rýzl and Rýzlová, 1962). This reduction to two alternatives further reduces sensitivity but this may be compensated for if subjects are more successful when they have only two alternatives to guess from. There is no evidence to show that the use of two alternatives is productive of more successful guessing; in Rýzl's case too it may be that he was fortunate in having found an unusually gifted subject or that he had discovered a good way of developing his subject's psi-capacity.

There were many other new directions of experimental exploration in the Duke University Parapsychology Laboratory besides the introduction of a new type of target cards. As has already been mentioned, Rhine started experiments in which the experimenter did not know what was the target card. The subject might guess through a pack of shuffled cards of which the order was known to nobody. It seemed that the percipient could correctly report a fact of the outside world which was not a piece of knowledge in someone else's mind. For such paranormal cognition, the words *telepathy* or *thought-transference* were obviously inappropriate. In the traditional nomenclature it would be called *clairvoyance*. In the type of experiment that had been used earlier in which someone is looking at the card when the percipient guesses it, we do not know whether the cause of the subject guessing right (if he does so to an extent that cannot be attributed to chance) is the knowledge in the other person's mind or the mere outside fact of the target card. In other words, we do not know whether to call what has happened 'telepathy' or 'clairvoyance'. We do not indeed know whether these are two different paranormal processes or whether they are merely two names we give to the same process under different conditions of operating. It seems better, therefore, to say simply that the successful subject is showing some form of *extra-sensory perception*. Even this more general term may be objected to on the ground that it implies that the process is some kind of perception. One may avoid this implication by coining an entirely new term which carries no implications whatever, and say that a *psi*-process is taking place. If, however, one uses the term 'extra-sensory perception', one is more likely to be generally understood.

From the results of experiments in which subjects could correctly name the target card when no one had normal knowledge of what the target card was, Rhine was led to ask whether there was really any evidence for tele-pathy (Rhine, 1945). If experiments in which an experimenter was looking at the card could be explained either by supposing that the subject knew the card directly or that he knew the contents of the experimenter's mind, the obvious experimental problem is to see how these two kinds of explana-tion can be distinguished. It is not so difficult to eliminate knowledge in the experimenter's mind, since this can be done by the simple device of not having the experimenter or anyone else know what the target card is. We can leave out the complication that arises if we try also to eliminate the possibility that the subject might succeed by foreseeing a future process of the experimenter's mind; that also can be provided for by a suitable design of experiment. It is more difficult to eliminate the external fact as a possible cause of the percipient's success. What is necessary is that there should be a correct response but no external target and no record of what is the correct response. It might be supposed that this aim could be achieved by arranging an experiment in which the experimenter merely thought of one of the target cards and the subject tried to guess which one he was thinking of. That would certainly enable one to do an experiment with no external target, but it would not fulfil another important requirement of a valid experimental design, that the sequence of targets be a random one. A succession of thoughts is demonstrably not random, however hard the thinker may try to make it so. The difficulty of designing a suitable experi-ment to demonstrate pure telepathy is to combine the requirement that there is no external target with the requirement that the succession of targets is random.

An experimental design that fulfilled these conditions was, in fact, suggested, and the experiment was successfully carried out by Dr Elizabeth McMahan at the Duke Parapsychology Laboratory (McMahan, 1946). Although four of her experiments showed only chance results, a fifth in which two groups were compared showed results which could not reasonably be attributed to chance. Even considered (as it must be) as the selected best result of a set of five experiments, the odds against the chance occurrence of these results is about sixty to one. This experiment demonstrated that it was possible for subjects to succeed in ESP tasks under 'pure telepathy' conditions, that is, when the only target was an item of knowledge in someone else's mind.

This was confirmed by an experiment carried out by Soal with a subject (Mrs Stewart) who had already shown success in ESP experiments (Soal and Bateman, 1954). This percipient succeeded under these conditions to an extent of about nine per cent above mean chance expectation over a series of one thousand guesses. This result also is beyond any deviation that could reasonably be attributed to chance.

There are two possible ways of interpreting these results. One may say that they establish 'telepathy' as a reality distinct from other kinds of ESP. Alternatively, one may say that they suggest that there is one single ESP capacity which can operate under a variety of conditions. One would say then that the tests now being discussed are not to be regarded as tests of a special capacity which we may call 'telepathy' but rather as tests of ESP under special conditions which we may call 'telepathic conditions'. It does not seem that there is any experiment by means of which we could discriminate between these two possibilities; they must rather be regarded as two possible ways of looking at the same facts. My own preference is for the second alternative, that ESP operates under a variety of conditions to which we may give different names without implying that they are different abilities. This alternative is not incompatible with the possibility that some ESP percipients may show their ability better under one set of conditions than under another; there is, in fact, a good deal of evidence that percipients do show such preferences.

The principal advantages of the card-guessing method of experimenting are those that result from the ease with which the results can be expressed as a number and the simplicity of the arithmetic that has to be used if one wants to make any deductions from that number. One may, for example, ask such questions as the following: 'How well has a given subject done in a particular experiment?' 'Has he done well enough to make it reasonably certain that his results are not merely accidental?' 'Has one subject A done better than another B, or is any difference that appears between their scores merely accidental?' 'Do the ESP performances of subjects show changes with time, e.g. improving with practice?'

For answering any such question it is necessary that we should be able experimentally to get a number that represents how far our subject (or subjects) has succeeded in an ESP task. In some cases we shall want two numbers, for example, if we want to compare the performances of two subjects. In other cases, as for that of how ESP performance varies with time, we shall need a series of numbers. It is not the case that we can only get the number or numbers we want for such purposes by means of card-guessing experiments, but that is one of the easiest tasks for representing degree of success by means of a number since all we have to do is to count the number of successful guesses (or hits) and compare it with the number we should expect if the hits were merely the result of chance. If we are using a pack of twenty-five cards with equal numbers of five different targets, we should expect our subject to get about five right answers each time he guessed through the pack. Unless he got appreciably more right than this we should not be led to look for any cause (ESP or sensory leakage) to explain his right responses. This expected number of five is derived by very simple arithmetic; it would not be easy to calculate a corresponding figure if the subject were trying to reproduce drawings. It would be by no means easy to say how many of the subject's reproductions would be likely by chance alone to fit the target well enough to be counted as hits.

The simplicity of the arithmetic of card-guessing does not, however, end here. There is a further question of how big a deviation from the most likely number of hits to be expected by chance is required before we can conclude that there is some cause at work which favours right guessing by the subject. When we say that we expect about five successes by chance in each series of guesses through the pack, we do not, of course, mean that we expect that, by chance alone, there will always be exactly five right. In some sets of 25 guesses, the number right might be 3 or 4 or 6 or 7. If our subject guessed through a very large number of packs and nothing except chance affected the likelihood of his being right, we should expect the average score to get nearer and nearer to five the more times he guessed through the pack. It would be, therefore, somewhat misleading to say that five is the number expected by chance or to call this number the 'chance expectation'; it may be called more correctly the 'mean chance expectation'.

It becomes a question of some practical importance to the experimenter in parapsychology how big a deviation from mean chance expectation in the number of hits can be taken as evidence that some other factor than chance is at work producing right guesses. He will not be surprised if a subject gets eight right in twenty-five guesses at ESP cards, but he will be surprised (and rightly so) if the subject gets twenty right, and he will begin then to think that, if his precautions against sensory leakage or other sources of error have been adequate, his subject must be using extra-sensory perception. But suppose the subject gets twelve right, would it be reasonable to suppose that this was merely a chance deviation from the expected average number?

This is the problem of the 'significance' of experimental results which will be discussed in more detail in Chapter VIII. Obviously it is a matter in which we cannot trust our intuitions in doubtful cases. The question of how big a deviation from mean chance expectation can be considered to be evidence against the deviation having arisen by chance must be settled by arithmetic based on probability theory, and the application of probability theory to the problem of how big a deviation would be likely to arise by chance is a good deal simpler for card-guessing experiments than it is for most other possible ways of testing ESP.

Both for quantification of results and for determining how strong is the evidence from a particular result, card-guessing has the advantage of needing relatively simple procedures. It has further obvious advantages in the ready availability of the necessary material (in the form of playing cards if not of the Rhine ESP cards) and of the ease with which a large number of results can be obtained in a short time. On the other hand, card-guessing experiments have disadvantages that become apparent to those using them. Both experimenter and subject are likely to become bored and fatigued by prolonged repetition of an activity without much interest, particularly since the task is the unnatural one of making choices when there is no rational ground for the choice made. This dislike of the card-guessing task is not felt by everybody, but many people who believe that they have ESP capacities complain that they cannot be expected to succeed in such an artificial task as card-guessing and feel that they would be able to succeed in an experiment involving a more congenial task. Certainly it might have been found that the card-guessing task was unsuitable for experiments in psychical research because nobody could succeed in it. In fact experiments of this type have proved to be unexpectedly fruitful, and no one seems yet to have found a task in which subjects do consistently better. The experimenter may regard the tendency of his experimental subjects to be bored by card-guessing as a challenge to his experimental skill, and he may succeed in counteracting this tendency by such devices as the avoidance of too-long sessions, the maintenance of a pleasant and informal atmosphere within sessions, by interesting his subjects in the problems to be solved, and so on.

Alternatively he may try other ways of experimenting which he hopes will be free from the objections urged against card-guessing. One of the first alternative methods he is likely to think of is the reproduction of drawings which will be discussed in the next chapter.

## References

BARRETT, W. F., GURNEY, E., and MYERS, F. W. H. (1883), 'First Report on Thought Reading', *Proceedings of the Society for Psychical Research*, i, 13–34.

GURNEY, E. (1889), 'Note relating to some of the unpublished experiments in thought-transference', *Proc. S.P.R.*, v, 269–70.

MCMAHAN, ELIZABETH (1946), 'An Experiment in Pure Telepathy', *Journal of Parapsychology*, x, 273–88.

RHINE, J. B. (1945), 'Telepathy and Clairvoyance Reconsidered', *J. Parapsych.*, ix, 176–93.

RÝZL, M., and RÝZLOVÁ, J. (1962), 'A Case of High-scoring ESP Performance in the Hypnotic State', *J. Parapsych.*, xxvi, 153–71.

SOAL, S. G., and BATEMAN, F. (1954), *Modern Experiments in Telepathy*, London, 1954.

# V

# Testing ESP by reproduction of drawings

In the search for a method of experimenting in extra-sensory perception that should be more interesting both to the percipient and to the experimenter than the card-guessing type of experiment, a natural choice is that of an experiment in which the task is to reproduce a picture drawn or looked at by an 'agent' who may or may not be one of the experimenters. Such experiments appeared early in the history of psychical research and they are still used. They have their own difficulties which seem not to be understood by many of those who complain of the general predominance of card-guessing experiments. The first of these difficulties is that, with rare exceptions, experiments in the reproduction of drawings have not proved very fruitful in showing ESP at work; the conviction of many experimental subjects that they could succeed better in reproducing a drawing than in naming a card does not seem to be borne out by a comparison of the results of these two kinds of experiment.

There is a further difficulty when one starts trying to measure how successful a subject has been in a drawing experiment. The agent, for example, may have drawn a vase and the percipient has made a half-circle. Do these figures sufficiently resemble each other for this result to count as a hit? This is a difficulty not present in the card-guessing situation where the number of targets and possible responses is limited. To answer the question in the case of drawing experiments, the experimenter will need the co-operation of a judge who does not know which drawings are meant as responses to each target figure; he may indeed use a number of such judges. These judges can give him an unbiased estimate of how many hits the percipient has scored, but the experimenter is left with the difficult question of how many hits the subject would have scored by accident if he had no capacity to be right by ESP: a vase is not a very unlikely thing for the agent to draw and a semicircle is not very unlikely for the percipient to draw; how likely is it that they will be drawn at the same time by mere accident? Once the experimenter starts asking questions like these, the arithmetical calculations he has to perform are much more complicated than those carried out by the experimenter in a card-guessing experiment. If he does not ask them, he is left with evidence of ESP that merely rests on his own impressions unless he is lucky enough to have a subject who can reproduce drawings in such detail that one can properly draw the conclusion from mere inspection that there must be some cause for this resemblance and that it could not be a mere chance effect.

Many discussions of the use of reproductions of drawings as a method of ESP testing seem to assume that all telepathic or ESP drawing is of this detailed type. It has, in fact, been rather rarely recorded and anyone who uses such a test of ESP is likely to find that his results are a set of drawings some of which somewhat resemble the target drawing but which need very elaborately designed systems of judging and of calculating success before one can be sure of whether there is any sign of ESP and, if so, how much it is.

In the first experiment done in the Society for Psychical Research on the reproduction of drawings, there certainly was such a degree of correspondence between drawings and targets that there could be no reasonable doubt that they were not accidental resemblances. These were the Blackburn-Smith experiments in which Blackburn looked at a drawing which had been prepared by one of the experimenters and Smith attempted to reproduce it by drawing. There were various defects in the experimental design, including the fact that Blackburn and Smith were in the room together at the time of the reproduction and could, therefore, have been communicating by means of some code. ESP experiments in which a friend or relative of the percipient knows the right answers before the response is given can never be sound evidence for the reality of ESP. It is not necessary that we should know how such a person could communicate with the percipient, or that we should have reason for distrusting the percipient or agent. The possibility of collusion must be ruled out by the design of the experiment. This does not, of course, mean that we should never do experiments in which, as in this case, two people say that they can communicate with each other by telepathy, only that we should not suppose that the results of such experiments can give very strong evidence.

Many years afterwards (in 1908) Blackburn wrote a statement in *John Bull* saying that he and Smith in collusion had hoaxed the committee and that their results were fraudulent. This statement was strongly denied by Smith. Such confessions are not uncommon in psychical research and must be treated with some reserve. While one must not be uncritically credulous of stories merely because they claim to undermine the marvellous, a case has been made out for believing that Blackburn's statement was correct, in particular the fact that Blackburn and Smith had previously given public shows of their allegedly telepathic powers in which it seems likely that they used trickery (Hall, 1964).

The question of whether the Blackburn-Smith series of experiments was fraudulent or not has no present-day importance. Neither this experiment nor any other of the early S.P.R. experiments contributes any weight of evidence for the reality of ESP as this evidence stands at the present time. The series is of some interest historically since it was one of the factors that, at the beginning, encouraged the early researchers to believe that telepathy was a reality. In this belief they were no doubt correct, although some of the grounds on which they at first held it may have been insufficient.

Although the investigators of Smith and Blackburn did not think that their experimental subjects were deceiving them, they did recognise the objection to experiments done with a single agent and a single subject. When they wanted to put forward a drawing experiment as evidence for the reality of telepathy when *Phantasms of the Living* was published a few years later, they chose another series organised by Guthrie which was not open to this objection (Guthrie, 1884). In this series, there were four different agents and two percipients; in some cases, agent and percipient were not previously known to each other. These facts obviously reduce the plausibility of the idea that agent and percipient could have been in collusion.

Specimens of the results are shown in Figure 2 (page 43). A casual scrutiny of them would suggest that the first pair shows such resemblance that it is unlikely that the target and reproduction are independent of one another, the second shows some resemblance but one could not be very confident that it was not accidental, whereas the third pair shows such close resemblance between target and reproduction that there is very great likelihood that the reproduction is a copy of the target. A large number of the reproductions of this series of experiments show resemblances of the same order of closeness as that of the third pair, so it was reasonable for the experimenters to conclude that, if the precautions against sensory leakage were adequate, the experiments showed strong evidence for some kind of ESP (they thought for telepathy).

Somewhat similar experimental results have been reported by other investigators, notably by Warcollier (Warcollier, 1938) and Upton Sinclair (Sinclair, 1930), but on the whole the experience of the eighty years which have elapsed since these experiments were carried out has shown that their highly successful results were exceptional. The experimenter who decides to use the reproduction of drawings as a method of ESP experimenting must be prepared for results which cannot be evaluated by simple inspection.

The kind of result likely to be found in practice is one in which a few of the drawings show some resemblance to their targets, but so little that it is a matter of opinion whether the target has had any influence on the reproduction or not; an optimistic judge might give many of these as possible hits while a more severe judge would reject them all. It is obviously unsatisfactory to have a method of assessment which depends on the personality of the judge. There may also be a few pairs in which there is undoubted resemblance although this resemblance is not so close or so detailed that one can be quite confident that it is not accidental. Let us suppose, for example, that the experimenter has drawn a rose and the

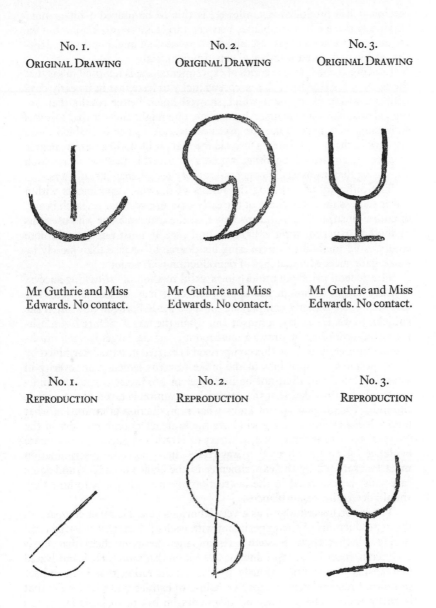

No. 1.
ORIGINAL DRAWING

No. 2.
ORIGINAL DRAWING

No. 3.
ORIGINAL DRAWING

Mr Guthrie and Miss
Edwards. No contact.

Mr Guthrie and Miss
Edwards. No contact.

Mr Guthrie and Miss
Edwards. No contact.

No. 1.
REPRODUCTION

No. 2.
REPRODUCTION

No. 3.
REPRODUCTION

*Figure 2*  Some results in Guthrie drawing experiments

percipient has produced a sunflower, is this to be judged a hit or not? Obviously there is a resemblance between target and reproduction but we are uncertain whether this resemblance is more than might occur accidentally, at least once in a number of experimental trials.

Looking at the Guthrie series of experiments, one is tempted to say that the Society for Psychical Research was lucky to have met in its early days with a drawing experiment which showed much better results than are typical of such experiments. Alternatively one might suggest that this was something of a misfortune for psychical research since it enabled those engaged in these experiments to avoid the real problems of assessing degree of success, and lured on other workers to use this method of research supposing that it was easier to get satisfactory results than it really was.

The difficulty of assessing the results of drawing experiments with a lower success rate than those of the early days of psychical research is not, of course, insuperable. It means only that the experimenter who uses this method of experimenting is likely to find that he must use a much more complicated method of discovering his degree of success than merely by looking for successful matches of reproduction with target.

The general principle underlying a valid method of estimating success is fairly simple although the application of it may be less simple. The essential point is that a comparison must be made between how often the subject draws, let us say, a mushroom when the target picture is a mushroom and how often he draws a mushroom when the target is not a mushroom. The details of how this comparison is carried out are determined by the experimenter. Any bias of the judge towards leniency or severity in awarding 'hits' will then not be in danger of producing a spurious indication of ESP. Provided that the essential precaution is taken of seeing that the judge (or judges) do not know what reproduction is meant for what target, leniency and severity will have the same effect on both sides of the comparison. At the same time, arbitrary or erratic judging might obliterate evidence for an ESP effect that was really there, so some discrimination must be exercised by the experimenter in the choice of judges, and some care must be exercised in the instruction given to judges as to how they should determine resemblances.

The unfortunate judge has a very laborious task. He must compare all the reproductions of the experiment with each of the target drawings and decide whether there is such a resemblance between them that he is inclined to record that reproduction as a hit on that target. He is motivated to take his judgments seriously by the consideration that if he misses significant resemblances he may be failing to extract evidence for ESP that is really there. The number of judgments he has to make is large, ten target pictures used with 100 percipients will require 10,000 judgments which must all be made by the same person (or persons). The experimenter cannot generally himself be judge since he cannot be sure that he does not know which pictures are meant for which targets. He must rely on his friends and colleagues to act as judges. For them, at least, the reproduction of drawings is not a trouble-free type of experiment.

As an example of an experiment on the reproduction of drawings of which the rate of success was so low that it required considerable effort to determine whether it was present at all, we may take the work of Whately Carington who did such an experiment in the early days of the last war (Whately Carington, 1941–2). His experiment differed from the early ones already discussed in the fact, that, instead of relying on one or more gifted subjects, Carington used as his subjects a large number of volunteers most of whom laid no claim to psychic gifts. Whatever method of experimenting is used, one has the choice between looking for good subjects or of applying the tests to a large group. One reason for Carington's choice of a large group was that he hoped to carry out a 'repeatable' experiment, that is, one of which the conditions could be exactly specified, and if carried out in the same way by someone else would give the same result. This hope was disappointed; there are probably too many imperfectly known conditions of psi-success for such a fully specified repeatable experiment to be yet possible, although it may prove to be an attainable goal sometime in the future. An obvious advantage of the use of the group method is that it is the only one available if we want to answer a number of questions about the distribution of psi-capacities through the population, between men and women, between the intelligent and the unintelligent, between the anxious and those free from anxiety, etc. Experiments on gifted subjects played a vital part in producing convincing evidence of the reality of psi-capacities, but when parapsychologists were able to regard that question as settled, they became more interested in the kind of question that can only be settled by experiments on groups of ordinary people. Experiments of that type have now, therefore, become common; they were relatively unusual when Whately Carington started his work.

Experiments on groups not selected for their paranormal capacities have the obvious disadvantage that the rate of scoring is likely to be relatively low and it therefore becomes necessary to adopt more complicated methods of assessing success. Also such results as are obtained will not be very dramatic and they may not be very strong evidence for the reality of the paranormal process under investigation. It is, I think, fair to say that Whately Carington's work on the reproduction of drawings did not produce any evidence for the reality of ESP that would have been by itself of value in producing conviction, although there was strong indication that ESP did have some effect in his experiments. They were, however, mainly important in drawing attention to curious and unsuspected characteristics of the ESP process which were afterwards fully confirmed by Soal's card-guessing experiments with Basil Shackleton which will be discussed in a later chapter.

In Carington's experiment, a picture was drawn by himself and hung in a locked room in his house during the night. His subjects were living near and far, some as far as the other side of the Atlantic. In each series of experiments, there was a different target picture for each of ten consecutive nights, and each of his subjects attempted all ten of the pictures.

He took one very proper precaution which had not been taken seriously by the early psychical researchers. In the Blackburn-Smith experiments it is recorded that the experimenter drew a picture 'at random'. This apparently means that he drew the first picture that came into his head. But there are few things less random than the processes of thought, and one cannot make a reasonable guess as to how likely it is that two people will think of drawing the same thing at the same time, especially if they are exposed to the same environment. There may, for example, be a case of mushroom poisoning reported in the newspapers which makes more probable the drawing of a mushroom by both experimenter and subject. To prevent such accidental coincidences causing a spurious indication of ESP, it is necessary that the targets should not be a product of the thinking of the experimenter but should be determined by some random process. The way that Whately Carington achieved this end was by making a random selection of a page in a dictionary and then drawing the first drawable object that was named on that page. There could thus be no rational ground for prediction as to what the target drawing on any night would be and no danger of a common influence producing parallelism between the drawings made by experimenter and percipients. There remains, of course, the possibility of common influences producing parallelisms between the drawings of different percipients on the same occasion so, if these are noticed, we must be very cautious about supposing that they are produced by ESP.

The judging of the drawings was done by the method already described, the same judge comparing all the reproductions and all the targets for a single experimental series without knowing which reproductions were meant for which targets. The instruction to the judges was that they should count as a hit any reproduction if it and the target with which it was compared 'unmistakably portrayed the same thing'. This was recorded as a mark of 1. A mark of 0 was given if they did not appear to portray the same thing, and a mark of $\frac{1}{2}$ could be given if the judge was doubtful whether a given pair should be marked as 1 or 0. The idea of these instructions was to make the judges' task as objective as possible but even the phrase 'unmistakably portray the same thing' is not entirely free from ambiguity. If the original was a rose and the reproduction was a daffodil, the judge might award a mark of 1 because both represented a flower, or 0 because they were not the same flower, or $\frac{1}{2}$ because he did not know whether to award a 1 or a 0. This unavoidable uncertainty is one of the factors that makes the judge's work difficult. Using criteria for judging that were either too rigid or too lenient might obscure real evidence for ESP. The judge can, however, console himself with the thought that errors of judging will not result in spurious evidence for ESP, since the judgment is made without knowledge of which are correct matches so any errors of judging will affect alike the hits on right targets and on wrong ones.

Whately Carington's first experiment of this type seemed to him to be yielding an odd result. Some of the matches seemed good but they were on the wrong targets, most often on a target that had not yet been drawn. This might have been a purely accidental effect, and no conclusion could properly be drawn from it. It did however suggest a possibility to be tested out in later experiments.

What Whately Carington suspected was that his experimental subjects were being influenced by paranormal knowledge of the targets exposed in his room, but that this knowledge was not necessarily of the target drawing which was exposed on the day they made their attempt at reproduction. A subject might, for example, make a drawing on Tuesday that seemed to resemble, not the target drawing exposed by Carington on Tuesday but perhaps the one exposed on Monday. It might even resemble the one that was going to be exposed on Wednesday, although the Wednesday target drawing had not, at that time, been drawn, and its subject matter had not been selected.

In order to test the truth of this suspicion, the question to be answered was not merely whether the drawings produced by the percipients were influenced by the target picture exposed on the night when the drawing was made, but also whether they were influenced by the pictures exposed on other nights of the experiment. For testing this possibility, Whately Carington carried out five experiments; the question he was now concerned with was whether percipients within any one experiment were more likely to make drawings resembling one of the target pictures belonging to that experiment than to make them resembling a target picture used in one of the four other experiments. To provide the required information, the judges now had to perform the more arduous task of comparing all the reproductions made in any experiment with all fifty target pictures of the whole series of experiments.

Whether there was a preference for the targets belonging to each percipient's own experiment could not be found out merely by casual inspection; the preference, if any, was not a very pronounced one. Whately Carington, however, did the arithmetic necessary to find out whether there was any such preference in his results, and he found clear indication that there was. In each of the five experimental series, there was an excess of hits on the percipients' proper set of targets. The total excess was thirty-eight, which does not indicate a very strong effect but it is unlikely to be an accidental one since a test of significance shows that this excess is of a size that would not occur by chance (i.e. without ESP or some other cause producing it) more often than about once in a thousand times.

While the evidence for some sort of paranormal cognition in this series of experiments is pretty strong, it would not, of course, be enough to give much support to the reality of ESP if we had no other evidence in its favour. One would then have to consider the possibility that this result was simply an example of a very unlikely chance having happened. But, since there is plenty of other evidence for ESP, the most likely explanation of Whately Carington's results is that they were due to ESP working in a rather odd and unexpected way. Their importance lies in the fact that this oddity of ESP causing hits on targets other than the one intended by the percipient has been abundantly confirmed in later experiments, particularly in those carried out by Dr Soal (see Chapter X).

So far, Whately Carington was using an experimental design which was rigorously correct but which imposed a heavy task on those he employed as judges. He later devised a simplification which relieved this burden on the judges but at the cost of sacrificing rigour. Instead of comparing hits on 'right and 'wrong' targets, he compared the frequency of objects drawn in each experiment with the frequency with which they had been drawn in his earlier experiments. These frequencies of drawings in earlier experiments were recorded in a catalogue, which Carington intended should be used by other experimenters and not only by himself. This may therefore be called the 'catalogue' method of assessing results (Whately Carington, 1944).

Let us suppose, for example, that a picture of a bear was the target in an experiment and that in 200 reproductions in that experiment a bear was drawn 10 times. Reference to the catalogue showed, however, that drawings of bears were liable to appear in experiments without bear targets once in 100 times. The expectation of a particular drawing being by chance a bear is therefore 1 in 100 (or 0·01), and the number we would expect to get in 200 reproductions would be 2. The observed excess of 8 above this expected number in the experiment we have imagined would, therefore, seem to be evidence of the causal influence of the presence of the bear target, i.e. of ESP.

At first sight this looks like an easier method of finding out how often percipients would draw a particular picture than that already described of counting hits on right and wrong targets. It would, however, only be a valid method if the catalogue responses had been classified by the same judge and at the same period of time, and that both experimental results and catalogue responses were derived from the same or a closely similar group of people. All of these factors might obviously affect the number of 'bear' responses: the judge because different judges might disagree in whether to classify as 'bear' a drawing of a koala or a shaggy dog, the period of time because the frequency of drawings of bears might be affected by such topical factors as whether the newspapers have recently been showing photographs of a baby bear born in the zoo, the social group because we have no grounds for assuming that bear drawings will be equally common among students and school children or among those who live and those who do not live within easy reach of a zoo. All these factors might affect the use of a catalogue in either direction; they might lead to an overestimation or an underestimation of the likelihood of a bear drawing appearing in an experiment whose results are compared with the catalogue. In either case they would make the comparison completely unreliable as a means of testing for the presence of ESP. I think that Whately Carington was mistaken in supposing that the catalogue method gave a reliable instrument for his own experiments and even more mistaken in thinking that it could be reliably used by other people.

Recent experimenters have not made very large use of the method of reproduction of drawings for ESP tests. They have probably been deterred by the difficulty of assessment of results and the common failure of such tests to yield the high scores that are hoped for. One exception to this tendency is the research of Dr M. C. Marsh in South Africa (Marsh, 1962). He did a well-controlled experiment on the reproduction of target drawings over a distance of 470 miles. He obtained a highly significant result with 133 hits on the targets used in the experiment as against 37 hits on an equal number of control targets.

A more recent investigation using this method was a carefully designed experiment carried out in 1967 by Sir Alister Hardy. The results of this experiment have not yet been published. It is clear, however, that they will not support the hope that the reproduction-of-drawings experiment is an easy road to striking success in demonstrating ESP.

## References

GUTHRIE, M. (1884), 'An Account of Some Experiments in Thought-transference', *Proceedings of the Society for Psychical Research*, ii, 24–42.

HALL, T. H. (1964), *The Strange Case of Edmund Gurney*, London.

MARSH, M. C. (1962), 'Three ESP Experiments Using Drawings as Target Material', *Publications of the South African Society for Psychical Research*, No. 5, 4–15.

SINCLAIR, UPTON (1930), *Mental Radio*, Pasadena.

WARCOLLIER, R. (1938), *Experimental Telepathy*, Boston (Mass.).

WHATELY CARINGTON, W. (1941–2), 'Experiments on the Paranormal Cognition of Drawings', *Proc. S.P.R.*, xlvi, 34–151, 277–334, and xlvii, 155–228.

WHATELY CARINGTON, W. (1944), 'Experiments on the Paranormal Cognition of Drawings', *Proceedings of the American Society for Psychical Research*, xxiv, 3–107.

# VI

# Other kinds of ESP experiment

Experimenters in ESP have explored a number of other ways of detecting and measuring ESP in addition to the methods of card-guessing and of reproduction of drawings. Partly their season for doing this has been that they have been dissatisfied with the older methods. Even without this dissatisfaction, there would be much to be said for trying to develop a variety of methods of attack on the problems of ESP. Only a sample of these attempts will be discussed here; the reader may himself think of something better than has yet been tried.

There are a number of considerations that the experimenter must bear in mind when he is selecting a method of experimenting in ESP. One that should not be overlooked is the usefulness for many purposes of being able to represent the degree of the success of the experiment by means of a number (see Appendix A). We may, for example, want to compare the success of one subject with that of another, or of percipients in one experimental condition with percipients in another condition, and so on. In trying to express results in a numerical form, the parapsychologist is doing what is also done in other branches of experimental science. It is sometimes said that psi is of such a nature that it eludes measurement. There may be a sense in which this is true, but degree of success in a psi-task can be measured. Also it must be measured if the experimentalist wants to be able to obtain definite answers to some of the questions he wants to ask. So of any new test of ESP, we must ask by what means we can attach a number to its results in order to indicate the degree of success in any particular application of it.

The ease with which a number can be assigned to indicate the rate of success is clearly an advantage of the card-guessing type of experiment. This is less easy in some other forms of experiment and it may not be possible in others. If the results of any test could only be evaluated in a non-quantitative way, this fact would seriously limit the usefulness of that test as a research tool.

Another obvious matter to consider in judging the value of a new experimental method is the question of how economical it is in experimental time. Other things being equal, the more information the experimenter can obtain about the ESP capacities of his subject or subjects in a given period, the better. A percipient may, for example, make a hundred guesses in a card-guessing experiment in the time he would take to make one drawing in a drawing-reproduction test. This suggests that, judged by this criterion of economy, the card-guessing test has a great advantage over the drawing-reproduction test. It is true that this advantage would disappear if there were such detailed correspondence between the drawing and the target in a reproduction test that one drawing gave the experimenter as much information as a hundred card guesses. Unhappily such detailed correspondence between target and attempted reproduction is not generally found in experimental practice.

Another choice facing the experimenter in which considerations of economy must enter is that between experimenting on a group or on an individual. It is obvious that a group experiment will be much more economical in experimenter's time than an individual experiment if both have the same rate of scoring. It is true that this advantage of the group experiment may disappear if, as is commonly the case, the individual experiment is carried out on a gifted subject who has a high rate of scoring. Even so, the group experiment may be preferred for other reasons, because, for example, it answers some question that cannot be answered by the results of a single individual.

Further, any useful experimental method should have a characteristic which I propose to call 'fruitfulness'. This means that it should be productive of good scoring when it is applied to a subject whose ESP capacity is good. That an experimental subject can succeed in some ESP tasks does not imply that he will succeed in any task that we can think up. If we devise a new ESP experiment, we may be demanding success in a task that no one can succeed in. This may be of interest at a later stage of research when we want to identify the limits of ESP performance, but it is of no use as a means of ESP measurement. We must test a new test by seeing how well people can succeed in it. It has always been one of the reasons for the attractiveness of the reproduction-of-drawings type of test that it has been supposed that it will prove much more fruitful than card-guessing; as has already been pointed out, this hope does not seem to have been fulfilled.

The method must also be as economical as possible not only in experimental time but also in the time spent in subsequent checking and evaluation. Card-guessing is very economical in checking since all that is required is the observation of whether a guess has the same symbol as the target. For reproduction of drawings, checking may take many hours of a judge's time for a relatively small amount of experimental information. This, however, is not all. Every quantitative experiment requires arithmetical work to estimate how well the subjects have succeeded and also to estimate the significance of any success obtained, i.e. how likely it is that the observed success might have been produced by chance. These processes of calculation can take up a lot of the experimenter's time, and, in choosing the type of experiment to be used, it is right that he should consider how to effect economy in this time. One way of achieving this end would be that he should have an experiment in which there was so much success that he would be under no necessity to consider whether the success could be accidental; it would be obvious that it was not. This is found in practice not to be easy to achieve. Even with a very high rate of success, it is difficult to avoid the necessity for some process of calculation; the experimenter may need to perform a calculation to justify the statement that his result is so good that it can be accepted without any mathematical argument as to whether it might be a chance effect.

One must not forget the necessity for a design of experiment that can be subjected to rigorous controls to eliminate the possibility that success might result from some other cause than ESP (such, for example, as unintended sensory communication). This may be called the requirement of 'rigidity'. Rigidity is more a matter of detailed design than of the type of experiment to be chosen; any type of experiment that could not be subjected to the requirements of rigidity would be unlikely to be considered at all by a serious experimenter.

In order to be useful an experiment should also be well adapted to answering as large a number as possible of the questions we are likely to want to ask in our research. In judging how suitable for research purposes is a particular type of experiment, one should ask such questions as: how could this type of experiment be used to test precognitive ESP, or the possibility of ESP hitting targets not intended by the subject (Whately Carington's 'displacement' effect), or to distinguish between success under telepathic or clairvoyant conditions, or the inhibition of psi-responses and the conditions under which such inhibition takes place, etc., etc. This quality in an experiment may be called its 'adaptability'. No doubt the two types of experiment already discussed are adaptable to some extent to all the questions mentioned above; some of the types of experiment to be mentioned later are not so readily adaptable. This may be a serious impediment to their usefulness as instruments of research.

I think one should also mention a requirement that may be judged trivial, that the experience of doing the experiment should be as pleasant as possible to the subject and also to the experimenter. Other things being equal, this is a point worth considering. It is not only a good thing to maximise happiness; it may also have reactions on the other criteria as, for example, on fruitfulness. A subject may be unable to give a good ESP performance because he is bored with the task he is required to do. It is an advantage of the reproduction-of-drawings experiment that subjects are much less bored by this task than they often are by the requirement to go on guessing five kinds of card. It may be argued that, in this case, the happiness of the experimental subject is purchased at the price of unhappiness of the person who has to act as judge, but any unhappiness of the judge is less likely to affect the fruitfulness of the experiment. In designing a new type of experiment, the pleasantness of the task is one of the points to be considered.

There is one other requirement of tests of ESP about which there has been much controversy and some misunderstanding. This is the condition of 'repeatability'. In an ordinary physical experiment, such as that of determining the acceleration due to gravity at the earth's surface, we have only to specify how the experiment is to be set up to be sure that anyone carrying it out will (within the limits of error of his observations) get the same result. Such an experiment is completely repeatable. No experiment in parapsychology is repeatable in that sense; one can specify the conditions in which one has oneself obtained a successful ESP result without any strong conviction that everyone else who tries will get the same result.

How much does this matter ? It is sometimes said that parapsychology will only be admitted as a science when its experiments are completely repeatable. So far as this is a question of the prestige of parapsychology it is obviously unimportant; it may be that there is an insuperable barrier to parapyschological experiments being repeatable in the sense in which physical experiments are repeatable.

On the other hand, it must be admitted that it would be a considerable experimental convenience if experiments in psychical research were as repeatable as physical experiments, or failing that, that they should be as repeatable as possible. Getting precise answers to questions raised in experimental psychical research is made more difficult by the fact that the results of an experimental set-up are somewhat unpredictable even for a single experimenter and still more unpredictable from one experimenter's results to another's.

It is, however, not altogether true to say that experiments in parapsychology are unrepeatable. If a given experiment is set up by one person with a certain result, we can at least say that other experimenters are likely to get the same result in the same situation. For example, Dr Schmeidler many years ago (Schmeidler and McConnell, 1958) found that, on average, those of her subjects who believed in the possibility of ESP (the 'sheep') scored better than those who did not believe (the 'goats'). A number of other investigators have asked themselves the same question; some of these have not got the same result as Dr Schmeidler has reported, but a considerable number have got her result. The experiment has proved itself not to be completely repeatable but considerably more repeatable than the more pessimistic writers about the repeatability of parapsychological experiments would suppose. It is not an unreasonable aim in experimentation in this subject to try to get experiments as repeatable as possible. Some of the ways in which this has been attempted will be discussed later. It must be remembered that the test of repeatability is not that the experimenter claims that he has, at last, designed a repeatable experiment (this claim has been too often made), but that the experiment has, in fact, been successfully repeated by a number of workers other than the original experimenter.

These basic criteria which I have set out above, provide us with standards by means of which the value of innovations in experimental method may be judged. A number of new methods of experimenting have been tried out in the recent past; more are likely to be explored in the future. It may well be that one will be discovered outstandingly better than those in current use; no such outstandingly superior experimental method seems to have been discovered yet.

One of the minor experimental innovations that has been introduced recently has been made by the Czech experimenter Dr Rýzl (1962). He has abandoned the five-target choice introduced by Rhine and used a two-target choice instead. This entails some loss of sensitivity, as did Rhine's change from fifty-two targets to five, but this will be unimportant if there is a resulting increase of scoring rate. In fact, Dr Rýzl's subject has shown much higher scoring than any recent experimental subject but it may be doubted whether this is due to the use of only two targets; Dr Rýzl has also introduced a method of training his subjects which may account for the higher scoring rate. It may, on the other, not be due to the method of experimenting but to the fact that the experimenter has been lucky in working with especially gifted experimental subjects. Whether the two-target type of experiment is generally fruitful must be found out by trying it in comparative experiments with five-target choices using a number of experimental subjects. If it proves to be an unusually fruitful method, it will have further advantages with respect to the third criterion since the arithmetic for a two-choice system is somewht easier than that for a five-choice system.

A more radical innovation in card-guessing experiments was made by Fisk when he introduced 'clock' cards (Fisk and Mitchell, 1953). These were cards bearing a picture of a clock face with an hour hand pointing to exactly one of the hours, the percipient guessing to which of the twelve hours the clock hand was pointing. The point of this new type of card was that it could be used as a means of differential scoring in which some credit was given for near misses as well as for an exact hit on the correct hour. It was hoped that such differential scoring would increase the sensitivity of the test. This is not necessarily the case. If the tendency of ESP is 'all-or-nothing', that is, to succeed completely or not at all, there will be no good result from counting partial successes, they will merely dilute the information given by successes. We can only tell whether there has been any gain in sensitivity by Fisk's method of counting partial successes by trying the method out. In the first experiments already referred to, there did seem to be some gain by the use of the differential scoring method, but, in a later series of experiments, a better result was found when only complete hits were scored than when partial successes were taken into account (West and Fisk, 1953). There is, however, no doubt that this method of scoring is open to the objection that it increases the labour of evaluating results. There seems to be no clear evidence that this increased labour is compensated for by a gain in sensitivity, so this method of experiment has not been used much by other workers.

Another experimental series by a method which has not been adopted by other people was that by G. N. M. Tyrrell in which a machine was used with five black boxes and the task of the percipient was to guess which of the boxes would contain a lighted lamp. The first part of this experimental series was defective since the correct box was chosen by the experimenter, and rigidity of design demands that the target series should be determined by some random method. With the experimenter choosing the target, we cannot predict how many of his choices will coincide with those of the percipient by chance alone; both may have a preference for the middle three boxes and a tendency to avoid the two outside ones. This fault in design was overcome when Tyrrell introduced a mechanical commutator into his circuit so that the target box no longer depended on his choice (Tyrrell, 1936). After a period of adaptation, his subject was successful with the commutator, and scored 178 hits above mean chance expectation in 4,200 trials. This excess of 4·25 per cent is good but not spectacular. The excess is highly significant—i.e. not of a size reasonably to be attributed to chance. Tyrrell's research design included another novelty in his use of mechanical recording of success and failure on a paper tape.

Although Tyrrell's work marks an important advance in showing that mechanical selection of targets and recording of results did not interfere with ESP success, his own machine is not likely to be used by any future research worker. Modern electronic devices provide more convenient machinery for mechanical ESP testing.

Another test which has not been used by other workers and which perhaps will prove to have no qualities to recommend it to other workers is my own 'picture construction' test of ESP. This was an attempt to combine the advantages of the card-guessing and picture-reproduction types of experiment (Thouless, 1966). In the first form of this test, the task of the subject was to combine four picture strips in such an order as to match a target which was one of the possible twenty-four permutations of the strips. My hope was that the creative character of this task would make it possible for those subjects to succeed who found ordinary card-guessing mechanical and boring, and that the rate of success would be high enough to compensate for the obviously small amount of information given by each attempt. The first aim was achieved; subjects found it a more interesting task than card-guessing. The second and more important aim was not achieved; so far subjects have only scored at chance level. If this is a characteristic of the test, it is of no use. It may, however, be the result of the fact that I as experimenter am now completely inhibited from getting positive psi-results. The final test must be to see whether other people can succeed in using this test.

In the hope that they will try, I add here as Figure 3 my latest form of this test. It is simpler than that previously published because I thought it better to use a system of pictures that could be easily visualised. I suggest that the targets should be the twenty-four pictures that can be made by the permutation of these strips taken three at a time. The percipient would be given all four strips and instructed to select three of them and to try to arrange them so as to match the target picture. If it turns out that this test continues unfruitful it must be forgotten, but if it works it might be a useful adjunct for the experimenter who wants to work with subjects who are strongly hostile to the idea of guessing cards. There is a one-in-twenty-four chance of accidental success so the arithmetic of evaluation is as simple as that of the card-guessing experiment unless one is tempted to follow Fisk in evaluating partial successes (which I do not recommend).

The most important recent innovation in ESP testing methods is that of the Russian group of experimenters of whom the best known is the late Professor Vasiliev, Professor of Physiology at Leningrad (Vasiliev, 1963). Their main method of experimenting was based on an observation made many years ago by Pierre Janet that he could put one of his patients into a hypnotic trance without her consent when she was at a distance and had no normal knowledge of his intention. Such hypnotisation without the use of any sensory signals was found by the Russian workers to be a reliable method of demonstrating ESP provided the experimental subject is one who has been frequently hypnotised by the experimenter. The evidence of ESP in the telepathic form (or 'mental suggestion' in Vasiliev's terms) is the coincidence in time of the experimenter's mental command and the falling asleep (or the waking) of the experimental subject. The special advantage of this type of experiment is with respect to the last criterion mentioned above, that of repeatability. The Russian experimenters were, in fact, able to answer criticism by demonstrating their experiment successfully before a critical audience. This would not yet be possible by using an experiment of the card-guessing or similar type.

On the other hand, the Russian 'mental suggestion' method has, to balance this advantage, certain grave defects with respect to other criteria which make it quite unsuitable for adoption as a standard experiment. It is not readily adaptable to a variety of parapsychological problems. It is a reliable indication of telepathy and was used by the Russians for testing the possibility of telepathic communication being screened by metal plates as one would expect if it depended on the transmission of any form of electro-magnetic wave. For this question it was a suitable method and it gave a clear answer; none of the screening methods used had any effect on the telepathic transmission. It is difficult, however, to see how the

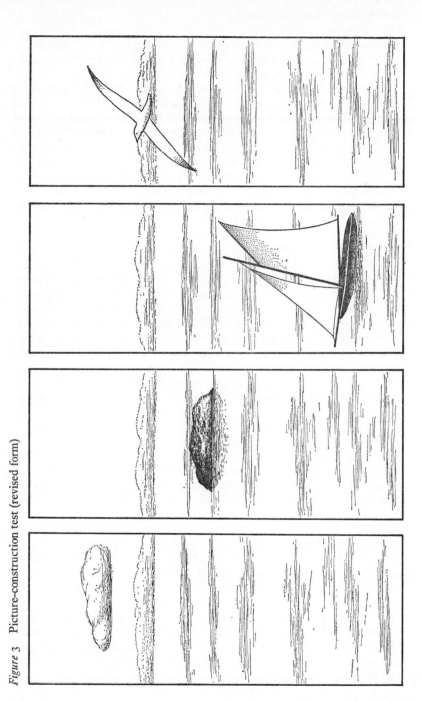

*Figure 3*   Picture-construction test (revised form)

experiment could be adapted to test ESP under clairvoyance conditions, or under precognitive conditions, or to answer any of the questions that will be discussed later, on chronological decline, displacement, psi-missing, etc. Apart from its lack of adaptability, the use of this method of experimenting as a standard one in parapsychological laboratories would raise the ethical question of whether subjecting percipients to a degree of hypnotic control that made them hypnotisable by the unexpressed command of the experimenter might not be injurious to the experimental subject. It seems very likely that that would be the case.

We may, therefore, recognise the work reported by Vasiliev as a solid achievement in experimental psychical research, and welcome it as a method well adapted to the solution of some problems, without considering that it is a possible form of standard experimental procedure for future research.

The last new method of experimenting which may be more widely developed in future is the use of computers as tools in experimental research. This use, already considerable, will no doubt increase in future. It is sometimes felt that mechanised target selection and response recording make it possible for the first time to devise a really rigid demonstration of the reality of ESP. This opinion is, I think, mistaken. Its underlying assumptions that machines cannot make mistakes and that human operators cannot be accurate within the required limits would seem to be both mistaken. Mechanical recording does not necessarily add anything to the confidence that one can feel in results obtained by a reliable human experimenter who has been careful to observe the experimental rules discussed in Chapter III.

The machine has, however, a great advantage over the human experimenter in the large amount of experimental data that can be obtained in a short time. If the machine can be made as error-proof as a careful human experimenter, and if the mechanisation of testing does not inhibit the ESP responses of the experimental subjects, mechanised psi-testing has obvious practical advantages. From results already obtained, it is apparent that there is no ground for the fear that mechanised testing necessarily inhibits psi.

An example of a successful ESP experiment using machinery for the presentation of targets (but not for their production) and for the recording and checking of responses is one carried out by Dr Kahn at Harvard (Kahn, 1952). The machine used in this case was a form of IBM called the International Test Scoring Machine; 177 subjects were used who made a total of 43,278 guesses with an excess of 271·4 hits over mean chance expectation. This is a highly significant result obtained under conditions which completely exclude the possibility of guidance by unintended sensory cues or other factor alternative to ESP. It makes clear that machine recording and presentation do not necessarily inhibit ESP. The rate of scoring is not high; the percentage excess of hits over mean chance expectation is about ·6. This compares unfavourably with the results obtained by Martin and Stribic (1940) in Colorado in a comparable experiment but with human operators, which had a three per cent excess of hits.

It would, however, obviously be wrong to draw from this single comparison the conclusion that machine testing is necessarily a relatively unfruitful method of psi-testing. A more hopeful prospect for machine testing is opened by the recently published work of Helmut Schmidt (1969). Dr Schmidt used a mechanised precognition test with three subjects selected by previous success in a psi-task. In a four-target task, his subjects succeeded at a rate of 1·2 per cent over mean chance expectation on a total of over 73,000 guesses. In the task of attempting to guess wrong, two subjects succeeded on over 9,000 guesses in getting 2·3 per cent below mean chance expectation. The significance of these results is very high.

A possible future use of machine methods in ESP experimenting is that they may provide a method of ESP training. It would be of great value to the research if we could discover reliable methods of training subjects so that they could voluntarily produce psi-responses. In ordinary learning tasks, learning is found to take place by rewarding correct responses; the reward for a human subject need be no more than giving him the information that he has been right. But such methods are not followed by learning in ESP tasks. There would seem to be two possible respects in which the situation of being subject in an ESP experiment might be unfavourable to learning. First, there is the fact that the reward of knowing when one is right does not normally immediately follow the right response, and, secondly, at a low rate of scoring only a small proportion of the hits are psi-determined. The remainder are accidental and it may be inimical to learning that a large number of accidentally right responses are rewarded as well as the occasional psi-determined right response. With machine testing it is easy to arrange that the rewarding information is given immediately after the response. If, in addition, one could achieve an experimental design so that the majority of the rewarded responses were psi-determined, one should have created a situation favourable to psi-learning. This, however, is an end for future research; it has not yet been achieved.

In addition to its possible usefulness for presenting or producing targets and recording results in ESP experiments, electronic machinery is likely to play an increasing part in the evaluation of results. Dr Pratt's study of the interrelations of response and targets in various positions in Soal's experiment with Mrs Stewart as percipient is a good example of a computer providing answers to parapsychological questions more complex than could be dealt with economically by a human calculator (Pratt, 1967). As was said earlier, economy of time spent in evaluation of results is one of the criteria by which an experimental method must be judged, and the amount of calculation that can be done in a given time may be enormously increased by computerised techniques. The complexity of mathematical treatment of results that is possible in a parapsychological research is much greater if the experimenter relies on a computer for this side of his activity. As experimenters do increasingly use computers in the future, it is to be expected that they will undertake experiments of a design more complex than was customary in the past.

I have tried to show here that there has been a good deal of activity in exploring new methods of ESP experimenting. If designs of the card-guessing type have remained the most commonly used basic method, this is not because there has been no search for substitutes but because so far nothing has turned up better on an all-round evaluation. The activity of exploring new methods will, no doubt, go on and it may, in the future, produce a new and better type of experiment than any of the existing ones.

## References

FISK, G. W., and MITCHELL, A. M. J. (1953), 'ESP Experiments with Clock Cards', *Journal of the Society for Psychical Research*, xxxvii, 1–14.

KAHN, S. D. (1952), 'Studies in Extrasensory Perception: Experiments Utilizing an Electronic Scoring Device', *Proceedings of the American Society for Psychical Research*, xxv, 1–48.

MARTIN, DOROTHY R., and STRIBIC, FRANCES P. (1940), 'Studies in Extrasensory Perception. III.', *Journal of Parapsychology*, iv, 159–248.

PRATT, J. G. (1967), 'Computer Studies of the ESP Process in Card Guessing: I. Displacement Effects in Mrs. Gloria Stewart's Records', *Journal of the American Society for Psychical Research*, lxi, 25–46.

RÝZL, M. (1962), 'Training the Psi Faculty by Hypnosis', *J. S.P.R.*, xli, 234–51.

SCHMEIDLER, GERTRUDE R., and MCCONNELL, R. A. (1958), *Extrasensory Perception and Personality Patterns*, New Haven and London.

SCHMIDT, H. (1969), 'Precognition of a Quantum Process', *J. Parapsych.*, xxxiii, 99–108.

THOULESS, R. H. (1966), 'The Picture Construction Test for ESP', *J. S.P.R.*, xliii, 422–7.

TYRRELL, G. N. M. (1936), 'Further Research in Extra-sensory Perception', *Proc. S.P.R.*, xliv, 99–168.

VASILIEV, L. L. (1963), *Experiments in Mental Suggestion* (English translation), Church Crookham.

WEST, D. J., and FISK, G. W. (1953), 'A Dual ESP Experiment with Clock Cards', *J. S.P.R.*, xxxvii, 185–97.

# VII

# Stage simulation of ESP

One reason for the doubt which some people feel about the experimental evidence for extra-sensory perception is that they have seen conjurors produce results which looked to them exactly like tasks performed by telepathy or clairvoyance. These being admittedly tricks, and the precautions against sensory communication seeming to the audience to be adequate, they are inclined to wonder whether any experimental set-up can really ensure that the ordinary senses cannot be used. Is not every experimenter in this field at the mercy of any experimental subject who is a skilful conjuror?

This, of course, is to overestimate the power of the conjuror, and it is a tribute to the skill of conjurors that people are so ready to overestimate their skill. But on the stage they impose their own conditions, and however adequate these may look, they are such as to leave loopholes for ordinary sensory communication. If these loopholes were apparent to the audience, it would be a poor trick. Many methods are available to the conjuror: substitutions of objects, communications from a confederate by means of a code or by using a small wireless receiving set, etc. (Goldston, 1934). In the conditions of an adequately controlled experiment, all such possibilities are eliminated. The experimenter determines the conditions, not the percipient. If the experimental precautions are adequate, the percipient may be the most skilful conjuror in the world, but he will find that he is working under conditions in which his skill cannot be exercised.

While this is true of a properly controlled experiment, it is not, of course, true of the psychical researcher's observation of an ostensibly paranormal spontaneous event taking place under circumstances not under his control. Then his judgment as to the reality of the phenomenon observed is vitiated by the impossibility of the continuous observation that would be necessary to detect skilful trickery. A good historical example of how this failure of continuous observation could lead intelligent and careful people to make erroneous reports as to what has really happened is provided by S. J. Davey's studies in 'spirit-writing' on slates (Hodgson, 1892). This should be read by all who want to understand how easily deceived one may be in reporting events that are under the control of some person other than oneself. From such errors the experimenter is saved by keeping the conditions of his experiment under his own control.

It is perhaps natural that most (though not all) conjurors should be inclined to imagine that every ESP experiment is a trick of some kind. They are accustomed to trick ESP and are inclined to approach any ESP performance as just another trick. I have heard that a British conjuror made the boast that he could succeed by trickery in the situation of the subject Basil Shackleton in the Soal-Goldney experiment. But he did not make his boast good. I understand from Dr Soal that when the opportunity has been offered him, he has made excuses for not trying at that time.

One must, of course, distinguish between the conjuror producing an apparent telepathy or clairvoyant phenomenon by trickery, and the fraudulent medium who performs a similar trick with the intention of imposing on his audience. The difference is a moral one. The conjuror would be infringing the ethical standards of his profession if he pretended that his results were due to anything but trickery; the fraudulent medium has no such scruples. The borderline between the two cases is not always as sharp as it should be. I have myself seen a performance of trick thought-reading which was advertised as a demonstration of telepathy and opened by the performer telling the audience that he had learned the method of using telepathy in a monastery in Tibet. He might have defended this introduction as being merely a part of the technique of showmanship but it is open to the objection that it blurs the dividing line between honest conjuring and fraudulent mediumship. A person wholly ignorant of conjuring methods might have been led to suppose that he had seen a genuine psi-performance.

The essential point of a good conjuring trick is that it shall lead the person who has seen it to report that something has happened which has not in fact happened. Generally the event as reported is one that is, in fact, impossible. For example, a well-known trick may be reported as follows: 'The conjuror held up a square piece of paper and cut a circular bit out of the middle of it. Then he crumpled in his hand the cut paper and the cut-out circle, and when he unfolded it the paper was just as it was at the beginning with nothing cut out.' This is plainly a physical impossibility. The report is incorrect since it mixes up what was seen and what was inferred. A correct report would be: 'I saw the conjuror cut a circle out of a piece of paper. Then I saw him crumple the piece of paper and the cut-out circle together in his hand. Then I saw him open an uncut piece of paper. I inferred that this uncut piece of paper was the same as the original paper that was cut.'

In performances of simulated ESP on the stage, it is also the case that the uncritical member of the audience will describe the performer as having done something that, in fact, he has not done. The report will, for example, be of the performer's assistant giving a description of some object held by the performer, although he could not see the object and no signals of any kind passed between them. This certainly is not an impossibility if we admit the reality of ESP, but it is unlikely to be a correct account of what happened. A report which included only what was observed and not what was inferred would not be of no signal having passed but of no signal having been noticed. A critical observer who is familiar with the literature of ESP would be likely to suspect that, in the stage performance, unnoticed signals did pass between the performer and his assistant because both the rate and the constancy of their success are higher than those commonly found in ESP experiments.

Some performances of simulated ESP are good spectacles, particularly those depending on the use of a memorised code which may easily lead the uncritical observer to suppose that he has seen genuine feats of extra-sensory communication. There are also trivial tricks which would not deceive any alert observer. One may, for example, prearrange the cards of an ESP pack so that the five symbols succeed each other in regular order, then invite someone to give the pack a thorough shuffle and undertake to guess each card turned up by someone else provided that, after each guess, one is told whether the guess is right or wrong. A surprisingly high rate of scoring can be obtained by this method; it depends, of course, on the guesser knowing that most of the sequences will be very imperfectly broken up by what the shuffler regards as a 'thorough shuffle'. As a trick, the method is crude and easily seen through; it is not to be supposed that any professional magician would think it worth performing. As a demonstration of ESP it is so obviously worthless that the most innocent experimenter would not be satisfied with its precautions. Yet an 'experiment' of this type was demonstrated at a scientific gathering in London, with apparently the implication that this was a sample of the ways in which experimenters in ESP were deceived. Any experimenter who allowed an experimental subject to provide his own pack of cards and who gave him information as to his success during his guessing would deserve to be deceived. But also he would not deserve to be called an 'experimenter'.

In Great Britain in 1949 there was a remarkable increase in public interest in telepathy stimulated by stage and broadcast performances by the Australian performers Mr and Mrs Piddington. Many people believed that these performers were genuinely demonstrating telepathy and even that their performances provided evidence for the reality of telepathy (Braden, 1949). These opinions were not shared generally by psychical researchers or by professional conjurors (Osborn, 1949). No doubt these performances had high entertainment value. In all cases, however, they were done under conditions of the performers' choosing and could not, therefore, be regarded as evidence of genuine extra-sensory powers. Although the Society for Psychical Research offered to make a test of the Piddingtons on its own premises and under conditions of the Society's choosing, this offer was not accepted by the Piddingtons.

Perhaps the feat which made the greatest impression on the public was one in which Mrs Piddington was in a dungeon of the Tower of London under observation and reproduced a sentence which had been chalked on a blackboard in the studio and read to wireless listeners. It is obvious that to make the performance entertaining, it was necessary that the sentence should be read to listeners before Mrs Piddington made her attempt at reproduction, but the fact that this was done would make the test worthless as evidence, however carefully the sentence may have been chosen to ensure that it was not pre-arranged. No examination of Mrs Piddington's clothes or hair seems to have been made to ensure that she had not a wireless receiving set concealed on her person.

Certainly no one could prove that these performances were not due to telepathy; that would be difficult to demonstrate anyway and impossible under the conditions of a public performance. So it was not unreasonable for anyone to maintain that he believed that telepathy was really used. What would be quite unreasonable would be to maintain that they provided any sort of evidence for telepathy, and many considerations led psychical researchers to hold the opinion that probably telepathy did not enter into the performance at all; the performances did not seem to be essentially different from known conjuring methods, and the Piddingtons were not willing to submit to test under strictly controlled conditions. Mr Piddington, himself, made no definite claim to be using paranormal means; he said the audience must be the judge. It is interesting to learn from Mr Braden's book that Mr Piddington had practised conjuring as a schoolboy and took it up again to entertain his fellow prisoners in a Japanese prisoner-of-war camp where also he distinguished himself by the skill with which he concealed parts of prohibited wireless sets on his person during inspections.

More puzzling to the audience than performances of trick telepathy are those of trick clairvoyance, such as demonstrations of 'eyeless sight'. A performer may, for example, allow both eyes to be covered with dough, patches of lint to be placed over the dough, a wide elastic bandage bound tightly over these, and finally three triangular bandages folded and tied over the top of everything else. With his head so swathed in bandages, he may copy sentences or diagrams written on a blackboard or pick up objects accidentally dropped on the floor. I have found even intelligent observers of such a performance who were convinced that the performer was really using ESP since he could not possibly see with his eyes so covered with dough, lint, elastic bandage, and triangular bandages. But in so describing his conditions of vision, we are mixing observation with inference. The three outer bandages are indeed seen throughout the performance; the other obstacles to vision are inferred because they were seen in place at the beginning and the end of the performance. The critical observer might wonder what purpose was served by the outer bandages since they add nothing to the difficulty of normal vision; if the performer could see at all, he could see between them. Such an observer might indeed be tempted to think that perhaps their purpose was to conceal from the audience what was happening during the performance to the other impediments to vision. These reflections would not, of course, affect his judgment of the performance as first-class entertainment. If he could guess how it was done, he would not have the illusion that he could do it himself.

If he were challenged to say what extra precautions he would take if he were performing an experiment to see whether this individual was really using ESP, the answer might well be that he would not take additional precautions but different ones, and that these would be of his own choosing and not chosen by the person to be tested. He might start by cutting out the three top bandages. If this did not cut out the apparent clairvoyance, he would try other methods of preventing normal sight, such as enclosing the head of the subject in a light-proof bag which did not interfere with breathing. He would only be satisfied of the reality of the performer's clairvoyant powers when they persisted under conditions chosen by the experimenter to exclude normal vision.

The fact that various forms of trickery are used in stage performances of 'telepathy' and 'clairvoyance' obviously does not imply that no stage performers have genuine ESP capacities. It may well be that, in some cases, what led them to take to these performances as a way of earning their living was the discovery that they had paranormal powers of reading other people's thoughts or of finding lost objects. Others may be led to the less reputable occupation of fraudulent mediumship for the same reason. In both cases, such individuals are likely to find their extra-sensory capacities are not reliable enough to be the sole means of getting their effects, so they may largely supplement them (or replace them altogether) by trickery. It might remain true that occasional successes were obtained by ESP; such successes, even though only occasional, might well make the performances considerably more impressive by adding to it an element of the inexplicable.

If there is anything in this idea, it would suggest one practical consequence for the experimental psychical researcher. He is always looking out for gifted subjects; the variety stage might be a good direction in which to look. It is true, of course, that he would have to be sure that his experimental precautions were adequate against any possibility of trickery on the part of his subjects. This, however, would be no new requirement; precautions should be adequate for this purpose in any ESP experiment. An example of a preliminary experimental investigation of the ESP powers of a stage performer is given in Appendix B.

There is a further possibility that may be worth consideration for future research. It would be a great convenience to experimenters if a reliable training for producing good ESP subjects were known. It is possible that we might get a hint of a possible method of training from the variety stage. There are some suggestions (not yet tested experimentally) that the use of a code for indicating objects, as is done in trick telepathy, may lead to the subject short-circuiting the code and naming the object directly by ESP. It is easy to see that this might happen if ESP is a possibility. The use of a code is laborious and this laboriousness would provide the percipient with a motive to short-circuit it if this were possible.

There are some indications that something of this sort may sometimes happen. There is, for example, a hint of it in Blackburn's account of the performances before a committee of the Society for Psychical Research in which Blackburn claimed to have communicated with the ostensible percipient Smith by means of a code: 'Smith and I, by constant practice, became so sympathetic that we frequently brought off startling hits, which were nothing but flukes.' These were apparently hits not determined by the code, but Blackburn's uncritical acceptance of them as 'flukes' is no more firmly based than would be the opposite conviction that they were evidence of the operation of ESP. Which of these they were could only be determined by a statistical enquiry into whether they exceeded in number or detail the amount of correspondence that could reasonably be attributed to chance. The fact that Blackburn found them 'startling' suggests that they may have been beyond reasonable chance expectation. Also it may be noticed that increasing 'sympathy' between the two operators might increase ESP between them, but not the likelihood of chance coincidences.

The suggestion that trick telepathy performances using codes might provide a good model for training procedures in ESP may prove to have nothing in it. But we do badly need a reliable training method and, for this end, it may be worth while for psychical researchers to explore rather wild paths as well as the more obvious ones.

## References

BRADEN, R. (1949), *The Piddingtons*, London.

GOLDSTON, W. (1934), *A Magician's Swan Song*, London.

HODGSON, R. (1892), 'Mr. Davey's Imitations by Conjuring of Phenomena Sometimes Attributed to Spirit Agency', *Proceedings of the Society for Psychical Research*, viii, 253–310.

OSBORN, E. (E. O.) (1949), 'The Piddingtons', *Journal of the Society for Psychical Research*, xxxv, 116–19.

# VIII
# Distinguishing between
# ESP and chance coincidence

When the first reports were made of successes in the early experiments on telepathy, suggestions that these were the result of unconscious whispering by the experimenter were not unreasonable. It is no longer a possible kind of explanation of the results that have been obtained in modern ESP tests since many of these have been carried out under conditions in which no explanation by unconscious whispering or other minimal sensory cues is possible. Obvious examples are those experiments in which the percipient calls 'down through' a pack of cards unseen by the experimenter until the calling is complete, or when his task is to predict the future order of a pack of cards which is afterwards shuffled.

Also an earlier possibility which is no longer a possible explanation is that apparently successful results are due to unconscious errors in recording. This could be an explanation of experiments in which the person recording the calls has knowledge of the target or in which the person recording the targets has knowledge of the calls. There are now a large number of successful experiments in which neither of these conditions is fulfilled, so recording errors could not have affected their results.

Unconscious sensory cues and recording errors can no longer be regarded as live alternatives to the ESP hypothesis by anyone with a good knowledge of the experimental literature. There remain two possible explanations to be considered: deliberate fraud by experimenters (to be discussed in Chapter XI), and that the whole appearance of positive results in ESP experiments is due to misinterpretation of what are in fact merely chance coincidences.

The possibility of explanation by chance coincidence arises from the fact that the evidence for ESP, whether spontaneous or experimental, is always an observed correspondence between some element of a person's behaviour and some event outside himself. The element of behaviour in question may be the naming of a card or a statement that the percipient's mother is ill. If the percipient's response is a correct one and the card named is also the target card, or if the mother does turn out to have been ill at the time of the statement, and if there is no possibility of sensory communication or rational inference having produced the correspondence, then we are left with the alternative that the correspondence was a result of ESP or that it was a chance coincidence. To make a decision between these possibilities, we must be able to estimate how likely is the explanation by chance coincidence; only if this is very unlikely can we safely conclude that the observed correspondence is due to ESP.

In the case of correspondence between a statement that the mother is ill and the fact of her being ill, only an uncertain and subjective estimate can be made. The likelihood of an accidental correspondence between the statement and the fact will obviously depend on such factors as how often the mother is ill and how often the daughter makes such despondent statements about her mother's health, as well as on how close in time were the onset of illness and the daughter's statement about it. In making an estimate of how likely is the coincidence explanation, we are likely to be hampered by the fact that we lack accurate information on these points so the estimate cannot be made definite.

This indefiniteness is not present if we want to make a similar estimate in the card-guessing situation. An application of elementary probability theory can give us definite answers to two questions. The first is that of how many guesses the percipient is likely to get right if he is merely getting them right by chance (the *mean chance expectation*). The second question arises only if he gets a number right which differs from mean chance expectation. Then we must answer the question as to how unlikely it is that the observed excess (or deficiency) of right guesses is the result of mere chance (the *significance* of the apparent success). Only if the likelihood of chance production of the difference from mean chance expectation is low, will the experimenter be tempted to look for a cause (such as ESP) for the observed deviation.

These questions face the experimental parapsychologist whenever he has carried out what looks like a successful ESP experiment. Let us suppose that, with adequate primary precautions, he has found that a percipient has guessed thirty right in one hundred guesses of the standard ESP cards. There are five equally probable target cards, so, if chance alone were determining the percipient's guesses, we should expect him to be right about one-fifth of the number of times he guesses and wrong in the remaining four-fifths of his guesses. Thus his mean chance expectation is twenty right in a hundred trials. This does not mean that, by chance alone, he would be expected to get exactly 20 right in 100 guesses; sometimes chance alone will give him 19 right, sometimes 21. He will also sometimes, although less often, get 15 right or 25. The experimenter will obviously not treat 21 right as evidence that any cause (ESP or other cause) is at work making the percipient give the right answers. He may well start being doubtful when the percipient gets thirty right; this is ten more than mean chance expectation. Is it so unlikely that an excess as big as this would occur by chance that one can reasonably conclude that it is not a chance effect but that some cause is at work favouring right guesses by the percipient?

This is the problem of the 'significance' of an experimental result. In order to answer it, the experimenter will have to do some arithmetic (at a not very advanced level) and he will also have to use some mathematical tables. It is not my intention here to give instructions as to how to carry out these mathematical processes; they will be found in any elementary book on statistical methods.

The general reader, who wants to understand what is going on in experimental psychical research, may well feel that the details of its mathematical methods are not his concern although he recognises that they are necessary tools for the research worker himself. On the other hand, the general reader may reasonably want to understand the problem of significance well enough for him to be able to make some sort of judgment as to the soundness of the conclusions that are drawn from experimental work. For this purpose, he will need to understand the language that the research worker uses in connection with this problem: what he means, for example, by saying that a given result is 'significant', and what he is indicating by the symbols that he uses to show degrees of significance: 'P $= 0.01$' or 'P $< 0.0001$'. No doubt the most direct way of getting to know this language is by carrying out the mathematical operations that lead to its use, but those who do not like mathematics may gain sufficient knowledge of it for practical understanding without doing this.

The problem with which tests of significance are concerned is that of how likely a given numerical result would have been if there had been no special cause (such as ESP) operating to produce it. As is explained at greater length in Appendix C, this is not the same as the problem of how likely it is that ESP produced the result. This is a question that is not answerable. If the likelihood of the result occurring in the absence of any special cause producing it (i.e. 'by chance') is large, there is obviously no reason to look for a cause; if however this likelihood is very small, it is reasonable to suppose that there was some special cause producing the result, and the lower is the chance likelihood, the more likely is it that some cause was at work. There is, however, no level of success at which the likelihood of it being a chance effect is zero, and therefore no level of success at which we can say that there is a certainty that ESP is indicated. But if the unlikelihood of a given level of success having occurred by chance is very great, we may say that we have 'virtually certain' evidence of a cause at work—of ESP if our precautions have been adequate to exclude the possibility of any other cause operating.

Sometimes the question as to how likely it is that some observed event will happen 'by chance', i.e. in the absence of any special cause producing it, may be answered by simple arithmetic. If an experimenter picks out a card from an ordinary ESP five-symbol pack and the percipient names it correctly, this might be expected to happen by chance alone once in five times. In other words, the odds are four to one against it happening if nothing but chance determined the rightness of the percipient's guesses. It is, in fact, not a very unlikely chance event and would not be good evidence of ESP or any other cause operating to produce right answers. We could draw no conclusion whatever from a percipient's success in a single guess.

If now the experimenter tries again and the percipient is again successful, the likelihood of two such successive right answers occurring by chance is considerably less; it would be one in twenty-five. The fact that the percipient guessed right twice would be better evidence that he was really able to get the card right. It will still not be very strong evidence; by chance alone it might have happened once in twenty-five times to a person with no ESP capacity. It is obviously not good enough evidence to create any strong conviction that the experimenter has found a good ESP subject, but perhaps good enough to encourage him to go on trying with the same percipient. How many times then would the percipient have to guess right in order to create a strong suspicion that he really had some capacity to get right and was not just having chance successes.

We should certainly strongly suspect some cause at work if the percipient guessed five times in succession and was right every time. A simple calculation shows that the probability of this happening by chance is very small; it is, in fact, $\frac{1}{3,125}$. We can express this by saying that the odds against its chance occurrence are more than 3,000 to 1.

The symbol P is conventionally used for the likelihood of a given level of success occurring by chance, and this is generally expressed as a decimal: $\frac{1}{3,125}$ expressed as a decimal is 0·00032, so for a succession of five guesses all of which are right, we may say that P = 0·0003 (approximately). This quantity P indicates the level of significance of the results. The smaller P is, the greater is their statistical significance.

Somewhere between P = 0·2 for one right guess and P = 0·0003 for five consecutive right guesses, the experimenter might consider that he had a value of P low enough for him to be justified in drawing a conclusion from his experiment. He would now say that his result was 'significant'; if P were larger than this limiting value, he would say that his results were 'not significant' which would be another way of saying that they do not prove anything one way or the other. The limit for significance is generally taken as P = 0·02 that is, the odds against chance occurrence of the observed rate of success should be not less than fifty to one.* With a P of

---

* The quantity P is normally calculated as the probability not merely of the chance occurrence of a deviation of at least the observed size above m.c.e., but of one of this size either above or below expectation. Scores below m.c.e. can also be evidence of ESP. In some experiments it is legitimate to consider only the chance probability of positive deviations, but generally it is safer to use the more severe criterion of significance and to consider the probability of chance deviations in both directions.

this size or smaller, the experimenter is justified in supposing that the excess of hits over mean chance expectation (or the observed deficiency) is not accidental; his conviction would, of course, be stronger if he obtained a value of P much smaller than 0·02. In neither case is he justified in feeling equally convinced that the cause of his result was ESP. There might be some other cause producing an excess of hits, such as some defect in his experimental precautions.

In the numerical examples already given, the situation was simplified in order to keep the arithmetic easy. We do not in practice concern ourselves with percipients who guess all right in the first five card guesses they give. If we found such a percipient we should not stop at that point to work out how likely was such a string of chance successes; we should be more likely to go on and see how well he went on succeeding.

The kind of problem we are more likely to meet in practice is that of the percipient who sometimes does better than chance expectation and sometimes worse but manages on the average to get about six right per pack over a series of thirty runs through the pack, so that he has a total score of thirty hits over mean chance expectation. Here we have to answer the same question as before: how likely is it that such an excess of right answers would happen accidentally, that is, by chance? It is the same question as before but it can no longer be answered by simple arithmetic. To get the answer it is necessary to carry out a combination of a not very difficult calculation with a reference to a mathematical table. What results from these operations is a value of P which has the same meaning as that already discussed.

Let us suppose, for example, that our experimental subject made four runs of 25 guesses each through standard ESP packs, and got 30 hits (10 above mean chance expectation). Should that be judged significant? None of us would feel much confidence in an intuitive answer to this question. In fact, calculation and reference to the appropriate mathematical tables shows that the odds against a deviation of this size or greater in 100 guesses is about 50 to 1 (i.e. P = 0·02). The observed excess is just significant.

It must be remembered, however, that this represents the odds against chance occurrence of a deviation of at least this size in a single series of four runs. If we went on testing this percipient on successive occasions and this remained his only considerable success, the judgment of its significance would have to be different. We should have to ask, not 'What is the likelihood of a single excess of this size turning up by chance?', but 'What is the likelihood of a deviation of at least this size turning up at least once in a number of occasions?' The answer to the latter question might be that it was not at all unlikely. If, on five occasions, the percipient had once managed to get 30 hits in 100 guesses, the likelihood of this happening by chance would be about 1 in 10; the result could not be considered to be significant. If the percipient had been tested on fifty occasions, the chance of at least one of these occasions producing a score of 30 hits would be about 2 to 1 in favour.

These facts in some cases obviously introduce a complication into the estimate of significance. If we are considering an isolated part of a series of experiments, we cannot make a correct estimate of its significance without taking into account the other results from which it has been selected. The ways of doing this and some of the problems arising from selection of results will be discussed in Appendix C.

$P = 0.02$ is a generally accepted conventional limit for significance. One must not, however, allow oneself to become superstitious about this figure. $P = 0.02$ is not to be regarded as a level of significance at which doubtful results change into certain ones. One must always consider measures of significance in relation to the purpose for which the experiment was carried out; what is a sufficiently convincing result for one purpose may be insufficient for another. It may be that all the experimenter wants to do in a particular experiment is to select a number of likely percipients for further experimentation. He may, in that case, be content to adopt $P = 0.1$ (odds of 9 to 1) as his limit of significance. By adopting such a generous limit of significance, he will have made it very likely that he will include some duds in his catch; he will, in fact, expect to get about a tenth of those originally tested into his sample, even though some have no real ESP capacities. He can, however, tolerate that number of non-scorers in his experimental group if he has managed to get also a number of real ESP subjects.

This experimenter will, however, naturally adopt a more severe criterion of significance when he reaches the next stage and starts using the experimental subjects already selected in order that their results may be used to decide some doubtful point in ESP theory, such, for example, as whether percipients succeed better with an experimenter they know than with one they do not know. He will not claim that he has obtained evidence on this point unless the significance of the difference between his two sets of scores reaches the limit $P = 0.02$, and he will be happier if the difference shows a significance level of $P < 0.001$. This will not be because he supposes that such significance levels give him certainty; he knows that chances with long odds against them do occasionally come off. His calculation is to assure him that he is very unlikely to have been misled by a chance difference in his scores. If it should happen that his conclusion is wrong, this is not an irreparable disaster; other people will repeat his experiment and fail to get his result. The point of being strict about criteria of significance is to make sure this does not happen very often. If all experimenters were lax about criteria of significance, they might all get different results and produce a confusion from which no firm conclusions could be drawn.

There is another class of experiment for which much more severe criteria of significance are commonly demanded. These are the experiments which have the special purpose of providing evidence as to the reality of ESP. In such experiments, the same test is repeated a large number of times under the same conditions until the deviation is so large that the odds against its occurrence in a chance series are of the order of many billions to one. There is obviously a case in such experiments for requiring a more stringent criterion of significance than would be necessary in the ordinary use of ESP experiments. It should be considered, however, that the use of a criterion of significance is only relevant to one source of error in drawing conclusions from an ESP experiment. It is quite erroneous to say that an extremely small value of P makes the conclusion that ESP is at work 'completely certain', one does not increase the certainty of one's conclusions by making the possibility of the chance occurrence of the observed results much smaller than the probability of other sources of error. Even the highly improbable explanation that the experimenter is lying about his results, is unlikely, with the most truthful of us, to be reasonably estimated as less than a million to one against. The sceptic who believes there is no such thing as ESP may agree that sub-atomic values of P eliminate chance as a reasonable explanation without thinking that the possibility of the experimenter being mistaken or lying is also eliminated.

It is sometimes suggested by those impatient of mathematical considerations that it would be better for psychical research to abandon the uncertainties of statistical experiments and to return to the safe road of qualitative observation of spontaneous cases. This is, however, to misunderstand the nature of the development that has taken place from qualitative observation to experiment. It is not that a kind of experiment has been developed that is 'statistical' and which therefore needs mathematical treatment that would otherwise be unnecessary. Statistical methods are procedures that have to be adopted in order to answer the question of whether the observed correspondences which are the basic data of psychical research are or are not such as can reasonably be explained as chance coincidences. This question arises in qualitative observations of spontaneous telepathy as well as in such quantitative experiments as card-guessing; the difference is that one cannot get a definite quantitative answer in the spontaneous case as one can in an experiment. Uncertainties in the application of statistical methods are not to be dealt with by a return to qualitative experiments but by using statistical methods with understanding and strict observance of their rules.

# IX

# Varieties of experimental design

In the biological sciences, there is a commonly used form of experiment in which a comparison is made between two sets of results (an experimental set and a control set), and the influence of some cause acting on the experimental set is deduced from a difference between the two sets of results. The essential point of the method is that the experimental results have been acted on by the cause under investigation while the control results have been obtained under otherwise identical conditions but without the action of that cause. One might, for example, want to find out whether a certain drug affected the likelihood of catching cold by arranging that an experimental group of people were given the drug and a control group of people, otherwise similar to the experimental group, were not given the drug, and comparing the number of colds caught in the two groups. Certain precautions would have to be taken to ensure that the two groups were 'otherwise similar', by, for example, getting the two groups by some random method of selection from the same larger group, and ensuring that they did not differ in mental attitude towards the experiment by giving both of them some substance which they supposed was the drug.

Some of the problems with which experimental psychical research is concerned are obviously problems of whether a postulated cause has or has not measurable effects, and are therefore problems which may be appropriately dealt with by designs of experiment involving controls. Such experimental problems are that of the reality of ESP, that of whether there are differences between the effectiveness of ESP in different conditions, and that of what differences are to be found between different groups of people with respect to their ESP.

The problem of the reality of ESP may be put in the form: do we find a measurable difference between scores obtained under conditions in which ESP might be operative and those obtained under conditions in which ESP could not be present? It is often felt that such a comparison between an experimental ESP result and a control set of results, would be preferable to the form of experiment in which ESP results are compared with mean chance expectation since it would seem to cut out the necessity for complicated arithmetic and make any results obtained more easily intelligible to the non-mathematical. It is sometimes asked why experimental psychical researchers have not made more use of this type of experiment.

In trying to answer this question, there are several things to be said. In the first place, the design of experiment in which such an external control is used has been much more commonly employed than the question suggests. Secondly, the advantages of this design of experiment are less than might be expected; no doubt its assumptions are more easily understood by the non-mathematical but it does not get over the necessity for arithmetic since the experimenter still has to find out whether the mean of his experimental observations is significantly different from that of his control observations. Thirdly, the difference between this design of experiment and the more usual one is less than is commonly supposed; results from experiments of the ordinary type, in which the number of hits on the target is compared with mean chance expectation, can also be displayed in a way that makes it clear that the experiment is internally controlled. When they are so displayed, one can evaluate the result by comparing the number of times any symbol is guessed when that symbol is target with the number of times it is guessed in what is, in effect, a control series of guesses when that symbol is not target. This does not involve any essential difference of principle from the more usual way of evaluating scores, but is a different road to the same result; it has the advantage of being somewhat easier to understand but it also has the disadvantage of involving the experimenter in more labour. Examples of this way of treating ESP data are discussed in Appendix D.

There are numerous examples in the experimental literature of experiments in which the number of hits on the targets aimed at is compared with an external control provided by the number of hits on some other system of targets which was not aimed at. No less than three experiments of this type were reported in the first volume of the *Journal of Parapsychology*. One of these was by an experimental psychologist Dr Dorothy Martin of Colorado State University (Martin, 1937). In ESP experiments with 39 subjects making a total of 76,525 guesses, Dr Martin found 17,759 hits on the target. This is 2,454 hits more than the mean chance expectation of 15,305. The experiment was carried out by the 'down-through' method in which the target cards are not seen by anyone until the end of the run. As a control of this experiment, Dr Martin checked the subjects' guesses against the reverse order of the pack used. This gave an average of 19·96 per cent hits which is very close to the mean chance expectation of 20 per cent; in the experimental series the percentage of successes was 23·2.

Whether one represents these results in the more usual way as showing 3·2 per cent more hits than mean chance expectation, or in the way appropriate to a control experiment as 3·24 per cent above the hits found when only chance is operating, this result is obviously highly significant. The second way of expressing the matter has some advantages, particularly in not depending on the probability statement that, on an average, with five targets, one-fifth of the guesses will be hits by chance alone. This statement is, in fact, true, but its truth may not be self-evident to everybody.

Another series in which experimental results were compared with a control series was carried out by Dr Soal with Mrs Stewart as his experimental subject (Soal and Bateman, 1954). This is of particular interest because of the high rate of scoring of this subject. The control was provided by checking each set of the subject's guesses, not against the pack used for that set of guesses, but against another pack used on the same page for another set of guesses. The result of this comparison is shown in Table 1. It will be seen that whereas in the experimental series Mrs Stewart obtained an excess of hits amounting to 6 per cent of the total number of guesses, an excess which is highly significant, in the corresponding control series in which only chance is producing hits, the excess is only an insignificant amount, about 0·03 per cent.

*Table 1 Comparison of number of hits in experimental and control series of Dr Soal's experiments with Mrs Stewart as percipient*

| | No. of guesses | Hits | | |
| | | Mean chance expectation | Observed | Excess |
|---|---|---|---|---|
| Experimental | 33,500 | 6,700 | 8,694 | + 1,994 |
| Control | 33,500 | 6,700 | 6,711 | + 11 |

Numerous experiments of a similar type have shown the same general result. These experiments provide the simplest refutation of the suspicion that the high scores found in ESP experiments might be the result of some fallacy in the probability theory on which is based the expectation that chance alone will produce an average of about five right answers per run of twenty-five cards.

As in a normal experiment in the biological sciences with a control, so also in a controlled ESP experiment, it is necessary to be sure that the cause under investigation is not affecting the control group as well as the experimental group. One of the early experiments of J. B. Rhine might have proved defective in this respect. As a control to compare with results indicating a positive ESP effect, Rhine (1934) made groups of twenty-five calls not trying to hit any particular pack. Afterwards he shuffled a pack of ESP cards and checked his calls against this pack. This is a situation in which we could be sure that ESP did not affect the control results only if we knew either that ESP could not work forward to a future event or that the absence of an intention for the cards to correspond with anything is enough to ensure that they will not correspond. We now have a great deal of experimental evidence that the first of these assumptions is false, and the second may also be false. Rhine seems therefore to have been lucky in getting almost exactly mean chance expectation in the number of hits in his control series, 801 hits in 4,000 guesses. From the standpoint of present knowledge, this is an inadequate control since it might have happened that it showed psi-determined correspondence. It is necessary that controls should be so designed that their results cannot be attributed to a psi-process. Only then can the presence or absence of a psi-process in an experimental series of guesses be deduced from the presence or absence of a difference between its results and that of the control.

An example of an inadequate control for the purpose for which it was intended is to be found in early work done by Coover on telepathy (Coover, 1917). In his experimental series, the experimenter looked at the card while the subject guessed it; in the control series, the experimenter did not look at the card. Both series were somewhat above mean chance expectation to an approximately equal amount. The design was obviously adequate for the purpose of finding out whether the experimenter looking at the card made any difference to an ESP performance, but not for the purpose for which it was intended, that of determining whether or not telepathy occurred (Coover was, of course, following the common assumption of his time that telepathy was the only form of cognitive psi). It may be that his total excess was accidental or due to some imperfection in his method of experimenting. It is also obviously consistent with Coover's subjects having succeeded by clairvoyance in both series since in both their score exceeded mean chance expectation. No one would suppose that these results contribute positive evidence of ESP, but Coover was clearly wrong in claiming that they provided positive evidence against telepathy. For this purpose, a longer experimental series would have been necessary with a more adequate control.

The type of ESP experiment so far discussed in the present chapter is that in which an ESP experimental result is compared with one obtained under control conditions from which the possibility of ESP is assumed to be excluded. This design of experiment is found principally in researches intended to contribute evidence as to the reality of ESP. There is another type of experiment which has a very similar design. This is the experiment in which two sets of results from the same group of subjects are compared, not because ESP would be a possible explanation of success in the one set and not in the other, but because the two sets of results differ in respect of some situation which may have a measurable effect on ESP scores. One may, for example, want to compare ESP scoring when subjects are informed as to the rightness of their guesses immediately afterwards and when they are told later or not at all, one may be concerned with finding out whether there is any difference in ESP scoring when subjects are given alcohol or some other drug and when they are not, one may want to compare scores when agent and subject are separated by a short distance and when they are separated by a great distance, and so on. There are a very large number of questions for the answers of which such a comparison must be made. It is perhaps the commonest design for those experiments in which one is trying to find out something about ESP and not merely to demonstrate its reality. Particular examples of experiments of this kind will be discussed in a later chapter.

The general pattern of such experiments is a familiar one since it occurs commonly in other fields than parapsychology; it is perhaps the most usual form of experiment in normal experimental psychology. Sometimes with the same single subject, more commonly with the same group of subjects, the experimenter makes two sets of experiments under conditions differing in some respect. The arithmetical question is then whether the scores obtained under the two conditions are significantly different, that is, whether the difference is greater than can be reasonably regarded as accidental. If the difference is significant, this indicates that the respect in which the two sets of measurements differ is one that affects the function which is being measured. It is less easy to interpret the absence of a difference between the two sets of measurements. It does not show that the variable condition has no influence on the function measured; only that if there is an influence its effect is less than the experiment is able to measure. In the case of an ESP experiment, such an absence of difference might be the result of ESP not being present in either set of measurements. Then, of course, no conclusion could be drawn as to whether ESP does or does not depend on the condition that has been varied.

Certain precautions have to be taken before a conclusion from an experiment of this type is fully justified. One necessary precaution is that of mixing up in time the two conditions to be compared. Such precautions were often neglected in early experimenting. It might be that an experimenter was investigating a subject who claimed clairvoyant powers. It was suspected that his apparent clairvoyant success was due to his receiving some sort of visual sensory cues so the subject's head was enclosed in an opaque bag, perhaps at the end of an otherwise successful session, and the successes were found to disappear. The conclusion was then come to that the apparent clairvoyant success was really due to visual sensory information cut out by the opaque bag.

This may have been the case, but a more elaborate experiment than this would be necessary to prove it. To draw conclusions from the introduction of a new condition on one occasion is to neglect what we know about the variability of ESP performance; the time of putting on the bag might have been a time when the subject would not have scored anyway particularly if this was towards the end of a session when chronological decline is liable to have set in. It must also be considered that the failure might be due to the novelty of the situation of being hooded. We know that there is often initial failure of ESP in new conditions which may be overcome by the percipient becoming habituated to the new conditions. A more prolonged experiment would be necessary to make sure that this was not the case here.

Not all experiments with comparison of conditions involve a new task but they are all subject to the uncertainties resulting from the spontaneous variability of ESP performance. This makes it necessary that the two conditions to be compared should be mixed up in all sessions of the experiment. If the two conditions are called A and B, the mixing up may be by some random process which will give such an order as AABAAABBABBBAAB. Alternatively it may, with less trouble to the experimenter, be in such a systematic order as ABBAABBAABBA. In either case, if there remains a significant difference between the total scores under conditions A and B, we can be sure that the difference is not due to the accident of one of the conditions having been used during a period of abnormally low scoring. If other precautions have been adequate, this difference in scores may now be taken to indicate a real difference in scoring rates under conditions A and B.

There are obviously certain problems for which this procedure of mixing up the two conditions within each occasion cannot be used. The experimenter may, for example, be concerned with the influence on ESP scoring of some drug. He cannot then drug and undrug his percipients in the course of a single experimental occasion. He can, however, still use the principle of mixing up the conditions by experimenting with each percipient on many occasions, each occasion being either with or without the drug. The conditions will then be mixed up between occasions and not within occasions. In subsequent calculations of significance, the experimenter will then have to use as his unit the result of each single occasion, not the result of each single guess.

A third type of problem which requires a somewhat similar design of experiment is one in which a comparison is to be made between two groups of people, not between two conditions of experimenting. Although such 'group-comparison' experiments are similar in design to 'condition-comparison' experiments, they differ in some respects from them. The experimenter might, for example, want to find out whether women showed a different rate of ESP scoring from men or whether introverts differed in ESP ability from extroverts. He obviously could not find an answer to these questions by the method of experimenting already described, for he could not change the sex or the temperaments of his experimental subjects in order to get the two sets of measurements that are to be compared.

There still will be comparison between two sets of measurements but these will be measurements from two different groups, not measurements obtained from a single group under two different conditions. This entails also a different way of comparing the measurements obtained. If we have ESP scores from a group of men and another from a comparable group of women, it will not do to find the difference between the total (or average) scores obtained from these two groups and to find that this is statistically significant. That would show that ESP was taking place in at least one of the groups, but it would be consistent with the possibility that ESP scoring was just as likely to be found in one sex as in the other. Let us suppose, for example, that the ability to score positively in ESP tests is rare in either sex but that it is just as likely that the rare ESP scorer is of one sex as the other. It might happen by chance that in the groups selected for our tests we have included a high scoring subject in the group of women but not in the group of men. This inclusion would result in the mean scores of the sample of women being higher than that of the sample of men; this difference would become significant if enough guesses were made by each subject. It would, however, signify a difference between the samples, not necessarily a difference between the populations from which those samples were drawn. It might be the case that men and women were alike with respect to their ability to make positive scores in ESP tests but that it happened by chance that we had included more good scorers in one of our groups than in the other.

In order to know whether any observed difference is significant in the only sense that matters in this enquiry, that is, in the sense that it signifies a real difference between men and women, a different method of statistical assessment must be used. It is necessary to employ one which uses the individual subjects (not the separate guesses) as unit. Instead of asking what is the total (or average) score of the two groups, we must ask such a question as how many men and how many women scored above or below mean chance expectation.

The principle underlying the method of assessment may be illustrated by data obtained by Dr Rao on boys and girls in an ESP task in which the targets were cards with words written in Telugu, an Indian language unknown to any of the subjects (Rao, 1963). It was found that the total scores of the boys in this task were significantly better than the total scores of the girls. This, however, proves only that ESP entered into the performance and to a greater extent in the sample of boys than in the sample of girls; it cannot be inferred that boys do better in the task than girls since the result might be due simply to the boy sample having accidentally included more individuals who happen to be better at the task. To draw any conclusion as to whether there is evidence of any sex difference, we must form a 'contingency' table showing the number of boys and the number of girls succeeding in the task. This is shown in Table 2.

Examination of this table shows that the boys scored considerably better than the girls. To ensure that this is a real indication of a difference between the populations from which the samples of boys and girls were drawn, the appropriate statistical method is what is known as the chi² test. Instructions for carrying this out will be found in any elementary book on statistical methods. A conservative estimate of chi² from Table 2 gives it as 9·6. This is ample for significance since reference to the appropriate mathematical tables shows that it corresponds to a P value of about 0·002 (odds of 500 to 1 against the production by chance of so large a discrepancy from expectation).

*Table 2   Comparison between numbers of boys and of girls scoring above and below mean chance expectation on Telugu targets\**

|  | No. scoring above m.c.e. | No. scoring below m.c.e. | Totals |
|---|---|---|---|
| Boys | 24 (18·2) | 5 (10·8) | 29 |
| Girls | 8 (13·8) | 14  (8·2) | 22 |

\* Numbers in brackets show number expected in each cell if tendency to success were equally distributed between boys and girls.

From this result one can conclude that the scoring difference observed is a characteristic of the two populations from which the boy and girl samples were drawn and is not merely a characteristic of the samples themselves. It does not follow that it would be true of all boys and all girls; it is a step towards that conclusion, but how general the indicated boy-girl difference is would have to be discovered by further research. The population from which Professor Rao's sample was drawn was only that of a school or schools within a particular town in the United States. That is itself only a sample of the whole world population of boys and girls; it may have had some special characteristic which made it easier for its boys to succeed in an unusual ESP task.

Nor does it follow that even within that restricted population, boys are better at ESP tasks than girls. Much research on sex differences has been carried out with indecisive results, and it seems unlikely that there are any general sex differences in performance. Rao himself is more inclined to attribute it to the boys and girls reacting differently to the barrier created by the use of a foreign language. This interpretation is rendered more likely by the observation that, if a similar table is made of the boy and girl successes on English targets, there is no significant difference when the chi² test is applied.

In order to know what conclusion can be drawn from a comparison of the experimental results from two groups of individuals drawn from two differing populations, it is necessary to use some method of assessment of statistical significance which treats all the results from any single individual as the unit. The simplest way of doing this is the one already described, making a contingency table of the individuals scoring high or low in each group and assessing its significance by the chi² method. This is not, however, the only way in which this end can be achieved. An alternative method is, for example, to use the method of analysis of variance as has been done in the later work of Dr Schmeidler (Schmeidler and McConnell, 1958) on the different scoring levels of 'sheep' (those who believe in the possibility of ESP) and 'goats' (those who do not). The significantly high value of the sheep-goat variance in this research is the same kind of result as that described above but reached by a different road.

The necessity in group comparison experiments for using a method of assessment in which numbers of individuals (and not total or average scores) are compared was not always recognised in early researches. This creates a difficulty in evaluating many of the researches in which groups were compared. The use of improper methods of assessment accounts, no doubt, for many of the contradictory findings in group comparison problems, for example, that of sex differences in ESP scoring. One main reason for the use of rigidly correct methods of determining significance is that we may reduce to a minimum discrepancies between the findings of different research workers. On the other hand, it may well be that, where incorrect methods have been used in assessing group difference experiments, the conclusions dubiously drawn would have proved to be well founded if a correct method had been used. When such results have been amply confirmed, it ceases to be important to consider whether the statistical methods originally used were adequate; the conclusions are justified by their proved repeatability.

The use of a contingency table whose entries are numbers of individuals and which is evaluated by the chi² method has now become the standard way of treating such group-difference results. It is sometimes referred to as determining the 'self-consistency' of the results. This term is somewhat objectionable since it seems to imply that this is a subsidiary test of such results, not, as it is, the main way of finding out whether the results really signify what the research is intended to investigate, the difference between ESP performances of two populations.

The present chapter has discussed three types of experiment with similar designs in which a comparison is made between two sets of results. These may be called: (1) the test of ESP with control, (2) the condition-comparison experiment, and (3) the group-comparison experiment. They have different purposes; the first is one way of investigating the reality of ESP, the other two are ways of finding out something about ESP. The last two are directed towards different problems of the nature of ESP and must be carefully distinguished since they require different methods of assessment.

# References

COOVER, J. E. (1917), 'Experiments in Psychical Research', *Psychology Research Monographs*, I, Stanford University.

MARTIN, DOROTHY R. (1937), 'Chance and Extra-chance Results in Card Matching', *Journal of Parapsychology*, i, 185–90.

RAO, K. R. (1963), 'Studies in the preferential effect. II', *J. Parapsych.*, xxvii, 147–60.

RHINE, J. B. (1934), *Extra-Sensory Perception*, Boston.

SCHMEIDLER, GERTRUDE R., and MCCONNELL, R. A. (1958), *Extrasensory Perception and Personality Patterns*, London and New Haven.

SOAL, S. G., and BATEMAN, F. (1954), *Modern Experiments in Telepathy*, London.

# X

# The problem of the reality of ESP

There have been other changes in attitude since the early days of psychical research besides the one already discussed, the shift of emphasis from anecdote to experiment. There has also been a change from exclusive pre-occupation with the task of obtaining evidence as to the reality of ESP to interest in the problem of what can be found out about ESP.

Must we not, however, be satisfied that something exists before we can be interested in finding out about its nature? Certainly no one is going to be interested in the research problems of something that he is quite certain does not exist; no zoologist is going to devote himself to study of the sex life of the unicorn. But something falling considerably short of certainty as to its reality is all that is necessary to give sufficient reason for pursuing the study of something as a research interest. Zoologists are more ready to investigate the abominable snowman than the unicorn although there is not complete certainty that the abominable snowman exists. Its existence may be judged sufficiently likely to make it an interesting topic of enquiry; so, at least, must also the existence of ESP and other psi-phenomena.

In planning an investigation, the experimental psychical researcher must choose whether he is going to try to convince sceptics by producing new and more rigid proof of the reality of the paranormal, or whether his experiments are to have some other aim, such as that of finding out about the characteristics of ESP. This is an important choice since generally an experimental design for one of these purposes is not suitable for the other. It is true that some experiments intended to produce evidence for the reality of ESP have, as a by-product, contributed important indications of new characteristics of ESP; the discovery of psi-missing and of displace-ment are examples. Generally, however, the condition of prolonged repetition of identical experiments which is needed for new evidence as to the reality of ESP is a condition unfavourable for studying the characteristics of ESP. For the latter purpose, the experimenter will need to try his experiments under varying conditions to discover how his subjects' scores change under these changes. Working in this way, the experimenter is not likely to get the impressive total scores that are needed in experiments to prove the reality of ESP.

One of the dangers to which experimental psychical researchers are exposed is that hostile criticism may divert them too much to the relatively unrewarding task of multiplying proofs of the reality of the paranormal. Some types of criticism seem to assume that proof of reality is always the aim of a parapsychological experiment and that it is reasonable to judge all experiments, whatever their ostensible object, by the extent to which they contribute to this aim. Such critics may suppose that they have made a case against the reality of ESP when they point out the failure of a particular experiment to prove the reality of ESP, although the experimenter himself may have made no such claim. It must, however, be admitted that experimenters do sometimes lay themselves open to this sort of criticism by not making it clear in their research reports exactly what was the object of their experiments. Sometimes even they discuss their results as if they were contributions to the total evidence for the reality of ESP, although the experiments were not carried out in a way appropriate for this purpose.

It is, of course, a fact about psychical research that there is a real question as to whether there is any reality in what it is investigating. Such a question is rarely a live one even in other fields of the biological sciences and only very exceptionally in the physical sciences. The 'abominable snowman' and the 'Loch Ness monster' are somewhat parallel examples from the biological sciences. The situation is even rarer in the physical sciences because generally the specifying of the conditions of an observation is sufficient to enable other scientists to repeat the observation.

There is, however, one parallel case in the physical sciences, that of 'ball lightning' (Silberg, 1965). It has been frequently reported that glowing balls have been seen during a thunderstorm. These are said to persist for some seconds or minutes and then either to explode with a loud bang or to disappear quietly. The people reporting these appearances have rarely been trained meteorologists and may generally be considered to be of doubtful reliability as reporters. The phenomena of ball lightning resemble paranormal phenomena in the fact that they cannot be produced at will. They have not been produced experimentally, and so far they have not been photographed.

It is plainly not unreasonable to doubt whether ball lightning exists at all, and many meteorologists remain doubtful. Yet the general tendency of scientific research workers has been neither to ignore the reports nor to try to test their validity by a rigid process of verifying the reliability of those who claim to have seen it. The tendency has been rather to consider that the evidence is sufficient to justify a research interest in the phenomenon, and to see whether a coherent picture of the properties of ball lightning can be built up from the reports, and how far a theoretical explanation of the reported phenomena can be constructed.

In the realm of the paranormal also, it may be suggested that the primary task of those who are engaged on research in the matter is not to produce such overwhelming evidence for its reality that hostile criticism will be silenced. Presumably the psychical researcher is already convinced

85

that the evidence for the paranormal is good enough to justify it as a research interest; otherwise he would not be engaged in psychical research. He may, in fact, think that the evidence is very much stronger than this, but he need not think that the demonstration of this evidence or the strengthening of it are matters of primary importance. He may think that it does not matter very much that there is hostile criticism; there may be some gain to psychical research that its findings are subjected to such criticism. Whether this is so or not, he may recognise that the criticism will not be silenced merely by accumulating evidence, and that it will be dangerous only if it diverts the research worker from his proper task of finding out about the nature of the paranormal to the less fruitful task of trying to defend its reality.

If it is admitted that the defence of the reality of the paranormal is not the primary task of the experimental psychical researcher, he must nevertheless be prepared to answer the question as to how strong the evidence is. The present chapter is an attempt to answer this question with respect to the reality of ESP.

An experiment which is to contribute any weight of evidence with respect to the reality of ESP must use other methods and other precautions than those used in the more ordinary type of experiment which is investigating the nature of ESP. Usually such experiments have involved many repetitions of experiments under similar conditions which would be an uneconomical and uninformative method for normal ESP research. One reason for large numbers of results under similar conditions is that experimenters aiming at producing evidence for the reality of ESP have felt that their evidence would be more impressive if the index of significance had an extremely low value. They may often have overestimated the importance of this; there is no real advantage in making the possibility of being misled by chance incomparably lower than the possibility of other sources of error.

They must also consider the possibility that other people may think the results are due to dishonesty on the part of the experimenter and have independent witnesses and procedures of independent checking to reduce this possibility. Such precautions would be unnecessary and hampering in the ordinary ESP experiment but they are appropriate here. The certainty of every experimental result is, as was pointed out long ago by Professor Sidgwick, limited by the honesty of the experimenter. It is unlikely that an apparently honest research worker will lie about his experimental results but the likelihood is not zero. The likelihood can, however, be reduced to a very small amount by adequate provision of independent witnesses and checking, and only those experiments which have been so safeguarded, and which also have been successful at a high level of significance, can be admitted as evidence for the reality of ESP.

There are a number of experiments which fulfil these conditions, and the choice as to which ones to cite is somewhat arbitrary. My own choice would not necessarily be that of other psychical researchers. In making the choice of experiments below, I have been guided by various considerations; partly by the extent to which particular researches have been accepted as of high evidential value, partly by the consideration that the researchers quoted should not be too remote from us in time, and partly by the aim of showing that successful experiments have been performed under different conditions and in different countries.

I have chosen the following five researches as examples of the strength of evidence for the reality of ESP:

1. The Pearce-Pratt series of experiments carried out at Duke University in 1933-4 (Rhine and Pratt, 1954).

2. The long series of experiments carried out by Dr Soal and Mrs Goldney with the high-scoring percipient Mr Shackleton in London in 1941 (Soal and Bateman, 1954).

3. An experiment carried out by Professor Lucien Warner in the thirties (Warner, 1937).

4. Card-guessing experiments carried out by Dr Rýzl in Czechoslovakia which have been witnessed or controlled by visiting investigators from other parts of the world (Rýzl and Otani, 1967).

5. A fully automated series of experiments carried out in 1967 by Dr Helmut Schmidt (Schmidt, 1969a, 1969b), then a research physicist at the Boeing Aircraft Research Laboratories (now Director of the former Duke University Parapsychology Laboratory at the Foundation for Research into the Nature of Man, Durham, North Carolina).

The first of the above series of researches on the reality of ESP was an early one in the Parapsychology Laboratory of Duke University, the design of which included precautions against the possibility of the experimenter cheating. It was carried out during 1933 and the following year with Dr Pratt as agent and a divinity student called Pearce as percipient. The percipient was sent by himself to the University Library and the agent was in another building, 100 yards away in some experiments and 250 in others. The agent displaced the cards one by one from an ESP pack at an agreed time without turning them over. At the end of going through each pack the cards were turned over and recorded by Pratt. The guesses were recorded by the percipient. In order to eliminate the possibility of cheating by agent or percipient, the precaution was taken that both placed their records in a sealed package which was handed to Professor Rhine before the two lists were compared. Under these conditions, success was obtained at a good rate. The total number of guesses was 1,850 of which one would expect a fifth (i.e. 370) to be right by chance. The actual number of hits was 558 which exceeds mean chance expectation by about fifty per cent. This is a highly significant result which leaves no doubt that some factor other than chance determined the hits. If this cause was not ESP, it must have been some kind of fraud not eliminated by the design of the experiment, since this design made impossible any accidental sensory leakage or accidental effects of recording errors.

A more elaborately safeguarded experiment was that of Dr Soal and Mrs Goldney which they carried out in London in 1941. These experimenters used 'open' packs, prearranged from lists of random numbers. There were five target cards with pictures of different animals; one of these was exposed to the agent in accordance with a code connecting each of the digits 1–5 with one of the animal pictures. The actual guess made by the percipient was the name of one of the pictured animals (lion, elephants, etc.). An earlier pilot experiment had shown that Shackleton seemed to be guessing, not the card at which the agent was then looking, but the card ahead of that; the experiment was planned to discover whether this guessing one ahead would continue.

The results of this confirmatory series of experiments are summarised on p. 149 of Soal's book (Soal and Bateman, 1954). A minor mistake in the totalling was afterwards discovered by Soal; the figures given here are the corrected ones (Soal, 1956). Over a long series of guesses (nearly four thousand in all) Shackleton showed continued success in this guessing of the card ahead, with the unusual scoring rate of seven per cent above mean chance expectation. Successes were made with a number of different agents; each experiment was observed by outside witnesses to ensure that the precautions were maintained and that a true record was made of targets and guesses.

One result of the combination of a high scoring rate with a large number of guesses in this experimental series is that the odds against a chance deviation of this size are very heavy. Soal's estimate of $P = 10^{-35}$ needs some correction since this was based on his original score totals but, even so corrected, the odds against chance occurrence would be of the order of many billion billions to one. Since the possibility of explanation of these results by chance is effectively eliminated by a much less extreme $P$ value than this; one might wonder whether this series of experiments was not longer than it need have been for the purpose of demonstrating Shackleton's ability to guess the following target card correctly. One must not suppose that a low value of $P$ gives an overall guarantee of the certainty of the result indicated, since it indicates only that the results were not produced by chance while it does not show that they were not produced by some other cause than ESP (e.g. by experimental error or by fraud). What gives this assurance is the adequacy of the primary precautions used, and this assurance is as complete in a short experimental series as in a long one.

If the sub-atomic value of $P$ reported in the Soal-Goldney experiments does not make these results more certain than they would be with a $P$ of, let us say, $10^{-6}$, it does allow one to make an answer to one possible objection to their interpretation as indications of ESP. This is the objection that this series of results might be the one accidentally positive result in an indefinitely large collection of ESP experiments performed elsewhere. Probability theory predicts that if one tried often enough to carry out an ESP experiment, any possible excess might turn up accidentally in an indefinitely long series of attempts. If, however, we ask how many experiments would have to be carried out before one could expect a deviation the size of the Soal-Goldney result to turn up by chance, the answer is that this number would have to be fantastically large, larger indeed than the whole history of the world would allow for. If one supposed that every inhabitant of the globe had done an unsuccessful ESP experiment every month during the last sixty million years, the necessary correction that would have to be made for the Soal-Goldney series being the selected best of all these experiments, would still leave it overwhelmingly significant with odds against its chance occurrence of many million millions to one. The Soal-Goldney result could not reasonably be attributed to chance even if this was the only evidence we had that pointed to ESP.

If, however, this or any other single experimental series were indeed the only evidence we had for the reality of ESP, the low value of P obtained in it would not, in itself, be ground for regarding this result as of any scientific importance. At best it would show that something very odd had happened, but if this oddity were never repeated it would not be a useful fact for scientific purposes; it would suggest no further step that we could take in order to understand it. The importance of this experimental series depends on the fact that it does not stand alone; it is one of a number of experiments with safeguards against the experimenters cheating which indicate the influence of ESP on the results obtained.

Another experiment of considerable importance as evidence is a relatively short one carried out by Professor Lucien Warner and reported by him in 1937. The experimenter was a psychologist who wished to make a decisive test on the matter. By himself acting as agent he could know that he was not cheating, and by using a percipient who had already shown success in ESP experiments he hoped to ensure positive results. This hope was fulfilled. Warner placed the percipient in a locked room on a different floor from the experimenter. In order to ensure that there was no involuntary indication from himself as to the nature of the target, he arranged that there was communication from the percipient to the experimenter and not the other way. In 250 guesses the percipient had 93 hits which is an excess of 43 over the 50 right guesses that would be expected if there were only chance correspondence between the percipient's guesses and the targets. Although the series was short in comparison with the others considered here, this excess was adequately significant with odds against chance occurrence of the order of a thousand million to one. There is, therefore, ample evidence for the presence of some cause favouring right guessing and the simple but adequate precautions seem to rule out any cause other than ESP. This experimental series therefore deserves an honourable place amongst those researches contributing evidence as to the reality of ESP.

The next set of experimental researches that will here be mentioned is that of Dr Rýzl of Czechoslovakia. Apart from its contribution to the problem of training in ESP, Dr Rýzl's research is of importance as an example of sustained high scoring which puts Dr Rýzl's subject, Pavel Stepanek, in the same class as Dr Soal's high-scoring subjects, Basil Shackleton and Mrs Stewart. It would be a disconcerting fact if all the high scorers in ESP experiments were figures of the past.

Rýzl's researches are scattered over the pages of the technical journals but the article cited (Rýzl and Otani, 1967) gives a table summarising the results up to that date. The method of experimenting has been that the percipient made a two-target choice as to whether a card in a sealed envelope had the white or the green face uppermost. The cards had been inserted in envelopes before the experiment, then shuffled and some of them turned before placing the envelopes in an outer cardboard cover. This ensured that none of the experimenting team knew which face was uppermost in any of the envelopes. The task was, therefore, an ESP operation not involving telepathy and therefore fully safeguarded against the possibility of information being unwittingly conveyed from the experimenter by such means as unconscious whispering.

The table given in the Rýzl-Otani article shows ten series of experiments with a total of 17,648 guesses and 10,117 hits. With a fifty per cent chance of accidental success, this means that the excess of hits was 1,293 over mean chance expectation. This corresponds to an 'index of success'* of about 14; this may be compared with the figure of about 9 which I have calculated from Soal's +1 results with Shackleton. The deviation from mean chance expectation in Rýzl's results is of such a high level of significance that they obviously cannot be explained as a chance effect.

Of the results reported in these tables, some were obtained in the presence of experimenters from outside, including Pratt, Blom, Beloff, and Freeman. The only series which did not show an excess of hits was that in which Beloff was present when 1,200 guesses were made with 65 hits below mean chance expectation (a significant deficiency).

While all the sets of experiments with outside experimenters present and in control are sufficiently safeguarded against the theoretical possibility of the results having been fraudulently produced by the main experimenter, the most completely safeguarded experiment is, no doubt, one carried out in November 1963 by Dr Pratt and Dr Blom in which Rýzl himself was not present and the organisation of the experiment was entirely in the

---

* This index is explained in Appendix A. In the case of a choice between two targets, it is a value double the percentage deviation from expectation.

hands of the visiting experimenters (Pratt and Blom, 1964). In this series, there were 1,600 guesses with 917 hits, 117 over mean chance expectation. The level of significance is very high, a P value of the order of $10^{-8}$. The result remains overwhelmingly significant if we take into account the fact that a series undertaken by Pratt alone and one by Pratt and Stevenson showed less striking results (Pratt, 1964). The odds against the occurrence of this rate of scoring by chance as the best of three experiments remains much more than a million to one.

At the time of writing, the most recent experimental confirmation of the reality of ESP is a research carried out by Dr Helmut Schmidt (Schmidt, 1969a, 1969b). This is of special importance since some critics of ESP have said that they reserved judgment as to the reality of ESP until its occurrence was shown by a fully automated experiment in which selection of targets was made by an automatic randomising device and all responses by the subject were scored automatically. These conditions were fulfilled by Dr Schmidt's machine. It might be argued that, even with such a machine, the reality of the results depends on the truthfulness of the experimenter and any witnesses of his records, but the advantage of automated selection and recording is that spurious results cannot be produced by any method of cheating by the subject or by errors made by the experimenter in target selection or the recording of hits. In spite of the rigorous conditions of Schmidt's experiment, his results were overwhelmingly significant.

The apparatus used in this experiment had four lamps of different colours. The task of the subject was to choose one of four keys to indicate his opinion as to which of the four lamps would light up when the key was pressed. Which light actually lit up was determined electronically. In the first experiment, this was not determined at the moment when the subject made his decision, so the task was a precognitive one. In another experiment a tape was pre-punched with a sequence of random numbers which determined the targets, so the task could be one of clairvoyance.

Schmidt used as his subjects three individuals who had given previous grounds for supposing that they could succeed in an ESP task; two of these were professional mediums. In the first series of experiments, a total of 63,066 guesses gave a preponderance of hits with odds against chance occurrence of about 2,000,000,000 to 1 ($P < 10^{-9}$). This, of course, effectively eliminates the possibility of it being a chance result, and the conditions of the experiment eliminate the possibility of any other explanation of the result than that of precognitive ESP. A later experiment with 20,000 trials gave a result of slightly greater significance ($P = 10^{-10}$).

Although this series of researches has provided additional proof of the reality of ESP, Dr Schmidt has not discovered a fool-proof method of ensuring that any experimenter can get positive ESP results by using it. Other parapsychological experimenters have got chance results with Schmidt's machine or with machines closely resembling it. The task of devising an experimental set-up by which any experimenter can be sure of getting positive ESP results remains a problem for the future. We cannot even be sure that it will ever be solved.

This is not, of course, a full list of researches that may be considered to supply evidence of the reality of ESP. There were many experiments well safeguarded and carefully carried out in the early days of the Society for Psychical Research, but these took place rather a long time ago. An excellent experiment was carried out at Groningen in 1926 by Professors of Physiology and of Psychology on a young man who obtained high scores in a task which involved pointing to a square on a board as determined by the experimenters in a room above using a random method of selection (Brugmans, 1921). There was also at Duke Parapsychology Laboratory another experimental series with safeguards against deception by the experimenter in the Pratt-Woodruff experiment which also showed a high rate of success (Pratt and Woodruff, 1939). One might also include the experiments reported by the Russian physiologist Vasiliev on the telepathic induction of the hypnotic state. These and many other carefully controlled experiments show, at any rate, that the appearance of experimental ESP is not confined to a few laboratories or to a short period of time. If the assertion of the reality of ESP is a conspiracy of dishonest experimenters, it is a conspiracy which extends widely in space and time and which includes a variety of people who seem unlikely to co-operate.

In considering the implications of this evidence, there is more than one question that we may ask ourselves. It has already been suggested that the important question for the experimentalist is whether it establishes a sufficient case for the reality of ESP to make it a reasonable matter for research investigation. I think there is little doubt that the answer to this question must be 'Yes'; there are few controversial issues on which the evidence in favour is stronger.

If one asks further whether the evidence is so strong as to compel belief, the answer is not so easy. It is clear that the evidence for ESP is strong, so strong that conviction of its reality can only be avoided by supposing that a number of apparently honest and reliable investigators are deliberately deceiving the world as to their results. This is certainly extremely unlikely, but not, in principle, impossible. If it were certain that ESP is impossible, one would have to prefer this improbability of a widespread conspiracy of deception to the impossibility of ESP, and to accept deception as the explanation of those successful results that cannot be explained by chance or by experimental error. That this is the case is the conviction of a number of critics of psychical research to whom it appears self-evident that extrasensory perception is as mythical as the unicorn. The point of view of these critics will be discussed in the next chapter.

# References

BRUGMANS, H. J. F. W. (1921), 'A Report on Telepathic Experiments Done in the Psychology Laboratory at Groningen', *Report of Premier Congrès International des recherches psychiques*, Copenhagen.

PRATT, J. G. (1964), 'Preliminary Experiment with a "Borrowed" ESP Subject', *Journal of the Society for Psychical Research*, xlii, 333–45.

PRATT, J. G., and BLOM, J. G. (1964), 'A Confirmatory Experiment with a "Borrowed" Outstanding ESP Subject', *J. S.P.R.*, xlii, 381–9.

PRATT, J. G., and WOODRUFF, J. L. (1939), 'Size of Stimulus Symbols in Extra-sensory Perception', *Journal of Parapsychology*, iii, 121–58.

RHINE, J. B., and PRATT, J. G. (1954), 'A Review of the Pearce-Pratt Distance Series of ESP Tests', *J. Parapsych.*, xviii, 156–77.

RÝZL, M., and OTANI, SOJI (1967), 'An Experiment in Duplicate Calling with Stepanek', *J. Parapsych.*, xxxi, 19–28.

SCHMIDT, H. (1969), 'Precognition of a Quantum Process', *J. Parapsych.*, xxxiii, 99–109.

SCHMIDT, H. (1969), 'Clairvoyance Test with a Machine', *J. Parapsych.*, xxxiii, 300–7.

SILBERG, P. A. (1965), 'A Review of Ball Lightning', *Problems of Atmospheric and Space Electricity*, (ed. S. C. Coronoti), Amsterdam and London, 436–54.

SOAL, S. G. (1956), 'The Shackleton Report: an Error Discovered', *J. S.P.R.*, xxxviii, 216–17.

SOAL, S. G., and BATEMAN, F. (1954), *Modern Experiments in Telepathy*, London.

VASILIEV, L. L. (1963), *Experiments in Mental Suggestion* (English translation), Church Crookham.

WARNER, L. (1937), 'A Test Case', *J. Parapsych.*, i, 234–8.

# XI

# Critics of ESP

The experimental evidence for the reality of ESP is obviously strong. It is indeed generally agreed that it would be strong enough to create conviction in any other field. There are, however, some who remain unconvinced by this evidence since they find its strength insufficient to outweigh the initial improbability of the organism being able to react to any information that has not come to it through the channels of sense. Those who are thus unconvinced may play a useful part in the development of the research if their doubts lead them to make criticisms that are soundly directed against real weaknesses in the supporting evidence for psi-phenomena. The ideal critic is one who is concerned to make an honest appraisal of the evidence and not merely with making a case against ESP.

Some critics fall far short of this ideal. In their anxiety to make a case against ESP, they may distort evidence, finding fault with experiments as not proving the reality of ESP while ignoring the fact that the experiments in question were not carried out with the intention of providing such evidence and that they would not be appealed to as evidence for the reality of ESP by any research worker in this field. The useful critic is one who recognises that the case for the reality of ESP rests on the strongest evidence provided by the best experiments designed to test this reality, and that, if this case is to be demolished, it must be by finding weaknesses in the evidence from these experiments.

There is a type of criticism, more concerned with establishing a case than with forming a balanced judgment, which is of no help to the research but rather tends to hinder it by diverting the energies of research workers into unprofitable controversy. There are, for example, critics who try to create bias against research findings by the use of such emotional language as 'fairy-land atmosphere' and 'simple credulity'. Still less are the ends of objective assessment of experimental results helped by those who try to create prejudice against psychical researchers by speculating as to unworthy motives for their opinions, or even by digging up or inventing discreditable episodes in their personal lives which have no connection with their experimental researches.

Such crudities are not to be found in the work of the two critics who will be discussed here: Dr G. R. Price of Minnesota and Professor Hansel of Swansea. Although these too sometimes seem to fall short of the stan-

94

dards of the ideal critic, one can, without agreeing with their conclusions, recognise that they are aiming at something essential to the work of psychical research, the testing of its foundations. If these are sound, they will survive the criticism of the honest critic, however searching this may be. Such a critic may also contribute to the research by making experimenters aware of unsuspected weaknesses in their experimental designs. This can be serviceable so long as it does not lead to an extreme preoccupation with experimental precautions which may produce types of experiment that are as unfruitful as they are elaborately safeguarded. Least of all is it desirable that sensitivity to criticism should mislead experimenters into the vain effort to create a new design of experiment that is impervious to all criticism, and away from the more profitable task of finding out about the nature of ESP.

Dr G. R. Price's criticism started from the very reasonable contention that, in a choice between the improbable and the impossible, we must choose the improbable (Price, 1955). Having been, at one time, a believer in ESP, Price changed his mind after reading Hume's discussion of miracles in which it is urged that we should always believe in the knavery or follies of others rather than in events that violate the laws of nature. He was convinced that the best ESP work cannot be accounted for by error and that the odds against their chance occurrence are overwhelming. Therefore one must consider the possibilities of fraud either by the experimenter or by one of those working with him. He takes Dr Soal's experiment as one of those most effectively cutting out all normal means of explanation, and discusses a number of different ways in which the results obtained could have been produced fraudulently. The actual modes of fraud suggested by Price would not be easy since they would involve memorisation of target orders and the use of codes. But Price argues that they would not have been impossible and, since they are merely highly improbable, they are to be preferred as explanations to ESP which he considers to be impossible.

There is, of course, here no assertion that anyone did commit fraud in these experiments. What is asked is the perfectly proper question as to whether anyone (including the experimenters) could have produced the results by fraud. This is a reasonable question to be asked about any experimental results (in other fields of research besides parapsychology) if the reported results seem improbable and the experiment is not easily repeatable. Unless special and unusual precautions have been taken, the answer to this question will generally be 'Yes'. This will not, in the absence of any ground for doubting the reliability of the experimenter, be a reason for rejecting the results of the experiments in question except for those who are convinced that they know the results are impossible. This conviction may be insecurely based but those who hold it will necessarily reject any experiments which point to such results.

Since Price's presuppositions would lead him to reject the results of any experiment in which experimenter fraud was possible, however improbable, there seems to be some inconsistency in his suggestion of a fraud-proof experiment with targets in sealed metal containers and with a jury of twelve prominent persons, all hostile to ESP. If we ignore the difficulty that such a design would seem likely to inhibit ESP, there remains the fatal objection that if this experiment were successful, it too would be inconclusive. It is true that the chance of twelve hostile persons entering into a conspiracy to deceive would be much less than that of two experimenters already favourably impressed by the evidence for ESP. But, although smaller, it would not be zero; if those twelve testified to an impossibility, those who agree with Dr Price would have to reject their evidence on the ground that even a high degree of improbability is to be preferred to an impossibility.

Professor Hansel also, in the *Journal of the Society for Psychical Research* and in a recent book (1966), has put forward a somewhat similar view. He is rather less emphatic than Price in his rejection of the possibility of ESP but regards its intrinsic improbability as too great for the existing experimental evidence to be sufficient support for its reality. In his opinion, the design of experiments has not excluded the possibility of their results having been fraudulently produced. He has also suggested how fraud could have produced the observed results in the Pearce-Pratt and also in the Soal-Goldney series of experiments.

With respect to the Pearce-Pratt experiment, Hansel points out that, although the percipient was seen to go into the University Library during the experiment, there was no one with him there and he might have left it and looked through the fanlight of Dr Pratt's door and so observed the target cards as they were recorded by Pratt. This is obviously a very unlikely explanation since the risk of his being seen would have been great, and it has been pointed out that the opinion that he could have seen the target cards if he had been looking through the fanlight is based on an incorrect plan of Pratt's room (Stevenson, 1967). It remains true that leaving the percipient by himself in the library was a defect in design of this experiment and leaves open the possibility that Pearce left the library and obtained knowledge of the order of the target cards by means normal but unknown. This is a theoretical possibility even if we think (as I certainly do) that nothing of the sort happened. A simpler explanation of the same kind would be that Pratt and Rhine were in collusion to defraud; the co-operation of Pearce would then not have been necessary.

In the case of the Soal-Goldney experiments, Hansel suggests that the successful agents might have memorised the card order and produced successful results by changing the coding cards so as to produce maximum scores. This too is not likely to be a correct suggestion; it would require a remarkable feat of memory, and it has been pointed out by Soal that even if it were carried out at maximum efficiency, it would not produce a deviation from mean chance expectation as great as that found in the Soal-Goldney experiments (Soal, 1960).

Although, however, the particular suggestions made by Price and Hansel as to how fraud might have produced the results found in these experiments may be erroneous, this would not affect the main point of their criticism. The point is: 'The impossible does not happen. ESP is impossible. Therefore ESP does not happen. If, therefore, any experimental results have been obtained under such carefully controlled conditions that they can be explained only by ESP or by fraud, the explanation by fraud must be accepted however unlikely it may seem to be.' The critic naturally prefers to be able to suggest how the fraud took place, but this is not essential to the argument.

Those who do not accept this argument will not deny its first premiss. That the impossible does not happen is a tautology which it would be nonsensical to deny. The second premiss that ESP is impossible may reasonably be doubted. Our intuitive judgments as to what is and what is not impossible may indeed merely be habits of thought expressing expectations based on what we already know. The history of scientific advance gives us many examples of such expectations which have been falsified, and those familiar with the history of science are not likely to feel much confidence in their intuitions as to what is and what is not possible. They will be rather inclined to look for a sounder guide in an experimental investigation of what does and what does not happen. What happens must belong to the realm of the possible, whatever may be our feelings as to whether it ought to happen.

But anyone so convinced of the reliability of his own intuitions about the limits of possibility that he can say with confidence that ESP is not possible will not be turned from this opinion merely by evidence derived from one (or more than one) highly successful experiment with new and more rigid safeguards against the possibility of fraud. Nor should he be so converted, for, however elaborate the safeguards, the possibility of collusive fraud is not reduced to zero. Even if Price's experiment were successful with its sealed metal containers and hostile jury, such a critic should still feel bound to prefer an extreme improbability to an impossibility.

We must consider then whether there is not another road to conviction as to the reality of ESP more sure than that of multiplying precautions against the possibility of fraud by the experimenter. I think there is a more hopeful way of achieving this aim which depends on the fact that the one person who knows with certainty whether the experimenter has cheated is the experimenter himself. So, if any person wanting to test the reality of ESP carries out a successful (i.e. highly significant) experiment with full primary precautions (against sensory leakage, recording errors, fraud by percipient, etc.) and he knows that he has not himself cheated, that experiment will be conclusive to him. It may be strong evidence to others as well, but will not be conclusive if they consider the remote possibility that the experimenter has cheated; that possibility will be closed only to the experimenter himself, but to the experimenter it will be closed absolutely.

In carrying out such an experiment I suggest that a simple design of experiment is to be preferred. Full primary precautions are compatible with a simple overall design. The complexities of the Soal-Goldney design were directed towards creating conviction that the experimenters could not be cheating and such precautions will be unnecessary in an experiment whose object is to convince the experimenter himself. It is interesting to note that Hansel's criticism of the Soal-Goldney experiment suggests as a possible means of fraud the five cards used for coding, which was a feature introduced to make it harder for any of the experimental team to cheat. This criticism might be met by the development of a new complication of design that would make the changing of the code cards impossible. This new complication might then, in its turn, be shown to have new possibilities of evasion. I think it is better to stick to simple experimental designs, and to eliminate the possibility of results being produced by the experimenters cheating, not by increased elaboration of design but by providing opportunities for critics to see whether they can, as experimenters, repeat the successes.

I propose to call this the 'Warner way', since it is the method which was followed by Professor Lucien Warner in the experiment described in the last chapter (Warner, 1937). In this experiment, Warner used a percipient who had already shown her ability in ESP, and, with fully adequate primary precautions, obtained a highly significant result. This provided conclusive evidence for the reality of ESP to Warner himself who knew that he had not cheated, and strong evidence for anyone else who believes in Warner's good faith. It is not, of course, sufficient evidence for the critic who believes that ESP is more unlikely than any alternative explanation. If he is to be convinced, it must be by doing such an experiment himself and doing it successfully. He might, of course, do it and not get a successful result and so find himself confirmed in his scepticism. He would, at any rate, have the satisfaction of knowing that he had taken the risk of being proved wrong. It is not clear how many of the more prominent of the critics of ESP have exposed themselves to this risk.

They may, of course, have wished to do so, but found it too difficult to get the co-operation of a percipient with a previous record of success. I suggest that it would be a good thing for parapsychological laboratories with a good percipient to refrain from the continuous experimenting with them which seems to inhibit their ESP performance. Instead they might be made members of a pool of potential experimental subjects who could be available for short series of experiments by those who were unconvinced of the reality of ESP but were willing to take part in experiments so designed as to give a good chance of success with adequate primary precautions.

It is often overlooked by critics of ESP that many of those who believe in ESP have come to believe in it by the Warner road; they have themselves obtained results under adequately safeguarded conditions and they themselves know they have not cheated. Against their conviction of the reality of ESP, arguments based on the possibility that experimenters carrying out the crucial experiments on ESP could have cheated are ineffective. Their conviction of the reality of ESP does not depend on these experiments.

Although we may doubt the assertions of those who tell us that ESP is impossible, we cannot reasonably deny that its occurrence seems improbable. We have deeply ingrained ways of thinking based on the physical sciences which lead us to expect that no information can pass from one mind to another without passing through the channels of sense, and that no information can be received about events in the outside world unless it passes through these same channels of sense. The type of explanation of transfer of information that science leads us to accept is one in which there is a continuous train of physical events between the thing informed about and the brain receiving the information. Although there is much that is mysterious about normal perception, it is a process that fits the ordinary scientific system of explanation if we ignore the problem of how a physical event in the brain is related to a conscious process. Leaving aside this problem with which science cannot deal, we may explain the process of visual perception as a continuous train of causally connected physical events, starting with a chain of electro-magnetic waves from the object which travel to the retina of the observer, there causing a chemical change which produces excitation in the retinal end-organs from which an impulse passes along fibres of the optic nerve to the visual area of the cerebral cortex. There is thus a complete chain of physical causation between the object seen and the brain of the person seeing it, so the pattern of events is one which is recognised as belonging to normal science.

This is plainly not the case in any form of extra-sensory perception. There is no discoverable chain of physical events linking the brain of the agent with that of the percipient in a telepathy experiment. It is true that telepathy can be dealt with in a way in which science has often dealt with an apparent gap in causation, by postulating a physical link where none appears. We may thus suppose that, in telepathy, some form of radiation passes from agent to percipient. In suggesting this, one is following a respectable tradition of stretching existing principles of explanation as far as possible to cover unexpected new facts. But this may not be the right way to deal with them; it may be that what is required is new principles of explanation. In the case of telepathy, Vasiliev has shown that, if there is a radiation carrying information, it is not screened by a thickness of metal plate which we should expect to screen electro-magnetic radiation of any likely wave-length (Vasiliev, 1963). This does not disprove the radiation theory of telepathy, but it does suggest very strongly that it is not in this

99

direction that we must look for an explanation. This suggestion is further strengthened by the consideration that any explanation in terms of emitted radiations can only be applied with great difficulty to cases of clairvoyance and not at all to phenomena of precognition since the percipient cannot be supposed to be receiving radiations emitted by something which does not yet exist. There is a strong case for considering that what is required for explanation is not a new application of present explanatory principles but rather the development of new explanatory principles.

The difficulty of such a development is considerably exaggerated by Price when he refers to ESP as a violation of nature and classes it with such events as miracles. This view, which treats an incompatibility with current scientific theory as equivalent to a breach of nature, seems to assume a somewhat superstitious view of natural law. A natural law is not a pre-existing system of rules which phenomena have to obey; it is a system of rules that the scientist puts forward to account for observed regularities. If an unexpected event occurs, it is not a breach of the law; it is an indication that the law, as at present enunciated, must be altered. Our expectations have been based on laws which are imperfect.

That any existing system of laws may be imperfect and in need of amendment is not an unfamiliar situation in the history of science; it happens at all those turning points in scientific development which have been called by Professor Kuhn 'scientific revolutions' (Kuhn, 1962). Examples of such turning points are the passage from Ptolemaic to Copernican cosmology, from Lamarckian to Darwinian views of organic development, from Newtonian to relativity dynamics, etc. In all these cases, expectations based on a currently accepted system of concepts and laws have been found not to accord with observation and have been replaced by a system of expectations based on a new set of concepts and laws; in Kuhn's terms, on a new 'paradigm'.

The situation which in the past has led to the overthrow of an accepted paradigm and its replacement by a new one, is the discovery in the course of normal research that some fact or facts revealed by research are not such as the old paradigm would lead us to expect. These may be called anomalies; examples are to be found in the failure of the Michelson-Morley experiment to detect ether drift due to the Earth's motion through space, Planck's discovery of unexpected irregularities in black box radiation (leading to the quantum theory), the discovery of diffraction fringes which amongst other things led to the general acceptance of the wave theory of light, and so on. In all science, the turning up of an experimental result that would not have been predicted from existing ways of thinking is important as a challenge to those ways of thinking. This is what gives ESP its theoretical importance; it is clearly an anomaly in the sense that it does not fit in with our currently accepted explanations of behaviour as influenced by the external environment only so far as this environment creates physical stimuli which act on our sense organs. The situation is one that the history of science would lead us to expect to be the starting point of a scientific revolution; it may be many years before the direction of this revolution can be clearly seen.

Kuhn's theory of scientific revolutions contains many illuminations of the problems of parapsychology; amongst others it suggests why we should expect to have critics who deny the reality of the phenomena reported in our experiments and why they will not be convinced merely by increased weight of experimental evidence. He points out that practitioners of normal science have always tended to resist new theories because these seem to throw doubt on what they are doing and on what they have already done. He also suggests that this resistance to change by normal science has its own value in emphasising the fact of anomaly when a new finding does not fit normal expectations. But this resistance has always led a number of the practitioners of normal science to refuse to recognise the necessity for conceptual change. They will not indeed abandon an old paradigm until a new paradigm is ready to take its place. We are, in parapsychology, far from the situation of being able to formulate a new paradigm. So we must expect incredulity to persist among our critics, and not expect that this incredulity will be overcome by mere increase of experimental evidence obtained under new conditions of stringency.

This does not mean that parapsychologists should now abandon experimental work and devote themselves to thinking out a new body of theory. It is not in that way that new paradigms have developed in scientific history. Rather it has happened that increased knowledge through research has shown increased discrepancy between what is observed and what existing theories would predict. Then, as these anomalies increase, at a certain stage of the resulting tension, someone comes along with a new paradigm which relieves the tension by showing that the apparent anomalies are, in the new way of looking at the field, no longer anomalies but are exactly what one would expect.

It seems to me that we are not yet at that stage of tension in parapsychology at which a new paradigm can be promulgated, and that we can only reach that stage by much more research. One obvious difference between parapsychology and the physical sciences is that expectations can be much more precisely formulated in the physical sciences and that one can therefore more precisely state the nature of the contradiction between what is observed and what is expected, and more easily formulate the nature of the paradigm change that will make this contradiction disappear. In order to get more precise research results in parapsychology we need more reliable methods of getting experimental results. The effort to get such reliable experimental results, whether by selection or by training of percipients, seems to be one of the most important immediate objectives of research in parapsychology.

In the meantime, the fact of anomaly is strongly indicated, not only in the experimental demonstration of the reality of ESP, but also in that of other paranormal phenomena which will be discussed later, particularly in precognition and psycho-kinesis. The situation is not one, I think, that invites us to theoretical speculation, but rather one that invites us to keep our minds open to the necessity for theoretical change and also to the fact that similar theoretical changes have taken place frequently during the development of science. It is not a situation that should surprise us or that should be seen as a threat to science. At the same time, it is not a situation that offers us much hope of being able to anticipate the nature of the paradigm change when it comes. What is required from us is flexibility of mind and readiness to accept paradigm change. When the time is ripe, the work of Kuhn suggests that the individual who introduces the new paradigm will be young or new to the field. Many of us are neither, so we should not be tempted to see ourselves as the Einsteins of parapsychology, but rather as having the task of preparing his way by increasing knowledge of the field.

## References

HANSEL, C. E. M. (1966), *ESP : a Scientific Evaluation*, London.

KUHN, T. S. (1962), *The Structure of Scientific Revolutions*, Chicago.

PRICE, G. R. (1955), 'Science and the Supernatural', *Science*, 26 April (abstracted *Journal of Parapsychology*, xix, 1955, 238–41).

SOAL, S. G. (1960), 'A reply to Mr. Hansel', *Proceedings of the Society for Psychical Research*, xliii, 43–82.

STEVENSON, I. (1967), 'An Antagonist's View of Parapsychology', *Journal of the American Society for Psychical Research*, 254–67.

VASILIEV, L. L. (1963), *Experiments in Mental Suggestion* (English translation), Church Crookham.

WARNER, L. (1937), 'A Test Case', *J. Parapsych.*, i, 234–8.

# XII

# The pattern of ESP

It has already been suggested that the main purpose of experimental research into ESP is not to provide more convincing evidence that ESP exists but rather to discover what can be found out about the nature of ESP. If ESP is a reality, the study of its events will be found to fall into a pattern. When we know enough of that pattern, we shall be able to make a guess at the rest of it, to construct a paradigm which is the conceptual system and set of rules within which ESP will fit so that it will seem no longer to be exceptional or surprising but to belong to the familiar order of things which we call 'Nature'.

We are far from that position yet. Bits of the pattern have emerged but they remain isolated bits of a pattern of which the whole is not yet perceptible. It is as if we had a large jigsaw puzzle of which only a few parts fit together but these parts remain isolated; we cannot see the larger pattern into which they all fit. Our task then is to try to fit together new bits of the pattern, in the faith that when enough little bits have been fitted together, the pattern of the whole will emerge.

Bits of the pattern are being all the time suggested by various researches which are published in the technical journals. A sample of these researches will be discussed in the present and following chapters. I shall not be attempting to cover the whole field but rather to give a representative sample of the experimental work that has made a soundly based contribution to still very incomplete knowledge of the total pattern of ESP. A conclusion can only be regarded as soundly based, either if it rests on data of high statistical significance which have been obtained under rigid experimental conditions, or if it has been amply confirmed by independent researches. We can, of course, feel more confidence in conclusions that satisfy both of these criteria.

There is no sharp dividing line between researches aimed at proving the reality of ESP and those directed towards finding out about its nature. This is especially true of the earlier experimental work, and it would be difficult to decide into which of these categories one should place the work of the Duke Parapsychology Laboratory reported in J. B. Rhine's first book (1934). In some respects the experiments took the typical form of experiments intended to prove the reality of ESP; there were numerous repetitions of observations obtained under identical conditions until values of P had become extremely small. At the same time, there were also variations of conditions, and the experimenters were alert to observe changes of response which occurred either spontaneously or as a result of these changes of conditions. As a result, there were a number of observations reported at this time which have been borne out by later work and which make a significant contribution to what we know of the general pattern of ESP responses.

It seems to be the case that some (but not all) of these early experiments were carried out under experimental conditions that were imperfect by modern standards. Certain defects in method were pointed out by critics both within and outside the laboratory, and where imperfections in method were seen to exist these were rectified. There is no good ground for supposing that any imperfections of method in early experiments did lead to spurious indications of success, but there is an element of doubt which makes the results of these experiments of uncertain value as evidence for the characteristics of ESP if they stood alone. They remain of great value as indicators of possible characteristics of ESP so far as these have been afterwards verified by later experiments carried out under more rigid conditions. There will be mentioned here a number of characteristics of ESP first suggested during the early Duke experiments which have received ample confirmation from the common experience of later experiments and researches carried out by the more rigid methods which became standard afterwards.

The first and most important of the early discoveries about the nature of ESP was that of the fact that looking at the target card by the experimenter (or agent) was not, as had been generally previously supposed, an essential condition for successful guessing by the percipient. One could, therefore, no longer refer to successful guessing by the percipient as due to 'thought-transference' or 'telepathy', and the more inclusive term 'extrasensory cognition' was substituted; later the more inclusive and less definite term 'psi' was suggested and largely adopted.

This was not, it is true, the first time that experiments had been done under the condition of the experimenter not knowing the right response, or the first time that success had been reported under such conditions. Success under clairvoyance conditions had, however, received little attention and the standard form of paranormal cognition had been regarded as that of one mind communicating with another ('telepathy'), although it was generally admitted that there might be an additional mode of paranormal cognition by 'clairvoyance'. Very often those who accepted mind-to-mind communication, rejected the possibility of clairvoyance. Experiments were generally done under conditions which could be explained by telepathy since the experimenter knew always what was the target object.

The experiments at Duke made a revolutionary change in this situation. Since subjects were found to succeed equally well in ESP tasks in which the experimenter did not know the target as with those in which he did, the way was obviously open to consider the possibility that such experiments did not involve two paranormal cognitive capacities 'telepathy' and 'clairvoyance', but only one which might be revealed under different experimental conditions.

If this surmise were correct, it would not follow that all subjects would be equally good under both conditions; even trivial changes of conditions of experimenting may produce differences in performance. It cannot, therefore, be regarded as evidence against the possibility of the equivalence of telepathy and clairvoyance that Soal's subject Shackleton was reported to be able to succeed when the agent looked at the target card and not when he did not. If this were a real inability to succeed under clairvoyance conditions, it might be an individual preference of the subject (or of the experimenter) for the telepathy condition of experimenting. On the other hand, it may have been merely an unfavourable reaction to the introduction of a new condition.

It cannot, of course, be properly said that the early Duke experiments proved the equivalence of what had been distinguished as telepathy and clairvoyance; they showed that the distinction was less firmly grounded than had been supposed, and they opened the possibility that both were the same paranormal capacity operating under different conditions.

Another ingenious modification of experimental conditions was made about the same time when some percipients tried to give wrong responses instead of right ones. The percipient Pearce, for example, succeeded in getting a score of 17 in 225 guesses when he was trying to score low (28 below mean chance expectation), whereas he was reported to be averaging about twice mean chance expectation when he was trying, in the usual way, to score high (p. 40).

The same variation in method of responding was tried with another percipient Stuart (p. 70). This subject scored 81 above m.c.e. (260) in 1,300 guesses with the usual aim of getting right, but only 182 hits (78 below m.c.e.) when he was trying to guess wrong.

There is nothing surprising about the fact that, if a subject can guess cards right, he can also, if he wants to do so, guess them wrong. What is interesting about these results is a fact pointed out later, that they show the subject having a much greater capacity to name the cards wrongly than to name them rightly (Thouless, 1935). It is true that both percipients showed about the same deviation below expectation when they were trying to guess wrong as they showed above expectation when they tried to guess right, but this is not the result that would follow if both kinds of guesses were being made with equal efficiency.

Stuart's 341 hits when he was trying to guess right can be accounted for by supposing that he knew the target card by ESP in 101 of his 1,300 guesses and got one-fifth of the remainder (1,119) right by chance. That would give him the observed number of hits (101 + 240 = 341). But his deficiency of 78 below mean chance expectation cannot be accounted for on the assumption that he knew 101 of the cards and could, therefore, deliberately guess them wrong, while for the remainder he guessed by chance one-fifth right and four-fifths wrong. A simple calculation will show that that would only give him a deficiency of 20 hits below mean chance expectation, about a quarter of the observed number. Further calculation shows that a deficiency of 78 would require that the percipient knew by ESP the nature of the target well enough to give it wrong about 390 times in his 1,300 guesses. Then if he gets right by chance in one-fifth of the remaining 910 guesses, this will give the observed number of 182 hits when he is trying to guess wrong (see Appendix A).

What seems to be indicated then is that the successful subject knows by ESP a certain number of the target cards well enough to name them correctly, but a much larger number of them are less accurately known and the subject can perform the easier task of naming one of the four symbols that the target card is not. In Stuart's case, it seemed that the latter task could be performed nearly four times as often as the other. One cannot feel very strong conviction that this is a genuine ESP characteristic; it does not seem to have been confirmed by later work but this may simply be because no later experimenter has thought it worth while to carry out card-guessing experiments in which the percipient is trying to guess wrongly. It is not intrinsically a very unlikely result and it seems unlikely to have been produced by any deficiency in the experimental conditions of the Stuart experiments. It must now be noted as a possible characteristic of ESP; whether it is important or not can perhaps only be judged when the whole pattern has emerged.

The next observation made in these early experiments is of undoubted importance, both in practice and in theory. This is the tendency of positive ESP scores to decrease with time. This has been called the 'decline' effect, or 'chronological decline'. This term does, in fact, cover more than one characteristic of the psi-response. There is first the type of decline within any single occasion during which a subject shows a lowering of score as the occasion proceeds, or during some division of the occasion, as, for example, between the first and the last half of each run through the pack of twenty-five cards. Let us call all such declines within a single occasion 'episodic declines'. It is characteristic of episodic decline that it is temporary; there is almost complete recovery of performance at the beginning of the next occasion or of the next run through the pack.

There is also, however, a more permanent decline which is found over a long period of experimenting. An experimental subject who showed promising positive ESP results in his early experiments very commonly shows declining scores which may reach chance level within a period of months. He may not recover his former ability to score positively even after a long period without experiments. This characteristic of ESP may be called 'long-period decline'.

It is not easy to give a date for the first discovery of the decline effects although they were first singled out as a significant feature of the ESP response by Rhine in his 1934 book *Extra-Sensory Perception*. They had, however, been noticed earlier. Of the Creery sisters, for example, it was reported that 'the average of successes gradually declined' (Gurney et al., 1886). A similar decline was also pointed out by Estabrooks in an early study of ESP (Estabrooks, 1927). Since then, decline effects (both episodic and long-period) have been found by so many workers that one must regard decline as one of the best attested and most often repeated observations in ESP research. It is true that a certain number of subjects (as, for example, Soal's subject Basil Shackleton) have gone on scoring over very long periods without measurable fall-off of score, but such cases are exceptional. The more general rule is that initial ESP success is followed by decline.

We commonly use the one word 'decline' both for the decreases in score that may take place within an experimental occasion and for the more permanent decreases that take place over a long period of experimenting. This must not be allowed to hide the fact that there are important differences between these two effects. While long-period decline is most inclined to attract attention because of the experimental inconvenience that is caused by a successful subject ceasing to be successful, episodic decline is perhaps of more theoretical interest because it is related to other discernible bits of the pattern of psi. It may, in fact, be regarded as a special case of the more general phenomenon of 'position effects' (Cadoret and Pratt, 1950).

The general principle of position effects is that a successful ESP subject may show tendencies to score in some parts of every experimental occasion while he may show chance results or even negative scoring in other parts of his session. Episodic decline may not only take place over the whole session, but also be a characteristic of the results of each run of twenty-five guesses; the first half of each run may be consistently better than the second half.

More detailed examination of run scores shows in many cases that decline is not the only relation of scoring to position within the run. There is often found also a tendency to an increase in scoring during the last five calls of the run so that, if the average score per segment of five calls were plotted on graph paper, it would show a U-shaped curve with the second arm of the U generally going less high than the first arm. This effect was called *terminal salience*, and a formula may be used to evaluate its amount. The index so given is called the *salience ratio*.

The run is an arbitrary division made within the experiment by a discontinuity produced at the end of the calling of a complete pack of cards.

Both the decline within the run and the terminal salience of the run must therefore be attributed to an effect on the subject's psi-response of a structuring which has been made within the experiment by the experimenter's way of carrying it out. One naturally asks, therefore, whether any other arbitrary division within the experiment would produce its position effects. This is found to be the case. When the percipient writes down his own guesses on a form in which each segment of five guesses is clearly marked off by a line from the adjacent segments, then (with adults, but curiously not with child percipients) the mean results of the segments showed significant terminal salience (Rhine, 1941).

Position effects were also first noticed early in parapsychological experimentation. In Rhine's first book *Extra-Sensory Perception* (p. 137 f.), graphs are shown demonstrating position effects within segments in Pearce's calls. The final mean segment curve shows a marked drop between the results for the first two calls of the segment and the last two. The curve is not U-shaped since the average scores for the fourth and the last call are the same. It looks as if both segmental decline and terminal salience may have been present, with the former predominating.

That ESP results may depend in regular ways on the structuring of the experimental task should not seem very surprising if we remember a very similar observation in memory experiments. If a subject learns a passage by heart, by the 'whole' method in which he repeats the whole passage many times in succession, it is found that, before learning is complete, the part best remembered will be at the beginning of the passage, the part next best remembered will be at the end, while the part least effectively learned will be in the middle. Thus the reproduction, when learning is incomplete, will be a U-curve of the same shape as that for ESP. I have little doubt that, if the passage were split up into verses, one would find optimal learning also at the beginning and end of each verse, corresponding to segmental terminal salience in ESP experiments. I do not think, however, that this experiment has been carried out for memorising tasks.

When position effects were first discovered, the interest felt in them was less in the fact that they revealed something about the pattern of psi than in their possible usefulness as an indication of the presence of ESP or other psi-process alternative to the direct evidence which would come from a significant positive deviation. It is obvious that position effects are evidence for some cause at work making the subject's responses correspond to some extent with the targets, since a merely random set of right answers would show nothing but accidental and non-significant internal consistencies of this kind. All position effects can be used as evidence for the presence of psi provided they were predicted before the particular set of results in question was examined for position effects. This prediction could be made as the result of a pilot experiment or from expectations aroused by some other set of experiments. It would be quite erroneous to notice a position effect in an experiment and then to work out its significance, and to regard that position effect, if significant, as evidence of ESP; that would be an example of the 'crumpled paper fallacy' (Appendix C). No competent modern experimenter would be guilty of such an error.

Episodic decline has a certain usefulness to the experimenter since it may provide him with indirect evidence of the presence of ESP; he is more inclined to regard long-period decline as just a nuisance since it prevents him from carrying out as many and as varied experiments as he would like with a gifted subject he is fortunate enough to have found. It is certainly a severe limitation to experimental work, and it would be easier to obtain answers to the unresolved problems of ESP if we had a reliable way of overcoming the tendency to long-period decline. This tendency is, however, also in itself of considerable theoretical interest. It is not what we should expect, because the more general rule in psychological experimentation is to find that the repeated performance of an activity leads to improved performance. This is what we call 'learning'. It is true that, within a single experimental occasion, we may find a falling off in performance which is attributed to 'fatigue'. This is parallel to the episodic decline in ESP experiments, but the long-period decline of ESP is obviously something different since it does not show the feature characteristic of fatigue that a period of rest leads to recovery of the lost ability.

The normal psychological activity to which long-period decline seems to be analogous is that of 'inhibition' in which there seems to be an active process within the organism preventing the repetition of a response, as, for example, when the response is coupled with some stimulus disagreeable to the responding organism. There does not, however, seem to be any obvious reason why a successful ESP response should be inhibited. Its results are not disagreeable to the person producing them. On the contrary, the percipient wants to be successful and is pleased when he is successful. At the conscious level, the situation seems to be typically one in which there should be reinforcement of the successful response which should lead to its becoming better over a period of time. If there is an inhibiting mechanism it must be an unconscious one; we must hope that future research in ESP will enable us to say more than this about it. Understanding of long-period decline will have both the practical advantage that it may lead to increased control and also the theoretical advantage of giving a new insight into the nature of ESP.

One possible theoretical implication of the tendency of ESP to become inhibited in the course of an initially successful series of experiments is that it seems to give some support to the speculation that ESP is a primitive form of cognition normally suppressed in favour of the more recently developed and more efficient perceptual system provided by the sense organs and the central nervous system. A successful ESP experiment would then be a situation in which this normal suppression has, in some way, been short-circuited; decline may be the automatic reinstatement of the normal suppression of the primitive psi-function. This speculation may give some hint as to the relation of the decline effects to the total picture of psi-functioning.

There are two further points about long-period decline on which the experimental records provide strong indications although neither has yet been made the subject of full-scale research. These are: first, the possibility that such decline may not be spread over all ESP performances but may be to some extent specific to the particular task which the percipient has already been carrying out; secondly, it seems very likely that long-period decline may not be merely something that happens to the percipient; it may also be that the experimenter is declining in his capacity to get positive results.

On the first of these points, a number of experimenters have had the impression that, if a subject has been successful in an ESP task but has dropped to chance results, he may start being again successful if he is given a new task. For example, in an experimental series with myself as subject, I carried out three tasks in card-guessing which differed in the degree to which I was accustomed to them (Thouless, 1949). On each of 144 occasions, one pack was guessed under 'down-through' conditions, one pack was guessed with the intention of the guesses corresponding with the order of the pack after a cut at a randomly determined point, while another pack was also guessed precognitively but in a more complex manner since the pack was thoroughly shuffled as well as randomly cut between the guessing and the check.

The first of these tasks was one that I had practised for a good many years with some degree of success, the second task was one that I had met at Rhine's laboratory about a year earlier and had used during that year again with some success, the third was a form of precognition task that I had never used before and which I thought would prove impossibly difficult. My expectation was that I would succeed in the familiar first task, probably succeed in the second more difficult task, but I felt sure that I could not succeed in the third task since this would require that I should foresee the result of the double process of shuffling and randomly cutting.

I made 25 guesses under each of these three conditions on each of 144 occasions. The results were at variance with all of these expectations. Under the first condition, I scored 62 less than the mean chance expectation of 720 hits, a significant negative deviation ($P = 0.01$). Under the second condition, the number of hits exceeded mean chance expectation to only an insignificant extent. In the new, and supposed impossible, third task, I obtained only chance results on the first 36 occasions but after that I began to score positively and ended with a significant positive deviation of 57 above mean chance expectation ($P = 0.02$).

A likely explanation of these results would seem to be that the first task, being familiar, was thoroughly inhibited to the point of negative scoring. The second, less familiar, task was also inhibited but to a lesser extent, while the third task, being novel, was not inhibited. The situation has changed now from that of twenty years ago; I am also now, I think, completely inhibited with respect to this third task.

When an experimenter has carried out a long series of successful experiments with a particular experimental subject and begins to find that he is scoring at chance level, he is inclined to say that the subject is suffering from long-period decline, and he begins to look for another percipient. This interpretation of the decline may, however, not be the true one, or it may not be the whole truth. It may be the experimenter who is showing long-period decline. This would not be easily apparent in the above situation; it might only show itself in the fact that the experimenter did not find it easy to get another subject to score successfully with him, and he might well attribute this difficulty to a shortage of gifted percipients, not to a change in himself.

Although I know of no systematic investigation of the relative parts played by the experimenter and the percipient in long-period decline, there are very numerous indications in the experimental literature which point to the experimenter as one factor in decline. Many experimenters who reported positive results in the early days of their researches have found that, after a few years of experimental work in this subject, they no longer have highly successful results, even perhaps no successful results at all. The most dramatic example of this was in Rhine's Parapsychology Laboratory at Durham, North Carolina.

In *Extra-Sensory Perception*, Rhine reported that the frequency of successful subjects and their rates of success were much higher than had been found anywhere else. This astonishing success rate seems to have continued during the first decade of the laboratory's work, but their later record is of success rates as disappointingly low as are found elsewhere. Critics of ESP sometimes suggest that the experimental conditions were lax in the early days of experimenting at the Duke Laboratory and that when these conditions were tightened up the early successes disappeared. If this were the case, it would be supposed that the early successes were due solely to the lax conditions, but the actual facts do not fit this simple explanation. It is true that, as experimenting went on, more rigorous conditions were introduced but the falling off of scoring did not coincide in time with the imposition of these stricter conditions. The Pratt-Pearce experiment, for example, took place in 1933–4 under the stricter conditions but it showed a high rate of success (over twelve per cent). The high rate of success seems to have gone on for some years after this. The later fall to levels of success only slightly above mean chance expectation appears to be, not a result of any change in experimental conditions, but an example of the setting in of the general inhibition of ESP scoring which we have called 'long-period decline'. If this is its explanation, it must have been the experimenters who were becoming inhibited since the experimental subjects were not the same individuals during the period.

No doubt the development of the inhibitory process was accompanied by, perhaps caused by, changes in the motivation of the experimenting team. Possible changes affecting motivation would be such factors as the falling off of the first enthusiasm which accompanied the conviction that they were breaking into a new area. Side by side with this falling off of the early enthusiasm, there may have been increasing boredom with the monotonous and repetitive task of routine experimenting, increasing ego-involvement with results, and so on. These are merely speculations as to possibilities; no systematic research has yet been done into the emotional factors determining experimenters' long-period decline.

Although episodic and long-period decline could not have been predicted as properties of ESP if they had not been experimentally demonstrated, there is nothing particularly surprising about them; we have other examples in experimental psychology of performances which fall off through fatigue or inhibition. The next discovery reported in the early Duke experiments was a much more startling one, that percipients pressed to continue in card-guessing after their scores had dropped to chance level, might begin to get fewer hits than the number one would expect by chance.

The first example reported of this was with the experimental subject A. J. Linzmayer (p. 62). After a session in which he was reported to have scored about forty per cent hits, he had dropped to about chance level but Rhine urged him to go on with the experiment which he reluctantly agreed to do. In successive series of 100 guesses, he scored 14, 16, 20, 17, 14; that is, 6, 4, 0, 3, 6 below mean chance expectation. No conclusion could, of course, be drawn from this single observation; the result might be accidental and not due to a real tendency to score below chance. Obviously one may, by chance alone, get groups of results below mean chance expectation as one can, by chance alone, get groups of results above mean chance expectation. The observation was, however, noted as an indication of a problem for future research. Later research has clearly shown that below-chance scoring is a genuine phenomenon and not a mere statistical accident; that such negative scoring effects may be real characteristics of ESP performance is shown both by statistical tests and also by their repeatability. It has also been found that negative scoring is not restricted to situations in which the percipient is urged to go on experimenting when he wants to stop, although some degree of negative attitude towards ESP seems to be a factor in some cases. Negative scoring has also been noted in some cases in which sets of scores have been compared in group experiments or between different conditions. It also seems as if some experimenters under some conditions habitually obtain significant negative scores. The matter of negative scoring is by no means fully understood although it seems clear that it is a genuine effect. The general term 'psi-missing' was used by J. B. Rhine for this and closely related effects (Rhine, 1952).

What makes psi-missing a somewhat surprising effect is the consideration that a percipient can only consistently make wrong guesses if, in some sense, he knows what the right guess ought to be. This strengthens the suggestion that an inhibitory process may be at work in psi-guessing, in this case not merely inhibiting the ESP response but converting it into a direction opposite to that consciously intended by the percipient himself. This would seem to imply that, in a group of experimental subjects of whom some are scoring at about chance level while others are scoring below the level expected by chance, it will be those who have the lowest scores who are showing most ESP activity. It is to be expected, therefore, that these low scorers will prove to have more in common with high scorers in ESP tests than with those who merely score about chance level. This is a problem which has not been much explored, but there are some experimental indications that this expectation is fulfilled.

There is another reported characteristic of ESP which, if it proves to be a genuine one, would seem to be related to psi-missing. This is the 'consistent-missing effect' reported by Cadoret and Pratt (1950). This is the apparent tendency in some subjects consistently to guess a wrong target, e.g. to guess 'cross' when 'circle' is target. This is not an unlikely effect and might indeed be the mechanism of psi-missing. The evidence for its reality is not, however, very strong. The only one of the experimental series they examined which showed the effect at all strongly was one carried out under defective conditions in which the percipient saw the backs of the cards at the time of guessing. Such indications need confirmation by experiments carried out under satisfactory conditions. Some of the experimental series found by Pratt and Cadoret to show the effect were carried out under perfectly satisfactory conditions, but none of these was at a sufficient level of significance to inspire much confidence. The consistent-missing effect may be, and most likely is, part of the pattern of ESP responses, but this needs confirmation. If the habit of showing the results of card-guessing experiments in a (5 × 5) matrix (showing all calls on all targets) became usual amongst parapsychologists, any published series could be examined for consistent missing; then we could quickly find out whether the effect exists and how common it is.

There were two other inhibitory effects noted in the early experiments at the Duke Laboratory which may be called the 'witness effect' and the 'change effect'. Both have been so fully confirmed by the common experience of later experimenters that it is not necessary to enquire whether the original experiments by means of which they were first detected were sufficiently safeguarded.

The witness effect was first reported in the case of the percipient Pearce (p. 76). The results of the introduction of visitors on nine occasions in 1932 and 1933 are shown. These ranged from William McDougall, Professor of Psychology at Duke University, to Wallace Lee, a magician. In each case, Pearce showed positive scoring before the visitor was introduced, a drop of score, sometimes to chance level, after the visitor came in, with a later recovery to a satisfactory level of scoring. A typical example is his reaction to a visit by McDougall on 2 February 1933. In 350 guesses before the visit he had scored 132 hits (38 per cent, i.e. 18 per cent over mean chance expectation of 20 per cent). During the first 125 guesses in the presence of McDougall, the scoring dropped to 33 (6 per cent over m.c.e.). The next 250 guesses, however, still with McDougall present, showed 105 hits (a rise to 22 per cent over m.c.e.).

What this observation suggests is that the introduction of a new person to the experimental session is likely to lead to a reduction or total disappearance of positive scoring, but that this is not a permanent effect since the percipient may become adapted to the presence of a new witness after a period of time. I know of no later systematic research on this effect, but it is constantly the experience of parapsychological experimenters that an observer who comes to look on has the disappointing experience of seeing no success. It may, therefore, be regarded as a finding that has had sufficient confirmation by common experience if not by systematic research. These early experiments also suggest that if the disappointed observer stays quietly looking on until the percipient has become adapted to his presence, the inhibition set up by his coming is likely to disappear and any former level of success to reappear in his presence. It is a common opinion amongst experimenters that such inhibition is particularly likely to occur if the observer is hostile to the experiment or to the percipient. There seems to be no certainty as to whether this hostility must be overtly expressed to be effective, or whether a concealed hostility also inhibits the phenomena. There seems to be no systematic research on these problems, but they are of both theoretical and practical interest.

Another inhibitory effect first reported by Rhine (1934) was that resulting from a change of experimental procedure. This may be called the 'change' effect. It was reported (p. 77) that any change in the experimental methods adopted with the percipient Pearce were likely to cause a drop in scoring rate unless the changes had been suggested by himself. Again the drop was temporary; after a period of low scoring, the subject recovered the ability to score under the new conditions. For example, the agent started looking at the target card after experiments carried out entirely under 'clairvoyance' conditions. In the first 175 guesses under this changed condition, Pearce scored 42 hits (a success rate of only 4 per cent over m.c.e.). In the next 175 guesses when he had got used to the new condition, the success rate went up to 34 per cent over m.c.e. (95 hits). In six other changes of task, a similar drop in scoring rate followed by recovery was recorded.

This reaction to experimental change has also been confirmed by later experimenters with other changes of task. Tyrrell, for example, in experiments in which the percipient (Miss Johnson) indicated which of five boxes would be lit up on opening, introduced a new mechanism (Tyrrell, 1935). Miss Johnson had been succeeding with an earlier and simpler type of machine, but her scores dropped to chance level when she started with the new one. But after a period during which she had only chance results with this new machine, she seemed to become adapted to it and scored 373 hits in 1,271 trials, an excess of 118·8 (or 9 per cent) over mean chance expectation. This excess is highly significant.

She was, however, still unable to score above chance level when a commutator was introduced into the circuit to make the choice of targets independent of the experimenter. In 500 trials under this condition, she scored 101 hits which is almost exactly mean chance expectation. Even when Tyrrell mixed up batches of experiments with the commutator in action with others in which it was not, Miss Johnson scored in those experiments in which the commutator was not in circuit but failed in those in which it was. A less persevering experimenter than Mr Tyrrell might well have concluded that the random choice of targets by the commutator eliminated the possibility of successful scoring, and might have inferred that the experimenter's choice of the target was essential to the percipient's right guessing.

This inference would, however, have been wrong since, after a holiday in September 1935, Miss Johnson became adapted to the experiment with commutator, and in 4,200 trials under this condition, she scored 178 hits over mean chance expectation (Tyrrell, 1936). This is highly significant ($p < 10^{-10}$) and corresponds to a success rate of 4·2 per cent, which is somewhat less than that recorded in the simpler conditions of experimenting but is sufficiently striking.

That change of task may produce a temporary inhibition of ESP response is only in apparent conflict with the finding already reported that, when a percipient has become inhibited with respect to an often repeated task, a change of task may result in a resumption of successful scoring. Both sets of observations may be included in the statement that either successful adaptation to a task or inhibition of ESP success in a frequently repeated task may be disturbed by the introduction of a new task. Both of these effects may be observed in succession in a single experimental series. In my own comparison of three psi-tasks already described, the new (complex precognition) task showed chance results on the first 36 occasions but significant positive scoring on the next 108 occasions.

The possibility of the newness of a task causing the disappearance of an ESP response is unfortunate for the experimenter in this field since it may mislead him as to the effectiveness of a change. It is a common device in experimenting to make some alteration in conditions which, on some hypothesis the experimenter wants to test, may be expected to eliminate the effect that is being studied. If the effect then disappears, the hypothesis is regarded as confirmed.

Although this method of experimenting is indispensable in psychical research, it must there be interpreted with caution. It may be the mere fact of change and not the character of the change that produces an alteration in scoring rate. When, for example, Soal introduced a few experiments under clairvoyance conditions into his series of telepathy experiments with Shackleton, he found that Shackleton dropped to a chance level of scoring and concluded that this percipient could not succeed under clairvoyance conditions. This may, however, merely be an example of a misinterpreted 'change effect'. To be sure that it was not so, it would have been necessary for Soal to persist with the clairvoyance condition of experimenting as Tyrrell did in his attempts to adapt Miss Johnson to the condition of working with a commutator in circuit.

## References

CADORET, R., and PRATT, J. G. (1950), 'The Consistent Missing Effect in ESP', *Journal of Parapsychology*, xiv, 244–56.

ESTABROOKS, G. H. (1927), 'A Contribution to Experimental Telepathy', *Bulletin Boston Society for Psychical Research*, v, Boston.

GURNEY, E., MYERS, F. W. H., and PODMORE, F. (1886), *Phantasms of the Living*, London (abridged edition, New York, 1962).

RHINE, J. B. (1934), *Extra-Sensory Perception*, Boston.

RHINE, J. B. (1941), 'Terminal Salience in ESP Performance', *J. Parapsych.*, v, 183–244.

RHINE, J. B. (1952), 'The Problem of Psi-missing', *J. Parapsych.*, xvi, 90–129.

RHINE, J. B. (1969), 'Position Effects in Psi Test Results', *J. Parapsych.*, xxxiii, 136–57.

THOULESS, R. H. (1935), 'Dr. Rhine's Recent Experiments on Telepathy and Clairvoyance', *Proceedings of the Society for Psychical Research*, xliii, 24–37.

THOULESS, R. H. (1949), 'A Comparative Study of Performance in Three Psi Tasks', *J. Parapsych.*, xiii, 263–73.

TYRRELL, G. N. M. (1935), 'Some Experiments in Undifferentiated Extra-sensory Perception', *J. S.P.R.*, 52–71.

TYRRELL, G. N. M. (1936), 'Further Research in Extra-sensory Perception', *Proc. S.P.R.*, xliv, 99–168.

# XIII

# More elements of the pattern

The characteristics of ESP described in the last chapter were all discovered by means of card-guessing experiments. This is not true of the next characteristic, 'displacement', which was first reported in a picture-reproduction experiment although afterwards it was confirmed in a card-guessing experiment. 'Displacement' was the name given to the oddity discovered by Whately Carington in the reproduction experiments already described in Chapter V (Whately Carington, 1940). It will be remembered that, in Whately Carington's experiment, the target was a picture hanging in the experimenter's room at Cambridge, while the percipients were people living at various places in Great Britain or the United States. The oddity of the results was that it seemed as if the percipients were often getting hits on the target picture exposed on some other night than the night of the guess, even on the targets for following nights although these were not yet drawn. This apparent displacement of the guess on to targets for other nights might have proved illusory. No conclusion could be drawn from this observation; it was noted as a possibility to be tested by a later experiment.

The opportunity for such testing came when S. G. Soal reported his failure to find evidence for ESP in card-guessing experiments taken by 76 subjects who made a total of 44,100 guesses between 1934 and 1939. Whately Carington made the suggestion that Soal should look for guesses scoring hits on the target before or after the one intended by the experimenter. To his surprise, Soal found that two of his subjects, Basil Shackleton and Mrs Stewart, did seem to be scoring on the cards turned up before and after the one intended; the remainder of his subjects showed no such tendency. That this was not merely an accidental occurrence was shown by the fact that both of these subjects showed displaced scoring in a long series of later experiments (Soal and Bateman, 1954).

These observations suggest that one of the possible characteristics of a psi-response is that it may not be directed on to the target intended but displaced to some other target. It is difficult to say how widespread such displacement is in parapsychological experimentation, since the records of experiments are, for obvious reasons of economy of printing space, not generally published in a form in which displacement would be apparent. For this purpose, one would require a record of all targets and responses in their proper time sequence; displacement cannot be inferred from a mere record of the number of guesses and the proportion of these guesses that were hits. Displacement is, therefore, not likely to be recorded unless the experimenter is specifically looking for it. Certain other experimenters did notice the fact of displacement in their own results after the effect had been reported by Carington and Soal. I was myself one of these, but the experiments were performed mainly to satisfy my own curiosity and did not include such precautions as would be necessary to provide evidence convincing to the sceptical (Thouless, 1942).

An important later confirmation of the displacement effect is provided by Pratt's computer analysis of results of card-guessing by Mrs Gloria Stewart (Pratt, 1967). This indicated that connections between guesses and surrounding targets may be much more complex than the simple displacement reported by Soal. It suggests indeed a complex web of causal connections between the percipient's responses and the cards that have been turned up in the neighbourhood of the target card. This is the kind of observation which is only reliable if one is sure that it is not a particular example of the 'crumpled paper fallacy' (Appendix C), of attributing to some cause a complexity which was not specified before the observation. That this is not here the explanation is indicated by the observation that this apparent relation of guess with neighbouring targets is only found when ESP is active (either positively or negatively) as indicated by hits or misses on the target.

The explanation that most obviously suggests itself for displacement is that, as in psi-missing, there is unconscious avoidance of the target. One may suppose that, if one postulates an inhibitory mechanism forbidding the direct appearance of a recognised psi-product in consciousness, this may be evaded by a psi-produced substitute for what would be consciously recognised as the correct psi-response (as, for example, to the intended target). If this is what displacement is in origin, it obviously ceases to be this in such a long series of experiments as that of Soal and Goldney on Shackleton, when the percipient knew he was guessing one ahead, intended to guess one ahead, and continued to do so. If it was merely an evasion of what was recognised as a psi-determined response, it should have disappeared as soon as the guessing one ahead was recognised by the percipient as a psi-performance.

It is natural to try to think of explanations but probably premature to expect to find them. Of this, and other elements of the pattern of psi, we may expect that we shall understand them only when more of the pattern is known. In the meantime we must note them as odd characteristics of psi that we can hope at some time to be able to explain.

Another interesting experimental revelation of a characteristic of the psi-process was the so-called 'sheep-goats' effect first pointed out by Dr Gertrude Schmeidler. This was from a group-comparison experiment in which the scores of subjects who believed in the possibility of ESP (the 'sheep') were compared with scores of those who did not (the 'goats'). Her finding was that the sheep scored significantly better on ESP tests than did the goats. Some of the early results were obtained by the method of comparing total scores of sheep and goats which is not an appropriate method for determining the significance in group-difference experiments, but this is unimportant since Dr Schmeidler's later results were assessed by the unquestionably adequate method of analysis of variance and the same difference was found (Schmeidler and McConnell, 1958).

In work reported by Dr Schmeidler between 1945 and 1951, she found that 692 'sheep', making 149,625 guesses, had 614 more hits than the mean chance expectation of 29,925. In the same experiments, 465 'goats', making 101,250 guesses, had 301 fewer hits than the mean chance expectation of 20,250. In other words, those who believed in ESP succeeded in getting a 0·4 per cent excess of hits while those who did not believe in the possibility of ESP had a deficiency of 0·3 per cent. This is, of course, not a high rate of scoring when we compare it with the kind of percentage score obtained by gifted subjects (as, for example, the 12 per cent above mean chance expectation recorded for Shackleton in the Soal-Goldney experiments). It does not, however, compare unfavourably with the rate of scoring found in other experiments with unselected groups of subjects. The large number of subjects employed in this experiment enables one to be sure that the results are not accidental. Calculation shows that the difference between the 'sheep' and the 'goats' is unquestionably significant (P = 0·00003).

This study is of special interest in the fact that there have been large numbers of attempts to confirm it. Not all of these have obtained the same result as Dr Schmeidler; some have been inconclusive because only a small number of subjects were used or because their significance was not assessed by a method appropriate for the purpose of testing a group difference. Their main result has, however, been in the direction of confirming Dr Schmeidler's finding. It seems highly probable that the difference in scoring rate between believers and unbelievers in the possibility of ESP must take a place amongst the assured items of knowledge about the pattern of psi-responses.

If this difference is regarded as well established, it remains doubtful exactly what difference it is between the 'sheep' and the 'goats' that makes them score differently. It may be their general attitude of belief or disbelief in the possibility of any paranormal means of obtaining knowledge, it may be their expectancy of success or failure in the particular task they have been asked to perform, it may be neither of these factors but rather some difference in their personalities which has the result both of causing them to believe or disbelieve and also to score positively or negatively. Some of the different researches which have followed Dr Schmeidler's have used different criteria for dividing 'sheep' from 'goats', and sometimes the differences in criteria may have led to conflicting results. More research will be necessary before we can be certain as to exactly what characteristic of the 'sheep' it is that makes them score more positively than the 'goats'.

It is not even certain in what direction is the causal relation between belief in ESP and positive scoring. One is inclined to talk as if Dr Schmeidler's results established that belief in the possibility of ESP caused the believer to score positively. It is, however, equally possible that the ability to score positively in ESP tests causes belief in the possibility of ESP. Those who score well may be those who have experienced psi-determination of knowledge in their daily lives and so find no difficulty in believing that it can show itself in a card test. If this were the explanation, it would not be the case that the 'sheep' score well because they are believers, but that they are believers in ESP because they have the ability to score well. The differential scoring itself between 'sheep' and 'goats' seems to be a well-established fact of the pattern of ESP; there obviously remains more to be found out about what determines this scoring difference.

Other group differences in ESP scoring level have been reported. One of the earliest was the report of Dr Betty Humphrey, who divided her subjects into a group of 'expansives' and 'compressives' by observing whether, in a free drawing, the object was made large enough to cover the space available or was restricted to a small part of it (Humphrey, 1946). Although the group as a whole showed no significant difference from mean chance expectation in their ESP scoring, there appeared to be a difference between the mean scores of the 'expansive' and 'compressive' subjects, the former doing rather better than mean chance expectation and the latter rather worse. In another experiment using a somewhat different type of ESP test, the opposite difference was found, the compressives scoring high and the expansives low.

Although this research had important results, its own detailed finding, of a real difference between the ESP abilities of expansives and compressives, cannot be regarded as very firmly established. Dr Humphrey reported the differences as significant but the test of significance was made by comparison between the total scores of each group. This is by no means conclusive since a spurious appearance of significance might result from the accidental inclusion of a larger number of ESP scorers in one group than the other. It is very likely that if the significance had been correctly assessed by a comparison between the numbers of individuals scoring negatively and positively in the two groups, the difference would have turned out to be significant, but we cannot be sure of this. Nor can we be confident of the correctness of this finding by its confirmation by later workers. So far as I know, the reported difference between the scoring of compressive and expansive drawers has not been confirmed.

Two more general findings of this research have, on the other hand, been amply confirmed. The first was that a set of ESP results which shows, as a whole, no significant deviation from mean chance expectation may be divided in such a way that there are two sub-sets, one of which shows positive scoring and the other negative scoring and these two sub-sets may be significantly different. This would, of course, be of no importance if the principle of division depended on the scoring; one could always divide a set of scores in such a way that half were below average and the other half above it. The important point here is that the division can be made on some principle which does not depend on knowledge of the scores, such as a difference between the temperaments or beliefs of the two sets of subjects, and a predicted difference is found between their scores.

The second point that has been confirmed is that such a division can be made on the basis of a difference in personality between the two sub-sets. It may be that the particular personality difference reported by Dr Humphrey may prove to have no consistent relation to ESP scoring, but her report has led the way to other investigations of the scores of subjects divided with respect to some characteristic of personality and significant differences in scoring rate of ESP have been found. Various psychological tests have been used for the purpose of investigating the relationship between test score and various traits of personality. Dr Schmeidler has herself used the Rorschach test in which the subject looks at standardised ink-blots and reports what he can see in them. The Guildford-Martin inventory was used by Nicol and Humphrey who reported that the subjects who were rated on the test as highly self-confident obtained a higher ESP score than the others (Nicol and Humphrey, 1946). Both Rao and Freeman have used tests of anxiety but the results show no consistent direction so we cannot be sure whether the tendency to anxiety is or is not related to ESP ability (Rao, 1965; Freeman and Nielsen, 1964).

Although it seems clear that the ability to score well in ESP tests is related to some measurable qualities of personality, the correlations found have not been close ones. That this is the case follows inevitably from the fact that neither traits of personality nor ESP ability can be measured reliably (in a manner free from a large factor of error). The low reliability of measurements obtained from such personality tests as the Rorschach is well known to experimental psychologists who treat measurements from them with considerable caution. When ESP average scores are in the neighbourhood of one per cent or lower, any measurement of relative ESP of different sets of subjects has an even larger error factor than the most unreliable psychological test of personality. The difficulty in this situation is that no high correlation or other measure of relationship can be found between any two variables that are subject to a large error factor in their measurement. It might be the case that a subject's ESP ability depended to a very large extent on the degree of his proneness to anxiety, and yet only a small correlation could be found between measurements of his anxiety level and his ESP ability because neither of these measurements gave reliable indication of the thing measured. If we are to go further along this way of exploring personality relationships with ESP ability, the parapsychologist must not only aim at finding more reliable ways of measuring personality traits than those generally available, but also better ways of getting fairly high scoring in a group of unselected subjects. This might be by discovering more fruitful experimental techniques, by developing methods of training in ESP performance, or in some other way.

One of the hopes that led to work on the personality correlates of ESP was that it might prove possible to select promising ESP scorers by the use of some combination of personality tests. This hope has, so far, been disappointed by the smallness of the correlations between ESP performance and the personality measurements available. No better way has yet been found of predicting who is going to be a good ESP subject than that of giving a group a preliminary ESP test and separating the high scorers. This is not a very satisfactory way since the amount of error in ESP measurements is so large that most of those selected by such a device are likely to be those who have scored high by accident rather than by ESP ability. Generally, therefore, experimenters testing numbers of subjects have merely taken a large unselected sample without preliminary separation of those who are expected to score well. For some types of experiment, however, it would be a convenience to have a good way of separating out those who would do well in ESP performance. At some time in the future it is to be hoped that a suitable battery of tests for this purpose will have been found.

Dr Humphrey's work, already referred to, was the first indication that the scores of a group of subjects which seemed not to differ from mean chance expectation might turn out to be made up of two sets of scores belonging to subjects who were scoring positively and to others who were scoring negatively, and that these two sets of scores might be significantly different. The same possibility of a mixture of positive and negative scoring producing an overall appearance of conformity with chance expectation may also be realised when the division is made between scores obtained by one method and another in the course of a single experiment. This is the 'differential effect'. It was fairly late in the history of experimental work in psychical research (from about 1950) that experimenters began to find that if subjects were given two contrasting operations to perform it was very likely that they would score positively on one of them and negatively on the other and that the difference between the two sets of scores might prove to be statistically significant.

The earliest report of such an effect seems to be that of Skibinsky who found that if the same six subjects were given ESP tests in which the targets were proper names and tests in which the targets were the ordinary ESP symbols, they scored significantly better on the ESP targets (Skibinsky,

1950). This was contrary to the expectation of the experimenter who supposed that the more meaningful and personal proper names would lead to better ESP scoring. His results seem rather to suggest that the more meaningful and personal targets led to more effective inhibition of ESP.

He gave his subjects a total of 299 runs (each of 25 guesses) on the 'names' targets, on which they scored 83 less than mean chance expectation (a score of −8 per cent). This is a deficiency which would occur only once in 60 times by chance alone so it is likely that there is here a real tendency to avoid the target. On the ESP symbols there was a score of 49 above mean chance expectation (+3·6 per cent). This might happen by chance about once in six cases so it cannot be judged significant. The difference of 11·6 per cent between scores on names and symbols is, however, more significant than is either score separately (P = 0·007) and must be considered to be strong evidence of a real difference between the scoring rate of the two tasks.

If it is a general rule that the use of two contrasting conditions in ESP experimenting tends to produce a negative score under one condition and a positive score under the other, this suggests that a design incorporating such a contrast may be a powerful instrument in the hands of the parapsychological experimenter. Although there were occasional reports of significant differences between results obtained from the same subject under different conditions, it was not until about ten years after Skibinsky's report that this method of experimenting was fully exploited.

In 1962, Sanders reported an experiment in which twenty subjects were given a precognitive ESP test in which they wrote down half of their guesses, while they called out the other half of their guesses which were written down by someone else (Sanders, 1962). They were asked, before the experiment, which of these two methods of recording they preferred. It was found that neither their total scores nor the difference between the written and called guesses was significant, but there was a significant difference between their total scores on the preferred way and the nonpreferred way of calling. Each subject made 100 guesses by each method of calling. The total score on the preferred method of calling was 26 above mean chance expectation (+1·3 per cent), while it was 44 below m.c.e. (−2·2 per cent); the difference of 3·5 per cent between these two sets of scores was clearly significant (P = 0·006).

This tendency of two contrasting conditions in ESP experimenting to produce a difference between the two sets of scores has been confirmed by many other workers, for example by Rao who used target cards printed in English with a contrasted set of target cards printed in Telugu (Rao, 1963). The contrasting conditions have been of various kinds: in experimental situation, in kinds of target, and (as in Sanders' experiment) in the direction of preference of the subject. Experiments of the last type have led to the use of the term 'preferential effect'. This term has been used interchangeably with 'differential effect', but it seems to help clarity of thought if the two terms are used differently. It is only in some differential experiments that the subjects' preferences are the differentiating criteria. When they are so used the direction of the effect of preference is variable, the preferred condition sometimes leading to the better scoring, sometimes to the worse. It seems best that the term 'differential effect' should be used as the general term for those experiments in which contrasting conditions give significantly different scoring rates, and to reserve the term 'preferential effect' for that sub-class of differential effects in which the differentiating condition is the subjects' preferences.

The differential effect has been well confirmed and there seems to be no doubt that part of the general pattern of psi-responses is its tendency to produce differences in scoring under contrasting conditions used within a single experiment. Understanding of why this differential scoring occurs must be left for the future; what it seems to suggest is that this is part of the inhibitory mechanism by which an overall positive score is unconsciously avoided by the subjects of the experiment, but the true explanation may be quite different from this.

On the practical side, the discovery of the differential effect is a convenience to the parapsychological experimenter since it takes him nearer to the ideal of full repeatability. If an intending experimenter asks how he may set up an experiment which he can be certain will give him positive evidence of psi, his adviser's reply must still be that it is impossible to specify a design of experiment which is certain to give him positive results, but that there is a very good chance of getting such results if he designs a group experiment in which the same subjects do ESP tests under contrasting conditions, and he examines the difference between their total scores under these two conditions.

Another part of the psi-pattern that has attracted attention in recent years is its apparent effect on the extent to which different scores (or sets of scores) differ from one another. The name 'variance' is given to a measure of the degree to which different scores differ from one another. A fuller discussion of variance and of the ways in which it can be measured and in which it can be compared with its expected chance value will be found in Appendix E. For the present we need only to remind ourselves that a chance determined set of run scores will not all be exactly 5 but may have such values as: 4, 2, 7, 5, 4 etc., and that such variation of score is quite consistent with the difference being purely determined by chance. It would be naïve to suppose that the differences were caused by ESP operating negatively on the second run and positively on the third. If, however, the run scores differed amongst themselves much more than this or much less than this, it would be necessary to look for a cause that was either intensifying the run differences or one that was making them more alike than they would be by chance alone.

There is no difficulty in finding a cause that could operate to make the difference between scores greater than would be expected by chance. We know, in fact, that in some cases such a cause does operate since we have evidence from such experiments as those already referred to on the differential effect and the group experiments of Humphrey and of Schmeidler that ESP results may be mixtures of positive and negative scoring. Where this is the case, the run scores are likely to differ from each other more than would be expected by chance, and this enhanced difference can be detected as an increase in the observed value of the run variance as compared with its expected chance value. A significant difference between the observed and the theoretical value of the variance can, therefore, be explained as the result of psi acting positively on some runs and negatively on others. Comparison between the observed and theoretical value of the variance has not, in fact, often been used as a criterion for ESP acting in different directions on different runs because, if this is happening, it can generally be established in other ways. A variance measurement would, for example, add no additional information to the finding that Dr Schmeidler's 'sheep' tend to score positively in ESP tests and that her 'goats' tend to score negatively.

It is, however, sometimes useful to be able to establish that, in a given set of measurements, the variance does not differ from its chance expected value. We then know that there is no evidence of ESP acting in different directions on different runs, and that it would be quite unjustifiable to suppose that a particular run showing a high score was made at a time when ESP was active and that a particular low score was made when ESP was being repressed. If, however, we can easily interpret the fact of an observed variance being greater than the theoretical 'chance' value, and even more easily the fact that there is no significant difference between them, it is not so easy to explain the observed variance being less than the chance expected value, i.e. different run scores being more alike than they should be. This also, however, seems sometimes to be the case.

The comparison between the observed and the chance expected values of the variance can be applied to other units of guessing than the run through the standard deck of twenty-five ESP cards. It can equally well be applied, for example, to the scores of groups of five guesses or to half-run scores. For these units the chance expected value of the variance will no longer be 4·0 as it is for the run scores, but it must be calculated in the way described in Appendix E for the particular unit used.

One of the earliest researches to use variance change as a measure of ESP was an investigation by J. C. Carpenter (1966) in which the variance studied was that of half-runs. He was concerned with the question of whether psi operated more strongly in the first half of each run (whether in a positive or negative direction) than during its second half. An affirmative answer to this question was suggested by the finding that the variance of the scores of the first half-runs was significantly greater than of the second half-runs. Carpenter also found that the variance of the units of five guesses declined from the beginning of the run to its end. What these findings indicate is that psi is more active either in making subjects guess rightly or in making them guess wrongly in the early part of each run than in its later part. This gives a wider view of the decline effect than the earlier way of regarding it as merely a decline in positive scoring.

The finding that the variance in ESP results may be greater than its chance expected value is of limited interest since it is merely another way of showing what had already been demonstrated by other methods, that psi may work both in the direction of making subjects guess more rightly than would be expected by chance and also in the direction of making them guess less rightly than would be expected by chance. Nothing new is added to the pattern of psi by the finding that scores may have a variance greater than the chance expected value.

A reported finding more difficult to explain is that of variances which are significantly less than the chance expected value. This means that scores are more alike than they should be if chance alone accounted for their differences. The idea of a cause making scores more alike than they should be is so strange that one naturally asks whether such reports may not be mistaken. The possibilities of other explanations of apparently low variances are discussed in Appendix E. Even when full account is taken of these, there seems to be good evidence that there is a real tendency amongst some subjects to produce run scores which differ amongst themselves less than they would if these differences were merely chance determined.

A number of research workers have reported finding sets of scores showing a smaller variance than would be expected by chance. Unfortunately those reporting this finding of low variance do not always report the mean rate of scoring of their subjects, so it is not certain whether the lowering of the variance was a separate effect or merely a secondary effect of low scoring. It is obvious that the expected degree of difference between scores will be less if all scores are low (as in psi-missing) than if they are centred round mean chance expectation. If the reported lowering of variance were merely a secondary consequence of below-chance scoring, it would be of no special interest.

That a lowering of variance can occur as an independent effect is, however, shown by a research carried out by D. P. Rogers in which average scores were at about chance level but the variance was significantly below chance level (Rogers, 1967). The research was intended to test a suggestion made by J. B. Rhine that low variance was due to a process of 'internal cancellation' by which the subject who began to score positively in the early part of a run would correct this by negative scoring before the run was finished. Rogers considered that he had obtained some evidence for this view in the finding that the scores obtained in the last five guesses of each run were significantly less than those in the rest of the run. In order to account for the run scores being more like each other than would be expected by chance it would be necessary that the amount of the negative scoring in the last segment of the run should be correlated with the amount of positive scoring that went before it. This does not seem yet to have been demonstrated. Although the reality of reduced variance seems strongly indicated, we do not yet know enough about it to know what part it plays in the psi-pattern. It may be, as has been suggested, that it is an unexpected and complicated part of the inhibitory mechanism by which a successful ESP subject hides his ESP success. On the other hand, further research may show that this effect has a different explanation.

A new and unexpected element in the pattern of psi was revealed in 1963 by the discovery by Pratt and Rýzl of what they called the 'focussing effect' (Rýzl and Pratt, 1963). The essential point of this is that the subject's responses, although partly determined by the nature of the target, may also be determined by which particular card he was guessing. This effect had not been noticed before and has not, as yet, been confirmed in other experiments since it could only easily be observed in the rather unusual design of experiment adopted by Rýzl. In the standard ESP experiment, a given card is always a particular kind of target (square, cross, etc. whichever may happen to be the design printed on it). Rýzl, however, used only one kind of card as target which was white on one side and green on the other. The subject had to guess which side of the card was uppermost. Any particular card could, therefore, be either sort of target and it was possible, in this design of experiment, to distinguish between the response to the particular card and the response to the target.

Under these circumstances, it was found that the subject (Pavel Stepanek) was not showing ESP uniformly for all the target cards but was showing a high level of ESP hitting on some of them, consistent psi-missing on some others, and consistently chance results on others. Since the cards were contained in opaque envelopes, one could also ask whether this consistency of response was characteristic of each particular card or of the envelope in which it was enclosed. The answer to this question was that it seemed to be determined by both, so the subject's responses seemed to be a resultant of three factors: the nature of the target, the particular card used as target, and the envelope in which the target card was enclosed. It must be supposed that ESP was operative in all three of these cases although it would only be guesses predominantly determined by the nature of the target that would be counted as hits in an ESP experiment.

Although the full range of the focusing effect could only be shown in an experiment of a design similar to that of Rýzl, some part of this effect could be seen in a standard card-guessing experiment if a record was kept of the guesses on each particular card in a pack. Such a record has not, so far as I know, ever been kept by an experimenter using the standard ESP pack. There has, however, been ample confirmation of the reality of this effect in the experimental setting in which it was first observed (Pratt and Roll, 1968). It remains to be found out how widespread it is.

The choice of the term 'focusing' to describe this phenomenon seems to have been unfortunate. There does not appear to be any analogy between the subject having his guess determined by the particular card or its enclosing envelope and the focusing of an optical instrument, such as the camera, in which the distance between lens and film is altered until a sharp image is made on the film. The essential point is that the subject's response is not determined by the intended target but by some other aspect of the guessing situation. This would seem to be another example of what has earlier been called 'displacement'. This was the term used by Whately Carington and Soal for the tendency of a subject to call, not the target card but some other card, as, for example, the next succeeding card. In the case of Rýzl's subject it would seem that he is displacing his guess from the target itself (in this case the colour which is uppermost) to the card which is used as target or to the cover in which it is enclosed. If the phenomenon reported by Pratt and Rýzl is looked at in this way, it would seem to be another example of an inhibitory phenomenon in ESP in which the direct evidence for ESP is suppressed by avoidance of the intended target while showing itself in a new unintended direction. It might perhaps be better to use the word 'displacement' for this phenomenon instead of 'focusing'. It could perhaps be called 'displacement to card' and 'displacement to cover' while the Carington–Soal type of displacement could be distinguished as 'target displacement'.

The last two chapters have been an attempt to describe the salient features of the pattern of ESP as they have so far emerged from experimental research. The choice is, of course, an individual one; other writers might have selected other findings for this purpose. No doubt there are other features already discovered that will be proved by later confirmation to be genuine parts of the pattern; I do not think that any of those I have picked out will prove to be wholly illusory although no doubt many will look different when more has been found out.

So far I have dealt only with experiments on ESP since this was the first topic in parapsychology that was experimentally studied and it remains the one on which the findings are most clear. But we must look beyond ESP to understand the experimental situation in psychical research. The next chapter will deal with that extension of ESP when the fact cognised is not a present but a future one. This is the form of ESP commonly called 'precognition'.

# References

CARPENTER, J. C. (1966), 'Scoring Effects within the Run', *Journal of Parapsychology*, xxx, 73–83.

FREEMAN, J. A., and NIELSEN, WINIFRED (1964), 'Precognition score deviations as related to anxiety levels', *J. Parapsych.*, xxviii, 239–49.

HUMPHREY, BETTY M. (1946), 'Success in ESP as Related to Form in Response Drawings', *J. Parapsych.*, x, 78–106, 181–96.

NICOL, J. F., and HUMPHREY, BETTY M. (1953), 'The Exploration of ESP and Human Personality', *Journal of the American Society for Psychical Research*, xlvii, 133–78.

PRATT, J. G. (1967), 'Computer Studies of the ESP Process in Card Guessing', *J. Amer. S.P.R.*, lxi, 25–46.

PRATT, J. G., and ROLL, W. G. (1968), 'Confirmation of the Focussing Effect in Further ESP Research with Pavel Stepanek in Charlottesville', *J. Amer. S.P.R.*, lxii, 226–45.

RAO, K. RAMAKRISHNA (1963), 'Studies in the Preferential Effect I, II & III', *J. Parapsych.*, xxvii, 23–32, 147–60, 242–51.

RAO, K. RAMAKRISHNA (1965), 'ESP and the Manifest Anxiety Scale', *J. Parapsych.*, xxix, 12–18.

ROGERS, D. P. (1967), 'An Analysis for Internal Cancellation Effects on Some Low-variance ESP Runs', *J. Parapsych.*, xxxi, 192–7.

RÝZL, M., and PRATT, J. G. (1963), 'The Focussing of ESP upon Particular Targets', *J. Parapsych.*, xxvii, 227–41.

SANDERS, M. S. (1962), 'A Comparison of Verbal and Written Responses in a Precognition Experiment', *J. Parapsych.*, xxvi, 23–34.

SCHMEIDLER, GERTRUDE R., and MCCONNELL, R. A. (1958), *ESP and Personality Patterns*, New Haven and London.

SKIBINSKY, M. (1950), 'A Comparison of Names and Symbols in a Distance ESP Test', *J. Parapsych.*, xiv, 140–56.

SOAL, S. G., and BATEMAN, F. (1954), *Modern Experiments in Telepathy*, London.

THOULESS, R. H. (1942), 'Experiments in Paranormal Guessing', *British Journal of Psychology*, xxxiii, 15–27.

WHATELY CARINGTON, W. (1940), 'Experiments on the Paranormal Cognition of Drawings', *Proc. S.P.R.*, xlvi, 34–151, 227–334.

# XIV

# Experiments on foreseeing the future

If by ESP a subject can, to a better than chance amount, guess the present order of a pack of cards or reproduce an already existing target drawing, can he also succeed in foretelling the future order of a pack of cards or the nature of a drawing that has not yet been made? There is a good deal of experimental evidence that some subjects can succeed in these tasks. The type of ESP that is involved is generally called 'precognition'.

The term 'precognition' is perhaps open to some objection on the ground that it implies that the capacity in question is a sort of 'cognition' or 'knowing'. Success in a precognitive task may, however, involve no 'knowing' in the sense of conscious awareness. The subject may simply give responses (such as naming cards or pictures) which show extra-chance correspondence with a future fact, although at the time of guessing he does not know that there is any such correspondence. It might have been better if some term had been chosen less definite in its implications than 'precognition'. Some time ago I suggested that the ability to carry out such tasks should be called 'promethic psi'. This suggestion has not, however, been adopted, so one will be best understood by using the somewhat misleading term 'precognition'.

One reason for trying experiments of this type is the large amount of anecdotal evidence that seems to point, at least in some individuals, to a power of foretelling the future. These reports are sometimes of unsought and unexpected premonitions of future events, perhaps trivial but more often of death or disaster. These may come as dreams or as premonitory experiences in waking life. Others of the reported precognitions are of a more deliberate kind carried out by special techniques used by individuals supposed to have special skills in foretelling. These techniques of prophecy or divination are found in various cultures in similar forms. They include looking at the viscera of animals or the flight of birds and listening to the rustling of leaves in the wind. These seem to be activities belonging psychologically to the same class as that of the Rorschach personality test in which the subject looks at ink-blots. An indeterminate perceptual situation allows the observer to see or hear something primarily determined by internal factors. Such an indeterminate perceptual situation might well prove to be favourable to the emergence of any psi-capacities that the diviner had. The techniques of divination also include the manipulation of cards, crystal-gazing, examining the lines on the palms of people's hands, astrology, and the interpretation of dreams.

In our own culture, these techniques have become disused or adapted to other purposes, and their use for foretelling the future is generally regarded as mere superstition. This is not because we are less interested in the future than were our great-grandfathers, but because we have more efficient methods of foretelling by rational inference than they had. We are using such processes of rational inference when meteorological methods are used for foretelling the weather, when sample polls are used to forecast election results, and in many other situations. The motivation behind these activities may be the same as that of the ancient diviner, the urgent practical demand to know what is going to happen, but its methods are different. They use rational processes of inference, the absence of which puts the activities of the diviner or the ancient interpreter of dreams into the class of ostensibly paranormal phenomena.

That these paranormal methods of foretelling the future are now regarded merely as superstitious practices should not deter the psychical researcher from examining them. He has more reliable methods of finding out whether such methods have any value than had either those people who originally believed in them or those who later discarded and condemned them. The simple disbelief of the nineteenth century is not necessarily a better guide than the simple credulity of earlier times. We must find out for ourselves whether there are paranormal (non-inferential) ways to foretell the future, and the most promising method of finding out is by the use of the powerful tool of experiment.

As in other lines of experimental research, the anecdotal evidence of the past can be used as a guide as to what seem to be profitable lines of experimental study. Precognition by means of dreams is a topic which is particularly rich in such anecdotal material. A familiar source of dreams which were regarded as precognitive is the Old Testament. One may also find guidance as to the experimental problems in such ancient sources as Bishop Synesius who died early in the fifth century. He believed that wisdom can come through knowing the future by means of dreams.

An earlier writer on dreams was the second-century Artemidorus (English edition, 1606). He particularly concerned himself with methods of dream interpretation. One of his observations that may provide a pointer for experimental research is his distinction between dreams that are speculative and agreeable to their vision and those that are allegorical and by one thing signify another. In more modern language we might refer to this distinction as that between dreams whose meaning is literal and those whose meaning is conveyed by symbols. Artemidorus said that the fulfilment of the first kind of dream comes soon after the dream while the fulfilment of symbolic dreams occurs some time after. Literal fulfilments of dreams are generally the only kind of possible fulfilment considered by modern writers, as when Dunne reports that he dreamed he was attacked by a mad horse in a narrow lane, and that the next day he was, in fact, attacked by a mad horse in a narrow lane (Dunne, 1927).

In a comparison between precognitive and contemporary spontaneous psi-experiences, Dr Louisa Rhine found that the former occurred much more commonly as dreams (in two-thirds of the cases) than did the latter. Most of the precognitive dreams reported by her were of the type with literal fulfilment as when a woman dreamed that she and her husband were sunning themselves on the beach at Miami when a girl walked past and kicked sand over her shoulder while remarking that she wanted to eat out that day. The fulfilment was that next day on the Miami beach a girl did walk past kicking sand over her shoulder and making the remark that had been made in the dream. There was also a smaller class (about one-fifth of the whole) of 'unrealistic' dreams in which there was an element of symbolism as when someone dreamed of trying to reach a baby who kept slipping away and the fulfilment was that the baby had an illness which proved fatal.

Neither in Dunne's book nor in Dr Rhine's collection are there any symbolic dreams of the kind in which the symbolism may not be apparent to the dreamer himself. This may not mean that such dreams do not now occur but only that they are less likely to be noticed unless they are specially looked for.

An example of the kind of dream in which the dream event is only a symbol of what is going to happen is given by Artemidorus as a dream in which the dreamer sees a swarm of bees and the fulfilment is that he receives some money. The precognitive dreams of the Old Testament, such as Pharaoh's dream of seven fat kine and seven lean kine, are also of this symbolic type. The possibility that if precognition takes place in dreams, this precognition might be of a symbolic and not of a literal kind, is one that should, I think, be borne in mind by the parapsychological investigator of dreams. The experimental investigation of symbolic fulfilments of dreams would be likely to be more difficult than the study of literal fulfilments; it might, however, prove to be more rewarding.

The problem of paranormal foretelling of the future did not engage much of the attention of the early psychical researchers. Some years ago, however, a great deal of general interest in the subject was aroused by J. W. Dunne's book (1927) reporting many of his own dreams of which he claimed to have had remarkable and detailed fulfilment. Others have tried to repeat Dunne's observations but have found only rare and doubtful correspondences between some elements of their dreams and later events, with insufficient grounds for a firm conclusion that these correspondences were not accidental.

This is the kind of situation with respect to spontaneous material that leads us to ask whether we cannot get more water-tight evidence by a well-designed experiment. An experiment directly concerned with dreams was not the first choice of parapsychologists since, although its difficulties could, no doubt, be overcome, the experiment would not be easy to design or to carry out. The mere finding of correspondences between dream and subsequent events would not be sufficient ground for concluding that the dream foretold the future. A certain number of correspondences might arise by chance and others might have a more normal explanation such as that the later events recalled dream elements that might otherwise have been forgotten. For the purpose of studying precognition in dreams, it would be necessary to arrange an experiment of more complex design. One might, for example, arrange an internally controlled experiment in which there were records of dreams by a number of different individuals and records of subsequent events in the lives of these dreamers. The judgment of correspondences would have to be made by judges who did not know which records of events belonged to which dream. So far as I know an experiment so designed has not yet been carried out.

Precognition in dreams is likely, however, to be the object of experimental study in the near future. Modern techniques of dream study open the way to such an investigation. The discovery of the fact that the activity of dreaming is accompanied by rapid eye movements (REMs) and that these can be detected by electrodes placed on suitable points of the skin means that a dreamer can be awakened at the actual time of the dream (Dement and Kleitman, 1957). The experimenter is, therefore, no longer dependent on the uncertain and highly selective memory of dreams that may remain after the final waking up.

Since there is so much anecdotal evidence connecting dreaming with psi-activity, the dream seems an obvious place in which to look for evidence of psi. There is now a research unit under Dr Krippner studying dreams by modern methods at the Maimonides Hospital in Brooklyn (Ullman et al., 1966). It has there been demonstrated that ESP of target pictures can occur both in naturally occurring and in hypnotically induced dreaming states. The more difficult quantitative problem of whether the efficiency of the psi-process is greater in the dreaming condition than in the waking state has not yet been solved. Nor has the research yet gone very far with the problem of precognition in dreams. There are, however, already interesting indications that the experimentally studied dream may also predict a future target picture, one not yet selected at the time of dreaming. This research continues and may be expected to yield further results in the future.

It may be a longer time before experimental parapsychology gets round to the investigation of such other reputed paranormal ways of foretelling the future as palmistry, astrology, or the examination of the viscera of animals. It is commonly found in experimental science that it is better to avoid the complexities of the conditions under which the matter to be investigated occurs in everyday life and to substitute a simple activity which depends on the same theoretical principle. The simple activity used for experimental investigation in this case was a card–guessing experiment in which the target was the future order of a pack of cards.

A simple form of this experiment is one in which an experimental subject records guesses for the twenty-five cards of the standard ESP pack, these guesses being intended to represent, not the present order of the pack, but the order that it is going to have after it has been shuffled and cut. These guesses are recorded, the pack is shuffled and cut, preferably at some randomly determined point, and the recorded guesses are compared with the target cards in their new order. If the number of guesses that are hits on the target card is significantly more than five, there is sufficient reason to conclude that there is some cause at work tending to produce correspondence between the subject's guesses and the new card order. If the design of the experiment provides adequate safeguards against the possibility of any other cause than precognition producing this correspondence, then the result must be taken as evidence of precognition.

Experiments concerned with the future order of a pack of ESP cards were carried out by J. B. Rhine in the early thirties (Rhine, 1938). A total of 49 subjects made 113,075 guesses on packs of ESP cards which were subsequently shuffled and cut by the experimenter. There was an excess of 614 right guesses over mean chance expectation which is a scoring rate of only 0·6 per cent. Since, however, the number of guesses was large, this excess was significant ($P < 0.00001$). This is sufficient to indicate very strongly that there was some cause at work making the guesses correspond more closely with the future fact than they would by chance alone.

It occurred to Rhine, however, that this cause might not be the ability of his experimental subjects to precognise the future order of the pack but the ability of experimenters unconsciously to shuffle the cards into an order to some extent corresponding to that already predicted by the subject. An experiment to test this possibility seemed to indicate that experimenters could perform this feat even when they had no normal knowledge of the order against which their shuffled pack would be matched (Rhine et al., 1938). Experiments in which cards were hand-shuffled and cut at a point chosen by the experimenter were therefore judged to be inadequate for the demonstration of precognition.

Later experiments in which the cards were machine-shuffled yielded an excess of 425 hits over mean chance expectation in 235,875 guesses (Rhine, 1941). This is an excess of only 0·2 per cent and is just significant ($P = 0.03$). This is evidence, but not very strong evidence, of some cause at work producing correspondence between the subject's guesses and the future order of the (mechanically shuffled) pack.

After experimental work on psycho-kinesis had started, the possibility was considered that success in this form of experiment might, even with mechanical shuffling, have an explanation alternative to precognition since the experimenter or the subject might be using PK to influence the shuffling machine to produce the observed correspondence. To eliminate this possibility, the shuffled pack was cut at a mechanically determined random point.

As has been pointed out earlier, a random cut made by some method that ensures equal probability of a cut at all points (including the zero point) completely gets rid of any possibility of a correspondence between the target order and the order of guesses being influenced by the order of the pack before the cut, since the average of all scores obtained at all 25 possible positions of cut will be 5 (exactly so with a closed pack, not significantly different from 5 with an open pack). The introduction of the random cut therefore makes machine-shuffling superfluous since the imperfections of hand-shuffling cannot produce a spurious indication of success if the subsequent cut is truly random.

The experimenter did not, however, use the ordinary method of obtaining a random cut by selecting from a table of random numbers by means of a throw of dice since it seemed to him possible that such a method of selecting the point of cut might also be influenced by PK. To eliminate this possibility, the shuffled pack was cut at a point determined by the temperature extremes reported in the Durham local paper at a predetermined later date (Rhine, 1942). This ingenious device has obvious practical objections. It necessarily causes delay in the preparation of the target order of the pack, and such delay may reasonably be expected to decrease the efficiency of any precognitive psi that may be operating. In the present experiment, there was a delay, sometimes of two days, sometimes of ten days, between the guessing by the subject and the target ordering of the cards. The results gave no direct evidence of precognition; in 57,550 guesses, the excess of hits over mean chance expectation was only 11. It cannot, however, be concluded that this disappearance of a positive deviation was a result of the introduction of the randomly determined cut. It may have been due to some other cause, such as a decline effect produced by continued experimenting or it may have been a product of the delay in checking caused by the use of the temperature readings for determining the point of cut.

Although the direct evidence for precognition by a positive deviation of right response over expectation disappeared in this series, there remained indications that precognition played a part in the results. These were provided by the observation of 'position effects', particularly the tendency for scores to be higher at the beginning and end of each run and of each segment of five guesses when the segments were clearly marked off on the record sheets. These have been called 'salience effects'. Obviously no such effects would occur in a merely random set of responses, so their occurrence, if it is not merely accidental, is indirect evidence for the influence of precognition on the responses in which it is found.

While significant position effects are an indication that some other factor than chance is determining the correspondence between guesses and the subsequent card order, they would not be convincing evidence if they were merely found in a single experimental series. Their occurrence might then only be an example of the 'crumpled paper' effect, that regularities will always be found, even in a chance series of events, if one examines them with a mind open to observe any apparent regularity. One could only be certain that such effects were not accidental if their first observation were made the basis for a prediction which was confirmed in a subsequent series of experiments. The reality of the salience effects in these precognition experiments was confirmed in this way.

A confirmatory series of experiments was carried out by Rhine and Humphrey (1942). In this series, 1,000 runs were made (25,000 guesses). Of these, 559 runs were made by a group of adults while 441 were made by children. The adults showed no evidence of their guesses being influenced by precognition either in their total score (almost exactly mean chance expectation) or in the salience ratio of their runs which was just about as would be predicted by chance. The children, on the other hand, scored 55 over mean chance expectation; an excess too small to be significant. They did, however, show run salience to a significantly greater extent than would be expected by chance ($p = 0.02$ if we take into account that this is the better of two comparisons). It appears from this experiment that precognition was effective in the children's performance but not in that of the adults.

The validity of this conclusion is not affected by the fact that the evidence is not of the direct kind that would be provided by a significant deviation from expectation of the children's scores but of the relatively indirect kind provided by a measurement of run salience. Indirect evidence is logically as good as direct evidence provided it is (as here) of a characteristic predicted before the experiment took place. No type of position effect would be found unless precognition were influencing the results. Indirect evidence is, no doubt, less psychologically effective in producing conviction but it is logically as effective in producing evidence that ought to convince.

These experiments produced good evidence that precognition took place under conditions of a random cut determined by a subsequent thermometer reading which eliminated any reasonable possibility of explanation by psycho-kinesis. The evidence is good but not overwhelmingly strong since the level of significance is not high; there is a possibility (although a remote one) that the result might be accidental. There would be some reason for hesitating to accept these experiments as evidence of anything so apparently improbable as precognition if they stood alone. There is, however, a great deal of confirmatory evidence of the reality of precognition by later experiments carried out by other workers. One of the most impressive of these is the recent experiment of Helmut Schmidt, referred to in Chapter VI, in which he obtained highly significant results in a mechanised precognitive task with four targets.

There is also evidence for the reality of precognition in experiments not primarily intended for this purpose. A recent example is to be found in an investigation by Honorton of the relation between precognitive scores and psychological estimates of creativity (Honorton, 1967). Those of his subjects who were rated as highly creative showed no significant difference from mean chance expectation in their precognitive scores, while those rated as of low creativity showed a deficiency in 32,650 guesses of 251 hits, a negative deviation of about 0·8 per cent. The difference between the scoring of these two groups was significant (P<0·03). This evidence of a relation between precognitive score and creativity rating, is also indirectly evidence of the reality of precognition since merely chance determined scores would not show any correlation with creativity or any other mental characteristic.

Much of the experimental work on precognition has been on unselected subjects with a low rate of scoring whose total results build up to a final result that is significant but not overwhelmingly so. If anyone who was doubtful about the possibility of precognition asked how strong is the total evidence for precognition from these experiments alone, the answer could not be a simple one. A completely satisfactory answer could only be given by balancing the results of these published successful experiments against the results of all the unsuccessful experiments that have been carried out, both published and unpublished. There would be considerable uncertainty in such an estimate unless it were backed by a more extensive research into all the published and unpublished work on precognition than has, so far as I know, yet been carried out. My own impression is that such a research would demonstrate a strong case for the reality of precognition, but this is merely an opinion which would rightly not be accepted as convincing by one who regarded precognition as an impossibility.

It is not, however, solely on experiments with unselected subjects showing a low rate of scoring that the experimental case for the reality of precognition rests. There are also (as in the case of contemporaneous ESP) experiments carried out with gifted subjects who have scored at a consistently high rate.

The first of these was carried out by Tyrrell with his subject, Miss Johnson (Tyrrell, 1936). In the course of the ESP experiment already mentioned (p. 55), Tyrrell introduced a modification in method which converted it into an experiment in precognition. In the original ESP experiment, Miss Johnson's task was to open one of five boxes which had been selected as target box by a key pressed down by the experimenter. The particular box selected as target was also determined by a mechanical commutator which produced randomised selection of the box which became target, and which also ensured that the experimenter did not know which of the boxes was target. This became an experiment in precognition when Mr Tyrrell required his subject to choose the box about half a second before the experimenter pressed his key and so made selection of the target box. That this instruction was obeyed was apparent since the time of the two keys being pressed was recorded on a tape which showed that the subject really pressed her key a fraction of a second before the experimenter pressed his.

This precognitive experiment showed success at a good and highly significant rate. In 2,255 trials, there were 539 hits which is 88 more than the mean chance expectation of 451. This is a scoring rate of nearly 4 per cent. The probability of chance occurrence is less than one in ten thousand, so the result is clearly significant. The design of the experiment is such that it does not seem possible that its result can be explained otherwise than by precognition.

Another experiment with a high scoring subject which has been considered to be evidence for precognition is that of Dr Soal and Mrs Goldney with the subject Basil Shackleton which has been described earlier (Soal and Bateman, 1954). This was not primarily intended as an experiment in precognition, but a precognitive explanation of the results was suggested by the fact that Shackleton's hits were not on the card that was then turned up but on the card that was to be turned up next. This was regarded by the experimenters as a foreseeing by the percipient of the future knowledge that the agent would have when he looked at the next card. They, therefore, gave the name 'precognitive telepathy' to the psi-capacity producing success in these experiments.

As pointed out in Chapter X, this experimental series showed a consistently high rate of success (7 per cent over m.c.e.) at a very high level of significance. The precautions taken were such that (unless we are willing to accept the fantastic hypothesis of fraud by the experimenters) there can be no reasonable doubt that Shackleton was performing successfully the guessing task required by this experimental situation and that his success was paranormal. It is by no means equally certain that he was displaying precognition. An alternative explanation for the main results of these experiments is that Shackleton was clairvoyantly aware of the next card on the pack as a contemporaneous fact and was not foreseeing the future event of it being turned up. Although there is ample experimental evidence to show that such non-telepathic psi-cognition of a contemporary event can take place (as in card-guessing experiments under down-through conditions), there are some indications that this is not the explanation of the Soal-Goldney results.

First, there is the fact that, in a short experiment in which the agent did not know which card was turned up (so that no telepathy, either precognitive or other, was possible), Shackleton did not succeed to an extent significantly above mean chance expectation. This, however, is not very strong evidence that he could not succeed in a clairvoyant task, since this may have been simply an example of the well-known tendency of changed conditions to lower scoring rates. A much longer series of guesses under these conditions would have been necessary to establish whether Shackleton could or could not succeed in a situation in which the agent would not know the target in the near future.

A stronger indication of Shackleton's success depending on precognitive telepathy was the finding that, when the speed of calling was doubled, the hits were made on the second card ahead instead of on the card immediately ahead. This is what one would expect if the subject were guessing ahead in time, but there seems to be no reason for it if he were merely becoming aware of the next card in the pack.

There was finally the result of a modification of the experiment which was designed to test between these two explanations. If Shackleton's successes were genuinely precognitive, he should still be able to succeed if, at the time of each guess, the next target had not yet been determined. This condition was not quite fulfilled by a modification of the experimental design in which the target for each guess was determined by the colour of a counter drawn from a bowl in which equal numbers of counters of five different colours were mixed up. Under these conditions, the percipient still scored on the target one ahead at a rate of 7·5 per cent above m.c.e. (about the same as his scoring rate with cards). This was not, however, a crucial test for the precognition explanation of the results since (as was pointed out by Soal), Mrs Goldney might already have picked up the next counter with her free hand when Shackleton made his guess so that there was a present fact which Shackleton might have cognised clairvoyantly.

Another set of experiments was therefore carried out to serve as a crucial test of the precognition hypothesis. Still using counters, the rate of guessing was speeded up to twice what it had been before, and Shackleton's hits were then on the target two ahead. Since Mrs Goldney had only two hands, the counter to be selected next but one must have been wholly undetermined at the time when Shackleton made his guess, so his success cannot be explained by ESP without foreknowledge. Under these conditions, his rate of success on the second target ahead was as high as it had been on one target ahead at the normal speed of calling. In 794 calls there were 236 hits, which is 9·6 per cent above m.c.e.; the odds against an excess of this size arising by chance is about 10,000 to 1.

This is strong ground for concluding that Shackleton could succeed under experimental conditions which excluded the possibility of explaining his success as due to ESP of a present event. The only other possibility would seem to be that his success was due to his paranormally influencing Mrs Goldney to choose the counter corresponding to the target already selected by him. In the next chapter, we shall be discussing the weighty evidence for psycho-kinesis, or the influence of human intentions on physical systems. If PK can affect the movements of objects, it is not unreasonable to suppose that it can influence the behaviour of other people. In the Soal-Goldney experimental design, however, precognition seems to be a more likely explanation of the results obtained than any alternative hypothesis, and the high rate of score and the high level of significance make them a weighty addition to the experimental evidence for precognition.

The experimental case for the reality of precognition has become much stronger in recent years, largely from experiments which had other objects than that of testing the reality of precognition. The precognitive design of experiment is a convenient one. For this reason, many of those engaged in psi-research (Schmeidler, Rýzl, Freeman, and Nielsen, among others) have elected to use the precognitive design of experiment and have found it no less fruitful than other methods of experimenting in ESP.

Taking into account these various lines of experimental evidence, it is clear that the case for the reality of precognition is very strong. Nevertheless many of those engaged in psychical research have been inclined to reject the evidence for precognition, not because they thought it was not strong enough but because it seems to them that non-inferential foreseeing of the future is intrinsically impossible. Certainly it is difficult to fit precognition into any rational system of expectations as to what can and what cannot happen. These difficulties have been well put forward by Professor Broad (1967). The essential point of the difficulty is that any case of precognition implies that an unknown future event (such as the order of a pack of cards after shuffling and cutting) influences a present event (the writing down of the card order by an experimental subject). But, at the time of writing down this card order, the results of the shuffling and cutting are non-existent and cannot be supposed to influence anything.

Essentially there is a conflict between the alleged facts of success in precognitive tasks and our ways of thinking about the time relations of causes and their effects. When there is such a conflict between ostensible facts and the expectations based on our ways of thinking, the conflict may be resolved by denying the reality of the ostensible facts. A better way would seem to be to accept such facts as are based on sound observations and to consider that our ways of thinking must be revised. This would seem to be the right way of dealing with the difficulty of precognition; if the facts of precognition are in conflict with our customary ways of thinking about time, then our ways of thinking about time need changing. This is a direction of speculation which has engaged many acute minds. It may be the case that none of the new ways of thinking suggested so far are a satisfactory solution of the problem. Nevertheless, it is to be expected that the solution will come some day. What is needed for the solution of the problem may be more original thinking; it may be more experimental knowledge about precognition. Probably both of these activities will be required.

While some psychical researchers have rejected precognitive ESP as impossible, others have speculated as to the possibility that all ESP successes are precognitive. It is plainly possible that an ordinary ESP card-guessing task might be successful because the percipient foresaw the position of the cards in the final check. If this were the case, it would not be necessary to suppose either the reality of telepathy or of clairvoyance, since all success would be due, not to receiving information from the agent's mind or from the cards themselves, but to a foreseeing of the final check. While this line of speculation is by no means closed, the present state of the evidence is against it. If this were the explanation of success in an ESP test, we should expect the rate of scoring to fall off rapidly as the time of checking was made at a longer interval after the guessing. Although there may be some relation between ESP success and time of checking, there is obviously not as close a dependence as we should expect on this theory.

A more serious objection to it is that success may be obtained when there is no future order of the pack to precognise. This can be ensured by a design of experiment in which only the number of successes is recorded, and there is no check of individual guesses which the subject can be supposed to foresee. Many successful ESP experiments have now been carried out under these conditions which seem to exclude the possibility that the percipient is not responding to a present fact but to one that lies in the future.

The present state of the evidence suggests strongly that precognition of the check is not likely to be the explanation of success in all forms of ESP experiment. It seems rather to be the case that the precognitive form of experiment reveals a special kind of ESP in which the target is a future event. This may be expressed in another way by saying that these experiments seem to show that ESP is not limited to targets existing at the present time but may be extended to targets which, in our ordinary way of talking about time, we should say are not yet in existence.

## References

ARTEMIDORUS (1606), *The Judgement or Exposition of Dreames* (English translation), London.

BROAD, C. D. (1967), 'The Notion of "Precognition"', *Science and ESP*, (ed. J. R. Smythies), 165–96.

DEMENT, W., and KLEITMAN, N. (1957), 'The Relation of Eye Movements during Sleep to Dream Activity: an Objective for the Study of Dreaming', *Journal of Experimental Psychology*, liii, 339–46.

DUNNE, J. W. (1927), *An Experiment with Time*, London.

HONORTON, C. (1967), 'Creativity and Precognition Scoring Level', *Journal of Parapsychology*, xxxi, 29–42.

RHINE, J. B. (1938), 'Experiments Bearing on the Precognition Hypothesis, I', *J. Parapsych.*, ii, 38–54.
RHINE, J. B., SMITH, B. M., and WOODRUFF, J. L. (1938), 'Experiments Bearing on the Precognition Hypothesis, II, the Role of ESP in the Shuffling of Cards', *J. Parapsych.*, ii, 119–31.
RHINE, J. B. (1941), 'Experiments Bearing upon the Precognition Hypothesis, III, Mechanically Selected Cards', *J. Parapsych.*, v, 1–58.
RHINE, J. B. (1942), 'Evidence of precognition in the covariation of salience ratios', *J. Parapsych.*, vi, 111–43.
RHINE, J. B., and HUMPHREY, BETTY M. (1942), 'A Confirmatory Study of Salience in Precognition Tests', *J. Parapsych.*, vi, 190–219.
SOAL, S. G., and BATEMAN, F. (1954), *Modern Experiments in Telepathy*, London.
SYNESIUS (1929), *A Discourse on Dreams* (English translation by A. C. Ionides), London.
TYRRELL, G. N. M. (1936), 'Further Research in Extra-sensory Perception', *Proceedings of the Society for Psychical Research*, xliv, 99–168.
ULLMAN, M., KRIPPNER, S., and FELDSTEIN, S. (1966), 'Experimentally Induced Telepathic Dreams: Two Studies Using EEG-REM Monitoring Technique', *International Journal of Psychiatry*, ii, 420–37.
RHINE, LOUISA E. (1954), 'Frequency of Types of Experience in Spontaneous Precognition', *J. Parapsych.*, xviii, 93–123.

# XV

# Psycho-kinesis

In dealing with precognition, we are still within the region of ESP; precognition may be regarded as ESP of which the target is a future event. A more novel direction of parapsychological research was started in the Duke Parapsychology Laboratory when J. B. Rhine and his colleagues started the investigation of what was called 'psycho-kinesis' or PK. Psycho-kinesis is the effect on the movements of material objects which has been reported to result from the thoughts or intentions of some person who has no physical means of influencing them. Gamblers often suppose that they can influence the fall of dice by 'willing'. Such a belief might be illusory; to discover whether it is altogether illusory or whether it may have some basis in fact is a task for experimental enquiry. These early experimental enquiries suggested that there was more in this conviction than common sense would suppose, and later research has strengthened the evidence for the reality of psycho-kinesis.

PK differs from ESP in the fact that there is relatively little anecdotal evidence of spontaneous movements of objects without contact in the presence of ordinary people whereas there is considerable anecdotal testimony to spontaneous telepathy. There are, however, a certain number of such accounts of ostensibly paranormal movements of objects as, for example, in the records of the 'poltergeist' form of haunting in which unexplained noises are reported and also mysterious displacements of objects. Sometimes these are said to have been observed in full light.

There is a general unwillingness to believe such accounts; the barrier to their acceptance is considerably greater than that against the acceptance of reports of telepathy. In some cases, this refusal of belief is, no doubt, fully justified. Sometimes there is misreporting by untrained and too credulous observers; sometimes poltergeist noises may have a purely natural explanation, such as that of earth movements along lines of fault. Another natural explanation that has been suggested for some poltergeist phenomena has been the activities of mischievous children or of notoriety-seeking adolescents.

Even, however, when due weight has been given to all these possibilities of normal explanation, there appears to be a residuum of poltergeist phenomena which cannot be explained as the result of any normal cause. One of the best-attested early cases was that of Derrygonnelly Farm, observed by Sir William Barrett (1911). All the occupants of this lonely farm were under the observation of Barrett while he heard loud knocks all around and saw a large pebble fall on to the bed.

A more recent case observed and recorded under satisfactory conditions was that of a young girl at the Scottish village of Sauchie (Owen, 1964). The usual phenomena of noises and movements of objects were reported to take place in her neighbourhood. Independent testimony of both furniture movements and noises was provided by the doctor of the family and the local minister, both of whom sat in her bedroom and heard noises of knocking and saw movements of a heavy linen chest. Evidence that the noises were not purely subjective was obtained by recording them on magnetic tape; this tape record was afterwards broadcast by the B.B.C.

Poltergeist phenomena are not the only spontaneous occurrences that suggest mental influence on material systems. There are also such incidents as clocks that are reported to have stopped or of pictures that have fallen to the ground at the time of a death. Any single incident of this kind, since it is unrepeated, can only be reported and not studied. A comparative study can, however, be made of a collection of such incidents. A study of this type has been made by Dr Louisa Rhine who shows that reports of such incidents are not uncommon and that they seem to form a consistent pattern (Rhine, L. E., 1963).

Movements of an object without contact are also reported as one of the phenomena of mediumship. Those mediums in whose presence such phenomena are reported to take place are often called 'physical' mediums. Unfortunately such effects can easily be produced fraudulently and have been found by commercial mediums to be an easy way of impressing the credulous. Certainly there has been much faking of physical phenomena amongst those fraudulently claiming to be mediums. This fact, however, does not give sufficient grounds for concluding that there cannot also be genuine phenomena of physical mediumship. Whether there are or not must be discovered by well-controlled observations. It is not even safe to conclude that, because a particular physical medium has been detected in fraud once or many times, she (or he) may not also produce genuine phenomena. If the medium earns her living by producing physical phenomena, she may find that these do not occur in a paranormal way with sufficient reliability to satisfy her sitters. So she may supplement (or replace) occasional unpredictable paranormal physical effects by more reliable normal ones which are equally impressive to her too uncritical sitters. The question that interests the psychical researcher is not whether a particular medium ever cheats, but whether she can ever produce movements without contact under conditions that are so well controlled that cheating was impossible.

There have, in fact, been a number of mediums who appeared to be able to produce movements of objects and the playing of musical instruments in the presence of competent observers who were satisfied that the conditions were such that fraud was impossible. An early case was Daniel Home who convinced Sir William Crookes that he was producing genuine paranormal movements of objects without contact (Crookes, 1874). Another physical medium studied by psychical researchers towards the end of last century was an uneducated Italian peasant woman, Eusapia Palladino. She cheated crudely and obviously when she had the chance of doing so, but disconcerted sceptical investigators by also producing striking phenomena under conditions of strict control. After reports of her cheating had made investigators very sceptical of the paranormality of her phenomena, she was investigated at Naples by three experienced and hard-headed investigators from the Society for Psychical Research who reported that, under conditions of control which made cheating impossible, she produced physical phenomena which included the raising from the floor in full light of a table on which the fingers of the medium rested, the hearing of raps and bangs, the seeing of lights, the feeling of cold breezes, etc. (Feilding et al., 1909).

A more recent case of a less spectacular kind was the very careful examination by Professor Winther and others of the medium Anna Rasmussen in Copenhagen (Winther, 1928). What was observed here were movements both of light and of heavy objects, various noises, including raps which were used for communication, and movements of pendulums. An experimental study was made of the pendulum movements, which seemed to indicate that these were to some extent influenced by the medium's intentions.

The importance of observations on poltergeists, physical mediums etc., from our present point of view, is that they create a strong prima facie case for the reality of paranormal movement of objects without contact. They would seem to establish a sufficiently strong case for it to be not unreasonable to submit this question to experimental study in the laboratory, even although the matter to be investigated might appear to common sense to be too unlikely to be worth serious study. The reward to be hoped for from such an experimental study is, as in the case of ESP, better grounds for an opinion as to whether such events do really occur, and, more importantly, better understanding of their nature if they do, in fact, occur. The first of these objects has, I think, been achieved; we can be reasonably certain that the movements within a physical system can be influenced by purely mental (non-physical) factors. The achievement of understanding of such events is still a long way off, further perhaps than in the case of ESP. Certainly there are hints of regularity in the pattern of PK events, but they will need a much more intensive experimental study before we can hope to be within sight of the goal of understanding them.

The paranormal effects which have been studied experimentally have been of a less spectacular kind than those reported in accounts of poltergeists and physical mediums. Most of the experiments have been made with the use of dice. Perhaps a part of the reason for this choice is that dice are commonly used as a means of gambling, and dice players have often a conviction that they can influence the fall of their dice by mental means. A laboratory test of PK can be regarded by the gambler as a scientific check on his intuitions. For the wider purposes of the research worker, dice have obvious advantages as a means of investigating PK. These are much the same as the advantages of card-guessing for ESP experiments; the ease with which a large number of results can be obtained in a given time, and the ease with which the experimenter can estimate what level of success he would obtain by chance and the strength of the evidence that a given result is not attributable to chance and must therefore (if precautions have been adequate) be attributed to the effect of PK.

Two kinds of experiments have been carried out with dice: those in which the object is to have a predetermined die-face fall uppermost, and 'placement' experiments in which many dice are thrown and the object is to make as many dice as possible come to rest on a particular part of the receiving surface. If the dice were hand-thrown, success in either of these tasks might obviously be the result of skilled throwing. To obtain evidence as to a PK effect, it is therefore necessary that the dice should be mechanically discharged over a rough surface.

There are possible sources of error in experiments with dice which may have affected some of the early results. The most obvious of these possible sources of error, in experiments aimed at getting a particular die-face uppermost, is the effect of bias. Dice in which the pips are hollowed out are considerably biased; the lightest faces are those with the most pips since it is from these that most material has been removed. So those faces (such as 5 and 6) with the most pips are the most likely to fall uppermost. This does not matter if (as is the case with all the more recent PK experiments) the design of the experiment is such that the mean chance expectation of success is not affected by bias. This, for example, is the case if each target face is aimed at an equal number of times.

Some of the early experiments were designed to eliminate the effect of bias by alternating sets of throws aiming at low targets with sets with high targets. Unfortunately, however, one of the most impressive of the results (that of Gibson, Gibson, and Rhine) did not conform to a design that eliminated the effect of bias (Gibson et al., 1943). This series included 144,792 throws with 25,189 hits. If it is assumed that the mean chance expected number of hits was one-sixth the number of throws, this would give a deviation of 1,057 hits over mean chance expectation which would be overwhelmingly significant. Since, however, the dice were not unbiased, and subjects selected their own targets and tended to favour higher targets, this assumption is not justified; mean chance expectation is likely to exceed one-sixth of the throws, and these figures do not, in themselves, enable us to judge whether or to what extent PK influenced the results.

This does not, however, entail that this experiment does not give evidence for PK. From the data given one can estimate the dice bias and the target preferences of the subjects. If the necessary allowance is made for these factors, this series of experiments still shows a significant excess of hits over mean chance expectation; P remains less than 0·00001 which is ample for significance (Thouless, 1947).

The problem of dice bias is of no present-day importance in PK experimenting. The modern experimenter uses unbiased dice. More importantly, he uses an experimental design which would make dice bias, if it were present, unable to produce spurious indications of PK. As already mentioned, a very simple way of doing this is to arrange that each die-face is target an equal number of times.

Another source of error in experimenting which must be eliminated is one already mentioned in connection with ESP experimenting, the possibility of systematic errors in recording. Some methods of recording results, as, for example, the experimenter simply writing down the number of hits and misses on each throw, produce the situation that recording errors are easy to make and difficult to detect. It is reasonable to suspect that, if recording errors are being made in such a situation, they are likely to be in the direction of increasing the apparent evidence for PK. It would be better for the experimenter to record the number of dice showing each face uppermost. This reduces the liability to error in recording, but not sufficiently for anything but a pilot experiment unless the falls are also recorded by a second experimenter who preferably should not know for what target each throw is being made.

The precaution of having the calls recorded by someone who is not informed as to the intended target is an adequate precaution against the possibility of systematic recording errors producing spurious evidence of PK. Even if there are mistakes in recording, these will be randomly distributed in a positive and negative direction. The possibility is also eliminated by the use of mechanical recording, by photographing the dice after their fall or by other mechanical means. It is also, of course, necessary that the targets are recorded by someone who does not know how the dice have fallen; this requirement is normally taken care of by the fact that, in a PK experiment, the targets are recorded before any throwing takes place.

The name used by early psychical researchers for paranormal movement without contact was 'tele-kinesis' or 'movement at a distance'. When investigation was started at Duke Parapsychological Laboratory, the term chosen was not this but 'psycho-kinesis' (mind-movement). This term suggests, as model for the phenomenon, the immaterial mind giving a push to the dice to make them fall in the intended way. This may be the right way of thinking about PK, but it may not. The right model for PK activity may be something quite different, something perhaps not yet thought of.

It might have been better to have chosen a name not pointing to any particular explanation. 'Psi' is intended as such a non-committal name. We could adapt the term to make a distinction between PK and ESP by using the term 'psi-kappa' ($\psi_\kappa$) for PK, while using 'psi-gamma' ($\psi_\gamma$) for the cognitive side of psi, as in ESP and precognition. This is, however, a suggestion for the future; at present, if we want to be understood we shall use the name 'psycho-kinesis' while reminding ourselves that the implications of this name may be misleading.

PK (or psi-kappa) is often referred to as the influence of the subject's intentions (or 'will') on the movements of the dice or other physical system used in the experiment. This too may be misleading since it goes beyond what is demonstrated by the success of a PK experiment. The situation is that a certain face has been chosen as target, the subject of the experiment has the wish and the intention that that face shall fall uppermost, so also presumably has the experimenter. If the experiment is successful, i.e. if the target face turns up significantly more often than could be expected by chance, we remain uncertain what exactly was the factor causing this success. We do not know whether it was the mind of the subject or of the experimenter; we do not know whether the mental factor was an intention on the part of one or both of these or whether it was a mere wish; we do not even know that the causative factor was not the mere fact of that particular face having been chosen as target. It would be possible to design an experiment to distinguish between these possibilities but the experiment would be a delicate one that would not be easy to carry out. Until the experiment has been carried out it seems better not to refer to a PK experiment as a demonstration of the influence of the human will over the movements of a physical system, but, more indefinitely, as a demonstration of the influence of mental factors of some kind on the movements of a physical system.

We may ask about PK the same two questions as were asked about ESP; as to how strong is the evidence that it really exists, and as to how much knowledge of its character has been contributed by experimental study.

The answer to the first question would seem to be that evidence as to its reality is now very strong although less extensive than that for the reality of ESP. The total amount of experimentation on PK has been considerably less than that on ESP and it has taken place at fewer research centres. If there is some hesitation in accepting part of the early evidence which may have been carried out under conditions that would not now be regarded as sufficiently rigid for the demonstration of a novel psi-effect, there is an impressive number of later successful experiments which were carried out under adequate conditions.

Most of these have been on groups of unselected subjects with a low rate of scoring, not on such high-scoring subjects as ESP research had in Pearce and Shackleton. In dealing with such evidence, it is proper to ask whether the appearance of success may not be due to the selection of successful experiments from a total number of experiments of which the unsuccessful ones do not get published. This is a theoretical possibility. My impression is that there have been sufficient successful PK experiments to outweigh any likely number of unpublished unsuccessful ones, but there is obviously an element of uncertainty in such an estimate.

Those who wish to know enough about the field to form for themselves an opinion as to how far the whole body of experimental evidence supports the reality of PK can do so by studying the scholarly and comprehensive account published in 1960 by J. G. Pratt (1960). This article has references to over one hundred reports on experimental investigations into PK from the technical journals. There is now also available to the student a fuller and more up-to-date account of the research into PK in the form of a book by Dr Louisa Rhine (1970).

In forming an opinion as to the strength of the evidence for the reality of PK, we are not limited to considering the evidence from the successful experiments on unselected subjects. We have also the more satisfactory type of evidence derived from an experiment yielding a decisive result under conditions of adequate witnessing and control. Perhaps the best single experiment of this kind is that carried out by Pratt and Forwald at the Duke Parapsychology Laboratory in 1957 (Pratt and Forwald, 1958). Mr Forwald has an impressive record of success in PK experiments of the 'placement' type in which the object is not to make dice fall with a particular face uppermost, but to make dice or other objects fall into a predetermined position. There is no reason for doubting that Forwald is a sound and reliable experimenter, but, since his experiments in Sweden were carried out on himself as subject, their results cannot be regarded as decisive for the demonstration of the reality of PK. For this purpose it is necessary that he should show himself able to repeat his successes in experiments supervised and witnessed by other parapsychologists. This object was achieved in a visit paid to the Duke Laboratory where he worked under the supervision of Dr Pratt.

An initial difficulty in this enquiry was the 'witness effect' already discussed in Chapter X. Forwald was used to working alone and at first showed only chance results when another person was present. This difficulty was got over by preliminary tests to discover whether there was anyone with whom he could work and continue to get positive results. Such a person was found, who acted afterwards as co-subject in the confirmatory experimental sequence and made an independent record of the results.

In this experiment, six wooden cubes were released electrically and rolled on to a horizontal surface marked off into two sides A and B. One of these sides was designated as target area for each release. The success of each release was measured, not by the relative number of cubes falling on each side of the dividing line, but by the difference between the average distances the objects rolled in the target and in the non-target direction. In order to eliminate any bias in the surface which would favour either direction, the sides A and B were designated as target areas an equal number of times in each set of ten releases; the subject's score was taken as the difference between the relative distances travelled by cubes in the A and B direction when A was target and in the corresponding release when B was target.

It was found in preliminary trials that scoring was predominantly on the difference between the first throw in each set for target A and the first throw for target B. It was decided, therefore, to make a separate evaluation for these first throws in the final confirmatory group of experiments. This selection of part of the data for separate treatment is, of course, perfectly legitimate provided that the selection has been decided on before the experiments to which it is applied are carried out, and provided that, in assessing significance, one takes account of the fact that one of two criteria is more likely to be fulfilled by chance than is one alone (in this case, a total significant score would also have been evidence of PK).

The final confirmatory experiment included fifty releases of the six cubes, directed towards each side as target (100 releases in all). Of these 100 releases, 20 altogether (10 towards each side) were first releases of a set, which previous experience suggested were particularly liable to show the influence of PK. The total result of this test showed a small difference in the expected direction which did not quite reach the level of statistical significance (P was about 0·07). On the other hand, the difference in the expected direction in the mean difference of first throws was a large one, strongly significant (with $P = 0·0002$). Even if we consider that this is the selected best of two results, the significance remains overwhelmingly strong, with $P = 0·0004$, that is, the odds against such a result occurring in a chance series would be more than 2,000 to 1; there can be no reasonable doubt that this is not an accidental result and the precautions taken render it very strong evidence of the operation of PK.

In view of the outstanding importance of this experiment, it is worth noticing that its conclusions have been carefully checked from the original records by Dr McConnell using more sophisticated techniques of assessment than had been used by Pratt (McConnell and Forwald, 1967). The result of this critical enquiry is a confirmation of the conclusions put forward by Pratt in his joint article with Forwald, and a confirmation of his estimate of the statistical significance of the result.

It remains, of course, true that, as in such outstanding tests for ESP as the Soal-Goldney experiment, this Pratt-Forwald result would be of little scientific interest if it stood alone. In fact it is one outstanding but not solitary case amongst a large number of experimental demonstrations of PK. It is in the context of these other successful PK experiments that its scientific importance must be judged.

Less is known of the general pattern of the PK response than of ESP. Certain characteristics of the ESP pattern have, however, been confirmed for PK. One of these is the 'position effect' discussed in Chapter X. As for ESP, there seems to be a tendency for scoring rates to decline within a session or any other unit into which the session is divided. When PK results are recorded on a printed form, there is a general tendency for scores to decline within each page of the record. On the forms commonly used in the Duke Parapsychology Laboratory, this resulted in a tendency to a decline in score from left to right and also from top to bottom of the page. If the page were divided into four quarters, the biggest difference would be that between the scores recorded in the top left quarter of the page (which were relatively high) and those in the bottom right quarter (which were lowest). This was referred to as the 'quarter distribution' (or QD) effect (Rhine and Humphrey, 1944).

This may be noted as a significant contribution to our knowledge of the pattern of PK. The aspect of it, however, which interested its discoverers was not so much the contribution it made to our knowledge of the pattern of psi, as the evidence it provided for the reality of PK. It was argued that no such consistent tendency should have been found in a merely random set of results such as these scores would be in the absence of PK or of some other cause affecting the correspondence between fall of dice and target. So it could be claimed that this result provided indirect evidence for PK.

This observation would plainly be of no value as evidence for the reality of PK if the QD effect were merely an oddity of the records which was noticed after the experiments had taken place. Such an observed oddity could properly be noted as an indicator of something to be looked for in a future experiment; it could not in itself be regarded as evidence of anything. What made the QD effect of importance as evidence was the fact that it was originally noticed in one set of results and was afterwards amply confirmed when other sets of results were examined. This made it clear that the effect was a real one, however it might be explained.

Such indirect evidence is, no doubt, less satisfying psychologically than the more direct evidence one can derive from the fact of the number of correct dice falls significantly exceeding the number to be expected by chance. Unless, however, it were supposed to be possible to explain these position effects as due to some characteristic of the dice falls or of the pattern of target selection, they must be admitted to be logically adequate evidence for the reality of PK. No consistent position effects would be found in randomly distributed records; if the design of the experiment excludes other explanations of departure from randomness than PK, then significant quarter distribution proves the occurrence of PK. The evidence from QDs thus gives useful support to the direct evidence from PK experiments in which there is significant correspondence between the intentions of the subject and the falls of the dice or other objects.

Other designs of experiment in PK have been used in addition to those involving the rolling of dice. Some investigators have used coins or other two-sided objects (McMahan, 1945). W. E. Cox, who originated the 'placement' method of PK experimenting, has also been fertile in the devising of other experimental methods including the use of clocks that might be accelerated or retarded by PK. In the experiments in Copenhagen already referred to, Professor Winther used pendulums as experimental material and it appeared that his subject could influence both the amount and the direction of their swing. Such material is, however, of little use for routine experimenting, partly because each observation necessarily occupies a very long time, partly because of the elaborate precautions that must be taken, when one is dealing with the detection of very small forces, to isolate the physical system effectively so that spurious results cannot be produced by air-currents or vibrations.

In the early days of psychical research, Crookes used a simple device in which a hinged board was apparently so acted on by psi-forces that its movements could be recorded on a smoked drum. This would be ideal PK material but, although Crookes reported success with other subjects besides the famous medium Home, other experimenters have not been able to repeat his success. If the experiment succeeded when Crookes was experimenter, it seems that it must have been because Crookes was a specially gifted PK experimenter.

Another promising line of PK experimentation which seems not to have been repeated by other investigators is Richmond's work on the action of PK on the movements of *paramecia*, microscopic organisms found in pond water (Richmond, 1952). Richmond tried to direct the movements of his paramecia into a quadrant of his microscope, the target quadrant having been selected by the turning up of a card when the observation started. He treated as success a movement into the selected quadrant or the one opposite, so there was a one-in-two likelihood of a chance hit. In 1,495 observations he obtained 927 successes. This is 179·5 (12 per cent) over mean chance expectation. Since this is a two-alternative task, this would correspond to the astonishing psi-efficiency index (Appendix A) of 24 per cent. In other words, Richmond appeared to be influencing his paramecia by PK enough to produce success in a quarter of his observations. This also would be an ideal form of PK experiment since the material is abundant and the observations are not difficult. Unfortunately, however, Richmond's success has not, so far as I know, been repeated, although others have tried his experiment. It appears that this result too must be attributed to Richmond's special capacity as experimenter in PK.

There is nothing intrinsically improbable in such individual differences existing between the success levels of different PK experimenters. We know that such differences exist between the amount of success that different experimenters can obtain from ESP subjects. Some experimenters, such as Soal, seem to be able to get successful results with many different percipients. Other experimenters are unable to obtain anything but chance results or negative deviations.

Apart from the demonstration that position effects occur in PK records as they do in the experimental records of ESP, not much work has been done experimentally in the direction of finding out about the nature of PK. A notable exception has been the work of Forwald on the influence of the physical material of test objects on psycho-kinetic results (Forwald, 1955, 1957). He found that, in a comparison between PK results with wood and bakelite cubes, the movement in the intended direction was such as to require the assumption of a force acting which was about the same on both kinds of cube. A later experiment in which these cubes were compared with wooden cubes coated with aluminium seemed to indicate that a greater force must be postulated to account for the PK movements of the aluminium-coated cubes while a still greater force would be needed to account for the amount of PK movement observed with solid aluminium cubes.

This is a praiseworthy attempt to open a very difficult group of problems that must be solved before we can be satisfied that we understand the nature of PK. These results must be confirmed by other workers before they can be accepted as part of the assured knowledge about psi. The method used by Forwald, in which he was both experimenter and subject, is obviously open to the objection that what seems to be discovered may be a product of the experimenter-subject's own beliefs as to what should happen. It must also be considered that Forwald's enquiry assumes a particular model of PK action, that of a force acting on the experimental objects in such a way as to determine where the die shall come to rest. There is no certainty that the right way of thinking about PK is in terms of a variable physical force. This is not an objection to Forwald's method of enquiry; the way of advance in experimental science is often that of testing an inadequate model and discovering that it is inadequate. That discovery may be, in itself, a step forward.

The present position with respect to PK is that we have very strong evidence for its reality. The next step would seem to be further experimental investigation of its nature.

## References

BARRETT, W. F. (1911), 'Poltergeists old and new', *Proceedings of the Society for Psychical Research*, xxv, 377–412.
CROOKES, W. (1874), *Researches in the Phenomena of Spiritualism*, London (republished 1953).
FEILDING, E., BAGGALLY, W. W., and CARRINGTON, HEREWARD (1909), 'Report on a Series of Sittings with Eusapia Palladino', *Proc. S.P.R.*, xxiii, 306–559.

FORWALD, H. (1955 and 1957), 'A Study of Psychokinesis in its Relation to Physical Conditions', *Journal of Parapsychology*, xix, 133–54, and xxi, 98–121.

GIBSON, E. P., GIBSON, LOTTIE H., and RHINE, J. B. (1943), 'A Large Series of PK Tests', *J. Parapsych.*, vii, 228–37.

MCCONNELL, R. A., and FORWALD, H. (1967), 'Psychokinetic Placement: I. A Re-examination of the Forwald-Durham Experiment', *J. Parapsych.*, xxxi, 51–69.

MCMAHAN, ELIZABETH, (1945), 'PK Experiments with Two-sided Objects', *J. Parapsych.*, ix, 249–63.

OWEN, A. R. G. (1964), *Can We Explain the Poltergeist?*, New York.

PRATT, J. G. (1960), 'The Case for Psychokinesis', *J. Parapsych.*, xxiv, 171–88.

PRATT, J. G., and FORWALD, H. (1958), 'Confirmation of the PK Placement Effect', *J. Parapsych.*, xxii, 1–19.

RHINE, J. B., and HUMPHREY, BETTY M. (1944), 'The PK Effect: Special Evidence from Hit Patterns, I and II', *J. Parapsych.*, viii, 18–60, 254–71.

RHINE, LOUISA E. (1963), 'Spontaneous Physical Effects and the Psi Process', *J. Parapsych.*, xxvii, 84–137.

RHINE, LOUISA E. (1970), *Mind over Matter : the Story of PK Research*, New York.

RICHMOND, N. (1952), 'Two Series of PK Tests on Paramecia', *Journal of the Society for Psychical Research*, xxxvi, 577–88.

THOULESS, R. H. (1947), 'A Method of Correcting Dice Bias in Evaluating PK Test Data', *J. Parapsych.*, xi, 231–5.

WINTHER, C. (1928), 'Experimental Inquiries into Telekinesis', *Journal of the American Society for Psychical Research*, xxii, 25–33, 82–99, 164–80.

# XVI

# The experimental study of survival

There are a number of topics in parapsychology which remain in the observational stage because no one has so far been able to devise experimental methods for their study. In others the evidence is mainly observational although attempts have been made to submit it to experimental control. Amongst the latter is one problem that has, from the beginnings of psychical research, been regarded as one of its key problems, that of the possibility of obtaining evidence as to whether human beings survive, in any sense, the death of their bodies. That there is survival in some sense is taught by all the religions; it is also supported by a good deal of observational evidence. Yet to many it has seemed so certain that human consciousness is a function of an intact nervous system that they have ruled out as impossible the idea that any consciousness could survive the death and corruption of the nervous system.

This is not a situation to be resolved by argumentation even on a philosophical level. Philosophical arguments for or against survival turn on the implications of language. It is not in this way that questions of fact can be settled. We cannot decide what is the case by considerations drawn from the socialised habits of thought which underly the implications of our language; rather we must be prepared to modify our habits of thought and our customary ways of using language in order to make them conform to whatever facts we may discover.

It is obvious that there is one kind of empirical evidence that could provide incontrovertible evidence of survival; this is the actual experience of our consciousness going on after our own bodily death. But we must wait for our death before we can know whether we have that experience; we cannot have it in this life.

Some people do, however, claim to have in this life an experience somewhat related to the post-mortem experience of continued conscious existence. This is what is called the 'out-of-the-body' experience (Green, 1968). This experience may occur while the subject appears to be asleep or unconscious but it may also occur in the waking state. Its distinguishing feature is the fact that the subject appears to be elsewhere than in his body, and the body itself may be seen as an object within his field of vision. Such experiences may seem to one having them, not direct evidence of the survival of death, but convincing evidence that he is of such a nature that survival is not an unreasonable expectation. They are not convincing as evidence of anything to other people than those experiencing them, since they rarely give verifiable information that would indicate that they were not merely hallucinatory. To give generally acceptable evidence of survivability it would be necessary that such experiences should be brought under experimental control. Such control has not yet been achieved.

The observational evidence for survival derived from the appearance of ghosts and other apparitions has not much force as evidence that people do survive their bodily deaths. There is much evidence that seeing a ghost is a genuine but rare experience, but little ground for supposing that a ghost is the surviving element of some deceased person. Even when what is seen is the apparition of some relative or friend who has recently died, there are strong arguments against the view that the spirit of the dead person is there as a visual object (Tyrrell, 1942).

More cogent evidence comes from communications ostensibly from the departed that are received through mediums. The *medium* is a woman or man who is considered to act as intermediary between a living human *sitter* and a once living *communicator*. The contact between the medium and communicator may appear to be direct as when the medium speaks by *direct voice*, that is, apparently with the voice of the communicator. More commonly there is another intermediary, ostensibly in the spirit world, called the *control*. There is some experimental evidence, obtained by Whately Carington (1935–7), that the controls are secondary personalities of the medium, although they may claim to be Red Indians, Greeks, Persians, and so forth. The control usually reports the presence of deceased relatives and friends of the sitters, gives messages from them to the sitters, and reports their answers to questions put by sitters. The medium may be in trance or semi-trance and may communicate what is said by the control either by word of mouth or by automatic writing or by some such method as spelling out by pointing successively to different letters of the alphabet.

There is no doubt that statements and answers to questions purporting to come from the departed are given in mediumistic seances and no reason for supposing (except in rare and purely fraudulent cases) that they are conscious fabrications by the medium. It has indeed been abundantly shown (in the case of Mrs Piper and other good mediums) that the information supplied about relatives of sitters unknown to the medium has gone far beyond the medium's normal knowledge. If their source was not the ostensible communicators, it would have to be attributed to the extrasensory capacities of the medium. Without a suitably designed experiment, it is difficult to see how a rational choice between these two alternatives can be made.

To suppose that the choice is simply between extra-terrestrial communicators and the medium's psi-capacities is to make the alternative too absolute. It is possible that both factors might enter into mediumistic communications as well as such other factors as the medium's own habits of thought and also the habits of thought and extra-sensory capacities of the sitters. If there is any factor of communication from the communicators, this may be diluted to any extent by such other factors, normal and paranormal. An answer to the key question of whether there is any evidence for communications from the departed in mediumistic material depends on the investigator's ability to filter out such an element from all such possible irrelevancies. If the question as to the reality of this element is answered affirmatively, there remains the further quantitative question of how large it is in comparison with other factors. A satisfactory answer to these questions demands more refined techniques of enquiry than mere attendance at mediumistic seances.

There may be real communication from the departed which is very imperfect as a result of dilution from such sources as the thought habits of the medium, the expectations of the sitters, and so on. The situation from the point of view of the communicator may well be as described by (ostensibly) F. W. H. Myers communicating by automatic writing through Mrs Holland: 'I appear to be standing behind a sheet of frosted glass—which blurs sight and deadens sounds—dictating feebly—to a reluctant and somewhat obtuse secretary' (Johnson, 1909).

In the same way, when Mrs Willett was the ostensible communicator through Geraldine Cummins, she referred to the communications as a 'mixed grill' composed of memories of the medium and the communicator, and spoke of herself as being in a sense compelled to select from the memories of the automatist (Cummins and Toksvig, 1965). If this was communicated by Mrs Willett, it is of special interest since her own experience in this life as a medium might have been a help to her in understanding the problems and difficulties of communication.

The evidence from communications received through mediums has appeared convincing to many people. Two lines of evidence may be distinguished: evidence by *recognition* and evidence by *information*.

The characteristic of evidence by recognition is that the sitter is convinced of the reality of the communicator by recognition of such personal characteristics as ways of speaking and even (in direct voice communication) of characteristic intonations. The feeling is that of being in direct contact with the deceased personality. Such experience of recognition seems understandably convincing to the sitter experiencing it. It can carry no conviction to anyone else, particularly when they remember how illusory experiences of recognition can be even in everyday life.

More commonly the evidence that convinces sitters of the reality of their communicators is their ability to give some identifying information. If someone were telephoning to us and we were uncertain whether he was the person he claimed to be, he might assure us as to his identity by producing such an identifying bit of information: 'I'm John Smith, you know, who used to ride a piebald pony called Peg.' If we are in doubt as to the identity of ostensible communicators, they may attempt to satisfy our doubts in the same way.

Not all information given in a seance is useful for identification; that part which can be used as evidence of identification is of very uneven value for that purpose. The informational content of a seance can be classified as follows:

1. Information that has no value as evidence because it is on matters that could be within the normal knowledge of the medium.

2. Information that is of little evidential value because, although true of the communicator, it is true also of many other people. Such information, for example, as 'Your grandfather died as an old man after a long illness' can be shown to be acceptable to a large proportion of sitters. On credulous sitters, it may have an effect disproportionate to its real value as evidence.

3. Information as to some particular fact known to the ostensible communicator which can be confirmed by one of the sitters or by some other person. This is the kind of information that obviously points strongly to the ostensible communicator being the person he claims to be. The evidence is not, however, coercive if we admit the possibility that the medium can get such information from the minds of the sitters by ESP. Information of this type is, of course, evidence of some kind of paranormal acquisition of knowledge, but not necessarily from other-world sources.

4. Information as to some fact (subsequently confirmed) which is known to the ostensible communicator but to no other person. This most striking kind of evidence does not often occur spontaneously although there have been cases. It is more easily arranged experimentally, as when a communicator tries to reveal the contents of a package he sealed before his death. In the early days of psychical researches such information was regarded as of very high evidential value since the early psychical researchers were inclined to regard telepathy as the only form of ESP to be considered. Since, however, we now know that psi-knowledge of an external fact is no more beyond the power of a gifted percipient than is psi-knowledge of another person's thought, this evidence is of no more force than is that of the third kind unless the possibility of the medium having acquired the crucial information by ESP has been in some manner excluded. This exclusion of the possibility of ESP can never be complete in a spontaneous mediumistic communication; it will be later considered how it can be achieved in an experimental situation.

Although it is, in principle, possible for authentic information of the third and fourth kinds to be explained by the sceptic as due to the medium's own extra-sensory powers, this explanation may appear, in the most striking cases, a highly improbable one since it assumes an ESP capacity in the medium greater than there is any other evidence for. The least that can be said for good spontaneous mediumistic evidence of survival is that it creates a strong prima facie case for some part of the communication coming from the ostensible communicator. Of recent cases which contribute strongly to this evidence, I should be inclined to pick out the 'Palm Sunday' case (Balfour, 1960) and the communications received by Geraldine Cummins ostensibly from Mrs Willett (Cummins and Toksvig, 1965).

If the most striking mediumistic utterances do seem to show evidence that they may come in part from an other-world communicator, it remains true that they seem to be diluted to an unknown extent by the psychological this-world factors already mentioned. In the less striking cases these factors may predominate to such an extent that one can feel no conviction that anything is coming through from the ostensible communicator. In all cases, correct information, from whatever source, is mixed with much misinformation, and evidence by recognition is confused by an admixture of uncharacteristic responses. While such misinformation complicates the problem of evaluating mediumistic evidence, it is not inconsistent with real activity of a communicator if it is considered that the communication is, at best, a composite product in which such factors as the thought processes of the medium may play a part. It must also not be forgotten that the communicator himself may suffer from defects of memory and some changes of personality after his bodily death.

It is clear that there are enough uncertainties in spontaneous mediumistic material to suggest the desirability of an experimental attack on the problem of survival. Either evidence by recognition or evidence from information may be made the basis for experiment. The first of such experimental enquiries to be considered here is the attempt of Whately Carington to reduce to experimental terms the problem of identification of communicators by recognition (Whately Carington, 1935–7). The essence of his method was to use the responses of communicators to psychological tests as a means of identifying them instead of relying on the subjective impression of recognition by the sitter. The intention was to discover whether what was ostensibly a single communicator would give, through different mediums, responses which were more similar to each other than were the responses of ostensibly different communicators. If it were found to be so, this would give reason for supposing that a communicator x coming through one medium was the same individual as communicator x coming through another medium. It would not, of course, prove that he was the individual he claimed to be, but Whately Carington had also the idea of a more extended experiment which would provide evidence also on this question (Whately Carington, 1950). He had a plan of doing psychological tests on living individuals, and after their death to see whether, as communicators, their responses to the same tests showed a significant resemblance to their responses during their life. This experiment was, however, never carried out.

In the more limited experiment on the resemblance of communicators coming through different mediums, Whately Carington thought that his case was proved. Further study of his numerical results showed, however, that this was over-optimistic; his positive results turned out to be the result of serious errors in Whately Carington's use of statistical methods (Thouless, 1937). When correctly evaluated, his results showed no more tendency for communicators to resemble themselves than to resemble other communicators. They provided no evidence that the different communicators were distinct personalities.

Whately Carington's experiment was a courageous and praiseworthy attempt to solve a difficult problem. There is no reason for taking its negative result as final. Other workers may repeat Carington's laborious plan of research by more fruitful methods and they may get more satisfactory results. No one seems as yet to have tried to follow the path laid down by Whately Carington; there seems here to be a field open for experimental research but it is not an easy one.

More commonly, parapsychologists have preferred to do experiments on identification of communicators by information. These have involved choosing the item of identifying information, generally by the use of a package containing information and sealed in the communicator's lifetime. Before discussing these 'sealed package' experiments, however, something should be said of another attack on the problem of survival which is, at least, semi-experimental. This is the system of 'cross-correspondences' which was reported in the *Proceedings of the Society for Psychical Research* from 1906 onwards.

If this was an experiment, it would appear to be one that was arranged from the other side of the grave. The general idea was that separate items of information were given through different mediums, items which were without significance when considered separately but fitted into a coherent whole when taken together. This feat was taken to be beyond the telepathic powers of the mediums concerned, and therefore to be evidence of a single mind acting on all the mediums, which mind had the necessary knowledge to arrange the connection between the items. The principal identifying characteristic of the items supplied was the amount of classical knowledge that was required for fitting them together; this knowledge was certainly possessed by the ostensible communicators: Verrall, Butcher, and Myers. I have not myself sufficient classical knowledge to judge the value of the evidence from the cross-correspondences, but some competent judges consider that they do demonstrate the unifying activity of the surviving mind of a classical scholar.

If this was an experiment devised by these scholars on the other side of the grave, I think it must be judged to be a badly designed experiment. It has provided a mass of material of which it is very difficult to judge the evidential value, and about which there are varying opinions. It reproduces, in fact, the defects of spontaneously gathered mediumistic material in a somewhat intensified form. A successful experiment should give a more clear and unambiguous answer to the question it is designed to answer than does spontaneous material; otherwise the experiment is not worth while. When judged by this criterion the cross-correspondences would seem to fail as an experiment.

The sealed-package experiments were attempts to make experimental the problem of identification by information. If the deceased person has put something into a package whose contents are known to no one else, then we have a specified bit of information which we may hope to recover from him through a medium after his death. A message was so sealed by F. W. H. Myers before his death, but the nature of the message was not afterwards discovered through a medium but only by opening the package. Sir Oliver Lodge left behind him a similar package but although there were many subsequent seances in which Lodge ostensibly communicated (in some of which I was the sitter) it proved impossible to get a plain statement from him as to what was in his envelope. When this was finally opened it proved to contain an account of a finger habit acquired from the five-finger exercises of his childhood which remained with him all his life and was, he said, known to nobody else.

It is not, perhaps, surprising that the communicator may find it difficult to remember the particular bit of information that he put into his sealed package. In this life, we use our material brains for the purpose of re-membering. If there is a disembodied communicator, he has lost this material brain which he left behind in his grave. He no longer possesses this convenient mechanism for the storage of information; the brain may not be essential for remembering and yet the loss of it may interfere with effective remembering. Some of us are in the habit of remembering appointments by writing them down in a pocket diary; we could, no doubt, have remembered them without the diary, but, since we have formed the habit of relying on it, we shall find it difficult to remember our engage-ments if the diary is lost. It may be so also when we lose our material brains at death. The task of remembering a specific memory may be a difficult one; if anything of the sealed-package type is to be attempted, it is important that the experimental material should be simple, striking, and easy to remember.

It is odd too that, in the experiments of Myers and Lodge, better success was not obtained by the clairvoyant powers of the medium. Too much weight should not be attached to this failure, but, so far as it goes, it suggests that the psi-capacities of mediums may be less formidable than they are commonly assumed to be.

It is true that certain writers have claimed that neither the Myers pack-age test nor that of Lodge were as complete failures as they were supposed to be, since the message delivered through the medium, although not identical with that enclosed in the package, had some relation to it (Salter, 1958). In the Myers package, for example, both the sealed message and the seance reproduction of it had something to do with love but one was concerned with the house where lived the lady whom Myers loved, and the other was concerned with Plato's *Symposium*. The resemblance is somewhat remote and one cannot say with confidence that it is not accidental.

The mere fact that there can be such discussion means that the experiments have failed in their main object, for the evidence they have produced has the same sort of uncertainty as that produced in ordinary non-experimental sittings with mediums. The point of doing an experiment is to do something better than this; it should produce evidence which approaches the ideal of an unambiguous proof that communication was received that could only be accounted for on the hypothesis of a disembodied communicator.

The failure of the Myers and Lodge sealed-package experiments should be considered as a challenge to the psychical researcher to design something better.

There are a number of defects in these two sealed-package experiments. First, there is the fact that, if they had been successful, there would have been no way of ensuring that this success was due to communication of information from another world and not to the extra-sensory capacities of the medium. Arguments could, no doubt, be put forward on both sides, but there is no experimental discrimination between the two possibilities. Secondly, the experiment is not repeatable; once the package is opened, the experiment is over. Those in charge of the experiment may be doubtful when to open the package. If it is opened too early, the experiment may fail although the communicator could have got through the correct message in a later sitting. If the package has been opened and examined there can be no later sitting. What one needs is to devise a task for which there can be an indefinitely large number of verifications without spoiling the experiment.

It was in an attempt to remedy these defects that I devised what I have called the *cipher test* (Thouless, 1948). This was intended to fulfil the following requirements:

1. That the information to be communicated should be simple and easy to remember.

2. That it should be of a hit-or-miss type; the answer should be either clearly right or clearly wrong.

3. The likelihood of hitting on the right answer by accident should be negligibly small.

4. It should be possible to try out any number of wrong answers without spoiling the experiment as it is spoiled by the premature opening of a sealed package.

5. The design should be such that a discrimination can be made between success through the medium's ESP and that which must be attributed to communication from the departed.

For the purpose of this test, I have prepared in cipher two passages in the *Proceedings of the Society for Psychical Research.*\* The passages are: INXPH CJKGM JIRPR FBCVY WYWES NOECN SCVHE GYRJQ TEBJM TGXAT TWPNH CNYBC FNXPF LFXRV QWQL and BTYRR OOFLH KCDXK FWPCZ KTADR GFHKA HTYXO ALZUP PYPVF AYMMF SDLR UVUB. The methods used for encipherment are described in the articles already referred to. The object of the test is to see whether, after my bodily death, I can communicate the keys by which the passages can be deciphered. It will not be my intention to communicate the content of the enciphered passages; that I have already forgotten. What is to be communicated is the keys required for decipherment: a passage from literature in the first case, and a pair of words in the second. The methods of encipherment are such that these keys cannot be discovered by any rational process.

This test seems to fulfil the first four of the required conditions mentioned above. It does not matter how many wrong keys are tried out; the passage will not be read by means of them and the subsequent reading of it by the right key is not prevented by these failures. The test may not indeed entirely get over the difficulty that imperfections of post-mortem memory may make it difficult for my disembodied spirit to produce the required keys. But this difficulty is made as small as possible by the simplicity of what has to be remembered and by the fact that any number of attempts to remember can be tested.

The design of this experiment also makes it possible to fulfil the fifth requirement, that of discriminating between explanation by the medium's ESP powers and by a surviving communicator. This possibility arises from the fact that any number of erroneous attempts at the key can be made without spoiling the test. Attempts can, therefore, be made to get the keys through mediums while I am still alive. Several such attempts have been made and all have been unsuccessful. If, therefore, the keys are correctly given by a communicator purporting to be me after my bodily death, the fact that they are so obtained and could not be obtained during my lifetime, will be a strong (though obviously not conclusive) ground for supposing that that communicator is indeed myself.

In order to carry much weight, this experiment should be carried out by a number of persons. There are difficulties in the preparation of enciphered material and, so far as I know, only one other person has made a similar test. It is satisfactory that Dr Ian Stevenson has devised a test on similar lines involving simpler material (Stevenson, 1958). What is

---

\* Vol. xlviii, pp. 258 and 342. There is also an earlier passage on p. 253 which is now withdrawn from the test because its method of encipherment proved not to be unbreakable by rational methods.

deposited in Stevenson's test is a combination lock, on which the combination has been changed by the person intending to communicate to a number known only to himself. The matter to be communicated is the number to which the lock must be set before it can be opened. This form of test has the advantage that the material is easily available and requires less labour in preparation than does a cipher. Already a number of individuals have contributed locks for this experiment.

All such experiments, derived from the original sealed-package tests, can go no further than establishing experimentally the fact of survival. The further problem as to the nature of what survives will be the next experimental problem in this field when the fact of survival is demonstrated.

Obviously the experimental study of survival has still a long way to go. There are promising leads as to possible directions of experiment. The path opened by Whately Carington, for example, still awaits further exploration. It would be a big breakthrough if anyone could devise methods of communication that did not involve a human medium, but there is no hint yet of how such a development could take place.

## References

BALFOUR, JEAN (1960), 'The "Palm Sunday" case: new light on an old love story', *Proceedings of the Society for Psychical Research*, lii, 79–267.

CUMMINS, GERALDINE, and TOKSVIG, SIGNE (1965), *Swan on a Black Sea*, London.

GREEN, CELIA (1968), *Out-of-the-body Experiences*, Oxford.

JOHNSON, ALICE (1909), 'On the Automatic Writing of Mrs. Holland', *Proc. S.P.R.*, xxi, 166–91.

SALTER, W. H. (1958), 'F. W. H. Myer's Posthumous Message', *Proc. S.P.R.*, lii, 1–32.

STEVENSON, I. (1968), 'The Combination Lock Test for Survival', *Journal of the American Society for Psychical Research*, lxii, 246–54.

THOULESS, R. H. (1937), 'Review of Mr. Whately Carington's Work on Trance Personalities', *Proc. S.P.R.*, xliv, 223–75.

THOULESS, R. H. (1948), 'A Test of Survival' and 'Additional Note on a Test of Survival', *Proc. S.P.R.*, xlviii, 253–63 and 342–3.

TYRRELL, G. N. M. (1942), *Apparitions*, London.

WHATELY CARINGTON, W. (1935, 1936, 1937), 'The Quantitative Study of Trance Personalities, I, II and III', *Proc. S.P.R.*, xlii, 173–240, xliii, 319–61, and xliv 189–222.

WHATELY CARINGTON, W. (1950), 'Survival of death', *Chambers's Encyclopaedia*, xiii, London.

# XVII

# Conclusions

There can be no conclusions to this book in the sense of a final report of what has been found out. We are at a fairly early stage of the process of finding out. To return to an analogy used in Chapter XII, it is as if we were engaged in solving a large jigsaw puzzle. Some bits of the puzzle seem to fit together and to make some sort of a pattern. We have as yet no idea of what the whole pattern will look like when all the parts are fitted together.

If our inclinations lie in the direction of speculative thinking, we can, of course, try to guess what the total pattern will be like. The usefulness of such guessing is likely to be limited by the fact that we may not yet have the ways of thinking necessary to give an adequate account of psi. The history of science leads us to believe that such new ways of thinking follow the discovery of new facts and new relationships between facts. It seems likely, therefore, that a more profitable activity for the experimental parapsychologist is to try to fit more and more bits of the puzzle together in the confidence that the pattern of the whole will emerge in the end.

Disappointment is sometimes expressed that this process of discovering the pattern in ESP is such a slow one. Often this disappointment is based on the belief that no progress is taking place. I think that this idea is mistaken, and a main purpose of the present book is to show that real progress has taken place during the experimental stage of psychical research although this progress has not been fast. There are obvious reasons for progress being slower than in the physical sciences. One practical reason is the relative shortage of experimental workers in the field of psychical research. A deeper reason is the relative difficulty in parapsychology of formulating expectations precisely in quantitative terms so that the experimenter can make the exact measurements necessary to find out whether the expectations are true or false. One may, for example, contrast the ease with which a schoolboy can find out in a physics laboratory how the intensity of light falls off with the distance from its source, with the great difficulty that parapsychologists have found in making quantitative measurements of the rate at which the efficiency of ESP varies with changing distance from the target (Osis and Turner, 1968).

The essential difficulty in the latter enquiry is the large element of uncertainty that dilutes any attempt to measure the efficiency with which ESP is working. This makes very uncertain any attempt to measure its relative efficiency at different distances. If one could work with subjects who scored at a consistently high rate, the problem would be no more difficult than that of discovering the law of falling off of the intensity of a physical radiation. One can try to overcome this difficulty by devising new designs of experiment in the hope of discovering one that is much more fruitful than any of the existing designs. A more hopeful direction would seem to be that of trying to discover some way of training subjects in psi-activities. This might be by some method analogous to the ordinary learning procedures of normal psychology or by some kind of meditational training. Alternatively one might hope to find a drug that produced reliable enhancement of psi-capacities. All these directions of trying for better psi-results have been tried by experimenters but, so far, without conspicuous success.

This task, of devising ways to increase the efficiency of experimental psi-performance, seems to be the most important immediate task of psi-research. Its purpose is not primarily to produce more convincing evidence of the reality of psi although this might well be one of its consequences. More important is the fact that it would provide the experimental parapsychologist with a means by which he could hope to answer the many questions in parapsychology whose answer depends on his ability to make exact quantitative comparisons.

I think we orient ourselves best towards parapsychology if we regard it not primarily as a means of achieving anything of practical usefulness or of attaining a new view of the world. Both of these results may follow from parapsychological discoveries. But all scientific research is essentially a puzzle-solving activity. Parapsychology presents us with a kind of puzzle particularly hard to solve. Experimentalists are people to whom an unsolved puzzle is an invitation to try to solve it. We do not know where we shall be led by the solution of the puzzles of psi, whether to a better world or a worse one, at any rate to a world that we shall understand more fully. There are still voices who assure us that there are no puzzles to be solved in this field. This is, however, no longer a reasonable belief. The research already carried out has made it clear that the problems are real; we seem still to be a long way from the solution of them.

## References

OSIS, K., and TURNER, M. E. (1968), 'Distance and ESP: a Trans-continental Experiment', *Proceedings of the American Society for Psychical Research*, xxvii.

# Appendix A

# The measurement of efficiency of Psi

One of the questions that we naturally ask about the result of any experiment in ESP or other psi-process is how well the subject is succeeding. This is a different question from that discussed in Chapter VIII of how significant his results are. If results are highly significant this means that they are very unlikely to have been produced by chance as is shown by a low value of P. But such high significance can be produced by a large number of observations of subjects scoring at a low rate or by a relatively small number of observations of a subject scoring at a high rate. The question of how well a given subject or set of subjects was scoring is a different question from that of the significance of their results and requires a different measure from any used as a measure of significance.

Those who report experimental results are often strangely uninterested in how well their subjects are scoring, and may be content to report that in a total of 2,725 guesses, a subject scored 52 hits over mean chance expectation, and that the significance of this result is given by the figure P = 0·01. The reader then knows how unlikely the results are to have been produced by chance; if he also wants to know how good the scoring was, he must work it out for himself.

Investigators who do not want to give their readers so much trouble often report their results as the average score per run of 25 guesses. The above result would then be reported as a run average of 5·48 (or 0·48 hits over mean chance expectation for each run). This way of presenting results is more informative; we can see at once that this represents a considerably lower rate of scoring than that of another subject who scores an average of 8·0 hits per run. It is open to the objection that not all ESP experiments are arranged in runs of 25 guesses, and that other psi-experiments may use runs of different length; the standard run, for example, in dice-rolling experiments of PK has been 24.

I suggest that a useful standard method of representing degree of success in all psi-experiments should be as a percentage score over (or below) mean chance expectation, and that all investigators reporting their experiments should give this index of percentage success for all their results as regularly as they now give the figure indicating the significance of their results. Then 52 hits over m.c.e. in 2,725 guesses would be expressed as a score of + 1·92 per cent which can be used more widely for the purpose of comparison with other psi-experiments than can the equally informative measure of run average as 5·48.

This index of percentage success is a practically useful device for indicating the degree of success in a psi-task. There are, however, theoretical objections to it which limit its usefulness as a measure of the relative degrees of success in tasks with different chance expectations of success, as, for example, ESP tasks with five kinds of target and those with two. The difficulty becomes apparent if we consider that in the ordinary ESP task with five targets, complete success in the task would be shown by the subject getting all his guesses right which would be represented by a success rate of +80 per cent. Complete success in a psi-missing task would be represented by a success rate of −20 per cent when he got none of his responses right. It would seem better that an index of psi-efficiency should represent these two extremes as + 100 per cent success and 100 per cent failure respectively.

The awkwardness of this becomes apparent when we try to compare, let us say, a 30 per cent success rate in a five-target task with a 30 per cent success rate in a two-target task such as that used by Rýzl. Do these indicate equal success in the two tasks? This seems unlikely when we consider that complete success in the two-target task would be indicated by +50 per cent, whereas in a five-target task it would be indicated by +80 per cent. This would seem to suggest that a given percentage rate of success in a two-target task indicates more ESP efficiency than would the same rate of success in a five-target task. The same question is raised in a comparison between a psi-hitting and a psi-missing task; how, for example, does a score of −12 per cent in a psi-missing task compare with a score of +20 per cent in a psi-hitting task?

It was in connection with this question of how to compare a psi-missing score with one in psi-hitting that I worked out what seemed to be a possible way of answering it in a review, in the *Proceedings of the Society for Psychical Research*, of J. B. Rhine's first book, *Extra-Sensory Perception*. If, in a five-target psi-hitting task, a percipient has more hits than the 20 per cent expected by chance, we may suppose that he has got a certain number of these right by ESP, while a fifth of those he has not got right by ESP will happen by chance to be hits. We want to be able to estimate how many of the hits he has scored are psi-determined hits, and how many are merely chance hits. Let us suppose that his ESP has given him a hit in 10 per cent of his guesses. In the remaining 90 per cent of his guesses he may be expected by chance to get four-fifths wrong and one-fifth right. So mere chance may be expected to give him 18 more hits, bringing his total score to 28 per cent (8 per cent over mean chance expectation). So the number of psi-determined hits would seem to be rather more than the observed excess of hits over mean chance expectation; in a five-target task it will be five-fourths of this amount.

The general formula for the index of psi-efficiency with any number of targets is $\dfrac{(h-100p)}{(1-p)}$ where p is the mean chance expectation of success on each guess (normally the reciprocal of the number of targets), and h is the observed number of hits in 100 guesses.

The proof of this formula, on the assumption that the effect of psi is to make the subject succeed in some guesses while he shows only chance success in the others, is as follows. Let m be the number of hits that are psi-determined in 100 guesses. The observed number of hits (h) may be supposed to be made up of these m psi-determined hits and $p(100-m)$ chance hits. So $h = m + p(100-m)$. From this equation we find, by simple algebra, that $h-100p = (1-p).m$ and $m = \dfrac{(h-100p)}{(1-p)}$. In the particular case of 5 targets, p is $\frac{1}{5}$, so this formula reduces to the form already given: m equals $\frac{5}{4}$ of the percentage of hits over mean chance expectation (i.e. of $(h-100p)$). This estimate of the percentage number of psi-determined hits may be used as a measure of efficiency in any psi-task. I propose to call it the *index of psi-efficiency*.

An obvious objection that may be made to this index as a general measure of psi-efficiency is that it would seem to depend on the assumption that a psi-reaction is of the all-or-nothing kind, that one either succeeds completely in it or not at all. It does not seem very likely that psi is of this character. Other assumptions can be made about the character of the psi-response which lead to the same formula for psi-efficiency. This formula does not, therefore, depend on the assumption that the psi-reaction is all-or-nothing although this is the simplest assumption to make.

We may, for example, assume that the effect of psi is to make it rather more likely that the subject will succeed at each guess; that at each guess his probability of being right is increased from the mean chance expectation of p by an increment $\Delta p$. Then his expectation of success in 100 tries will be $100(p + \Delta p)$ instead of the 100p predicted by chance alone.

On this assumption it is natural to take as one's measure of psi-efficiency the relative size of this increment $\Delta p$ which is contributed by psi. If there is no psi-component in the subject's success, $\Delta p$ will, of course, be zero, and the index of psi-efficiency should also be zero. If the subject's success is complete, h will be 100 and $\Delta p$ will have the greatest value that it can have, $100-p$. Since this is its value for complete success, the index of psi-efficiency should then be 100 per cent. This can be secured if we make the index of psi-efficiency the percentage of the distance between 0 and $(100-p)$ that $\Delta p$ has been increased by psi. That is, the index of efficiency will be $\dfrac{100\Delta p}{(1-p)}$ which is the same as $\dfrac{(h-100p)}{(1-p)}$. This is identical with the index of efficiency calculated on the other assumption that psi is an all-or-nothing response.

One can, of course, make other assumptions about the nature of the psi-response, such as that psi acts only on some of the subject's guesses and that its action on these is, not to make them certainly right, but to increase the probability that they are right. Any such assumption is a combination of the two assumptions already discussed and will lead to the same index of psi-efficiency. This index does not, therefore, depend on the particular assumption of the all-or-nothing character of psi, but is valid for that or for the enhanced probabilities assumption or for any combination of these.

The purpose for which a research worker is most likely to want a measure of rate of scoring is merely for indicating how well a particular subject is succeeding in a particular psi-task. For this purpose, the index of psi-efficiency would seem to have no advantage over the more easily calculated index of percentage success. One does, however, need something more than this as a measure of psi-efficiency when we meet problems which involve comparisons between the efficiency with which two psi-tasks with different chance expectations are carried out. The index of psi-efficiency enables one to answer, for example, such a question as that raised earlier of how a success rate of 20 per cent over m.c.e. in a psi-hitting five-target ESP task compares with a score of 12 per cent below m.c.e. in a similar psi-missing task. Expressed in terms of estimated psi-directed responses, these scores would show an index of psi-efficiency of $\frac{5}{4} \times 20\%$ (i.e. 25%) in the psi-hitting task, whereas in the psi-missing task, a 12% deficiency indicates $5 \times 12\%$ (i.e. 60%) as the estimated number of psi-determined responses. That the number of psi-determined responses in the psi-missing task should be considerably larger than in the corresponding psi-hitting task is not difficult to understand since it is an easier task to say what a card is not than to say what it is, and the percipient's psi can more often succeed in this easier task.

The index of efficiency worked out here is the one used in the present book. It is not the only one possible and it may not be the one finally selected for use by experimental parapsychologists. Since this book was written, Dr Helmut Schmidt has suggested a different measure which he calls the 'psi quotient' (PQ).* This is obtained by taking the square of the critical ratio (that is of the ratio of the deviation from expectation to the standard error), dividing this by the total number of calls and multiplying by 1,000. Thus $PQ = \dfrac{1,000 \ CR^2}{N}$. If a subject made 1,600 calls in an ESP experiment with 384 right guesses (64 over mean chance expectation), the PQ of this experiment would be $\dfrac{1,000 \ (\frac{64}{16})^2}{1,600} = 10$.

Other formulae based on information theory have been suggested.

---

* Schmidt, H., 'The Psi Quotient: an efficiency measure for psi tests', *Journal of Parapsychology*, xxxiv, 1970, 210–14.

Which of these will survive is a question for the future. My concern here is to point out the need for having some measure of how well psi is working in a particular experiment, and of distinguishing this problem from that of the statistical significance of the result of the experiment.

# Appendix B

# The case of Marion

One example of a stage performer in 'telepathy' who has been tested experimentally is the late Frederic Kraus, whose stage name was 'Marion'.* Unlike the Piddingtons, Marion definitely claimed to have ESP capacities, and showed himself very willing to submit to investigation under conditions determined by the experimenter. On the stage, he gave demonstrations of finding hidden objects, reporting the contents of sealed envelopes, etc.

Under test, he showed no ability to succeed in the ordinary type of card-guessing experiment, but showed considerable power of finding hidden objects under conditions in which, at first sight, there seemed to be no sensory cues. Soal concluded, however, that this success was not due to ESP but to a use of sensory cues unwittingly supplied by other people present in the room.† This conclusion was based on the observation that if all the people who knew the position of the hidden object were totally concealed from Marion, he no longer succeeded.

These experiments, although they were carefully carried out, suffer from a defect of design which prevents them from being conclusive evidence that Marion was guided to his successes by visual observation of others present. The number of experiments in which Marion was prevented from seeing the sitters was small. These were often at sessions when no successful experiment had been done or after other experiments when the session was drawing to a close. There is much experimental evidence of the extreme variability of ESP performance; the same experimental subject may succeed on some occasions and fail on others, and the rate of scoring is particularly liable to fall off at the end of an experiment or of a series of experiments. One cannot, therefore, conclude from a drop in scoring rate when a new condition is introduced (such as concealing the sitters under a blanket) that the new condition has prevented scoring; it may be that the drop in score would have taken place at that time anyway.

The only satisfactory design of experiment for testing whether a particular condition affects score is one in which experiments with and

* Marion, F., *In my Mind's Eye*, fifth imp., London, 1950.
† Soal, S. G., 'Preliminary studies of a vaudeville telepathist', *University of London Council for Psychical Investigation (Bull. III)*, 1937.

without the condition are irregularly mixed up. If, in a reasonably long series of such mixed-up experiments, the experimental subject persistently scores when he can see the other sitters but not when they are covered up with blankets, then we can reasonably conclude that covering the sitters with blankets prevents the subject from succeeding in his task; presumably he is not using ESP. Since, however, such mixing up of the conditions was not done in Soal's experiments with Marion, the indications of these must be regarded merely as suggestive and not as conclusions. The possibility that Marion was succeeding by ESP in Soal's hidden-object experiments remains open.

In 1945, Dr B. P. Wiesner and I were able to make an experimental study of Marion which led us to a different opinion as to his ESP capacities from that of Dr Soal. In preliminary experiments (in which we had also the co-operation of Mrs Goldney), we found that Marion could succeed at a high rate on a type of card-guessing experiment in which he picked a red card from a number of black ones. The cards were shuffled before laying them out so that no one in the room knew which the right card was. Marion looked at the backs of the cards but did not touch them either during the experiment or before. This experiment was not, in itself, sufficient evidence of ESP since Marion could see the backs of cards, but the result encouraged us to go on with the investigation since Marion was succeeding in a task in which Soal had found that he failed in his series of experiments.

This experiment could be regarded as no more than an indication that Marion might be guided by extra-sensory perception. He had to see the backs of the cards. It might be that this seeing of the backs was, for him, a necessary condition of ESP, but it might also be an indication that he was guided in some way by sensory cues. Certainly he was not doing so in any obvious way. He was never allowed to handle the experimental cards, so he could not bend or mark them; the only pack he handled was one used for preliminary practice but never for the experiments themselves. The possibility that he obtained access to the experimental cards and marked them in our absence was ruled out by the fact that he succeeded equally well with fresh cards brought by me from Cambridge.

His use of ESP could obviously not be established by card-guessing experiments in which Marion could see the backs of the cards; it was necessary to confirm their indication by other experiments less open to objection. The natural solution was to try the standard card-guessing experiment with the ESP cards used at Duke, but he succeeded in this task no better with us than he had with Soal.

His most striking success was guessing the number (from 1 to 7) on which Wiesner and I were concentrating while he was in another adjacent room from which he could not see us. In 240 trials, Marion succeeded 82 times, which is more than twice mean chance expectation (34·3). This is a highly significant result which would not occur by chance more often than once in a million million trials. It is clear that Marion could succeed in this task, whether by ESP or some other means.

We hoped to be able to clinch the matter by training Marion to succeed in this task with increasing distance until any possibility of sensory leakage was completely excluded. This hope was disappointed; the effect disappeared when the door between the two rooms was closed. When the door was closed, only 16 successes were obtained in 110 trials, which is about mean chance expectation; it was clear that the closing of the door stopped the success. It might be that the shut door cut off some unsuspected sensory cues, or it could be that the increased isolation from the experimenters was a factor unfavourable to Marion's ESP.

We had no opportunity to do further experiments to decide between these alternatives; shortly afterwards Marion went to America. We hoped that he would visit the Laboratory at Duke while he was in the United States, but this projected visit was never carried out.

From the positive result of this experiment and from what we saw of Marion's performance in other experiments, Wiesner and I were inclined to the opinion that Marion had considerable ESP abilities which enabled him to perform a limited range of tasks. It is clear that our work with Marion did not provide convincing evidence that this opinion was a right one. We should have felt more confidence in it if we had been able to get him to succeed at greater distances from the experimenter, or if our findings had been confirmed by other investigators at the Duke Laboratory or elsewhere.

It remains, I think, a probable conclusion from the Marion experiments. If it were right, there would remain many puzzles. Although Marion succeeded with us in some tasks, neither the level of success nor its reliability was such as would be required to make a convincing stage performance. Was it the case that, although he may have used ESP in stage performances, he supplemented it by trickery, or were the stage performances all trickery? He himself denied that he used any trickery on the stage. An alternative suggestion is that an audience witnessing a stage performance is so uncritical that its members will be convinced by a level of success which appears unconvincing when it is recorded and subjected to statistical test. Or it might be that Marion did use ESP for his stage effects at a higher level than we could obtain under test conditions because he was stimulated to better ESP performance by the reactions of an admiring and uncritical audience. This last possibility is a challenging one for the experimenter; how can he supply the factor of uncritical admiration in his experiments to see whether this is the determining factor in a reliably successful performance? It was only at a late stage of our investigation that we considered this problem, and our efforts to provide enthusiastic and uncritical audiences were not successful; uncritical enthusiasm does not easily occur spontaneously in academic circles, and it is not easy to simulate it effectively in the situation of experimental research.

This experimental series with Marion obviously did not succeed in the object of providing a convincing demonstration as to whether he had or had not ESP capacities. The indications that he may have had such capacities were, however, sufficiently strong to give some support to the suggestion made in Chapter VII that the variety stage may be one of the places in which to look for potential ESP subjects.

# Appendix C

# The estimate of significance and some of its pitfalls

The problem of how successful an experiment in ESP had to be before it could be regarded as sufficiently convincing evidence was one that early engaged the attention of the more mathematically minded of the psychical researchers, particularly when they started considering the question of how far evidence could be obtained from prolonged experiments with subjects showing a low rate of scoring. In the second volume of the *Proceedings of the Society for Psychical Research*, there are contributions to this problem by Richet, Lodge, and Gurney.* The answers they gave to this problem are of little present-day use since they were inclined to see it as a question of how probable it is that a given level of success was due to telepathy. There can be no definite answer to this question since its answer must depend on the question of how likely it is that there is any telepathy. If there were certainly no such thing as telepathy, the likelihood of any particular result being due to telepathy would be zero, however high its score. Since we cannot give a definite figure to the likelihood of there being any telepathy, this question can have no definite answer.

More recent developments of statistical methods by Pearson and Fisher have reformulated the question to be asked: not 'How likely is it that the observed level of success was produced by ESP?' but 'How unlikely is it that success at the observed level would have occurred by chance alone (i.e. in the absence of any cause tending to produce correspondence between guesses and targets)?'† To this question a definite answer can be given. The way to the answer is through some mathematical reasoning, but the meaning of the answer can be understood without mathematics.

The answer to the question as to how unlikely it is that an experimentally observed excess (or deficiency) of hits in an experiment on psi would occur by chance is conveyed by the symbol 'P', which expresses the likelihood that a deviation equal to or greater than that observed would turn up by chance in a series of that length. It is well to be clear as to the exact meaning of this symbol 'P' since there is some confusion about it. Writers who should have known better have referred to it as the odds in favour of ESP or whatever other psi-capacity the experiments have been

* Gurney, E., 'Researches in Thought-transference', *Proc. S.P.R.*, ii, 1884, 239–64.
† Fisher, R. A., *Statistical Methods for Research Workers*, London, 1930.

176

designed to measure. This, however, as we have already seen, is a quantity that cannot be determined since it depends not only on the adequacy of the precautions taken to exclude other possibilities of success but also on the likelihood that there is such a capacity as ESP to which likelihood no definite value can be given. If a man were found lying dead in a wood with a round hole running from his chest to his back, we could not determine the probability that he was killed by a unicorn merely by examining the characteristics of the hole and considering the very low probability of the hole having been produced in any other way. We should also have to take into account the likelihood that there really are such animals as unicorns. If we know they do not exist, the probability of the man having been killed by a unicorn would be zero, however strong might be the evidence that he could not have been killed in any other way.

Other writers have referred to P as if it measured the 'odds against chance' and they may refer to P as the 'anti-chance probability'. It is not correctly described in this way either. If an experimental design excluded all possible causes from affecting the result, then any observed discrepancy, however large, must be a chance one. If the value of P is low, then we must say that, in this case, a very unlikely chance has come off.

Even more objectionable is the idea that we are measuring the probability that an observed discrepancy from expectation was 'caused by chance'. 'Chance' is not the name of a cause; it is a word we use for the absence of cause. If a gambler weights his dice so that six is most likely to fall uppermost, then if he gets three sixes we may say that this result was caused by the bias he introduced into his dice. But if he throws unbiased dice under conditions which exclude the possibility of any cause favouring sixes (even PK) and he throws three sixes, we should say that the three sixes turned up 'by chance', not that they were 'caused by chance' as if chance were a cause like bias which produced specific effects.

What the symbol P really means is the probability of the observed discrepancy from mean chance expectation occurring in a series in which there was no special cause operating to produce the observed discrepancy. If the difference between this meaning and that of a 'probability against chance' seems obscure, it may perhaps be clarified if we consider a simple case in life outside the laboratory where the same distinction may be made.

Let us suppose that a man is being tried on a charge of murder. The man denies his guilt and the judge reminds the jury that experience shows that if a man has committed murder, the probability of his saying that he is not guilty is 0·9, that is, nine out of ten guilty prisoners deny their guilt. When the judge says that the probability of his saying 'not guilty' if he were guilty is 0·9, this is plainly not the same thing as saying that the probability of the man's guilt is 0·9. The probability of his guilt remains unknown until other evidence is examined.

This imagined case would be more closely analogous to the problem of statistical significance of a parapsychological experiment, if we suppose that the accused man has been given a 'truth' drug which makes very small the likelihood that he would say 'not guilty' if he really was guilty. The judge might now be able to say that the chance is only 1 in 100 that the accused man would not be telling the truth when he pleaded 'not guilty'. Now P = 0·01 and the fact that the man said he was not guilty would be strong ground for believing that he was innocent. It would still not be the case that it meant that the odds were 100 to 1 against his guilt; examination of evidence about the crime might give these odds a very different value.

This distinction is by no means hair-splitting, it has serious consequences for the use of estimates of P in practical research. Any use of P that is based on the idea of it as the 'odds against chance' is likely to be erroneous, and gross mistakes in the estimate of significance of research results have been caused by this error.

In order correctly to estimate how unlikely it is that a particular result would be produced by chance, it is sometimes necessary to consider not only the particular result with which one is concerned but also the whole set of results from which it has been selected. Let us suppose, for example, that a subject made 100 ESP guesses and obtained an excess of 10 hits over m.c.e., the ordinary calculations would show that this was just significant (P = 0·02). If, however, the subject had been tested on ten occasions and this was the selected best of the results obtained on these ten occasions, it would no longer be significant. The likelihood of getting by chance alone an excess of ten hits over m.c.e. at least once in ten attempts would be ten times 0·02; P would therefore be 0·2 which is not small enough for significance. That the appearance of significance may disappear when one makes this correction for selection may be easily understood if one reflects that any level of deviation from expectation is likely to arise by chance if one tries often enough.

The general rule is that if an experimental result is the selected best of N experiments, the likelihood of its deviation having arisen by chance will be N times the value of P that would have been applied to this result if it had been an isolated observation.

Those who are interested in why this is the proper correction for the significance of the selected best of a number of results will find that this is an approximation although a very close one in most cases. The method is as follows. If the probability of the chance occurrence of a given deviation (or a greater one) on a single occasion is P, then the likelihood of its chance non-occurrence is $(1 - P)$. The chance that it will not occur in N repetitions of the experiment is, therefore, $(1 - P)^N$. From this it follows that the chance of its occurrence in N repetitions of the experiments is $[1 - (1 - P)^N]$. This quantity is found to be almost exactly equal to N.P unless either N or P is unusually large; if either of them is large, the exact formula can be used.

Applying this correction does not, of course, always lead to the disappearance of significance. A single good result which is the selected best of a number of others may still be significant after the correction for selection has been applied. The indication then is that the subject showed genuine ESP on one occasion although he may not have shown it on others. This also is a significant finding.

It is sometimes asked why, if it is necessary to make this correction for estimating the significance of the selected best of ten sessions with a single subject, should we not also take into account all the other experiments that have been done on other subjects by other experimenters. The answer to this question is that the necessity for the correction for selection depends on what the experiment is trying to find out. If we are trying to find out something about the ESP performance of a particular subject or group of subjects, and if only one of the experimental sessions appears significant, then the correction for selection must be made if the experimenter is to get the correct answer to the question with which he is concerned, but for the purpose of that correction he will be concerned only with the set of experiments made on that particular subject or group of subjects.

If the experimenter had been concerned with finding out how much this particular set of experiments contributed to the general evidence for ESP, then indeed it would have been necessary to consider also the number of unsuccessful experiments that have been performed by other people. But he knows the answer to this question without any calculation: the average ESP experiment contributes virtually nothing to the general evidence for ESP; that was not its aim. In the particular case of an experimental series (such as the Soal-Goldney series) in which the aim was to find out about the reality of the occurrence of ESP, it would make sense to ask how good this evidence would be if this were considered to be the selected best of all the ESP experiments in the world. The answer to this question was discussed in Chapter X.

There are other, somewhat less obvious, consequences of the fact that the significance of an experimental result depends on the size of the sample from which it has been selected. One of these is the fact that we can only rely on an estimate of significance as a measure of how unlikely is the chance occurrence of some characteristic of our results if we had decided to examine that particular characteristic before the experiment was done. If we apply the estimate to some characteristic that was only noticed after the experiment was done, we must consider that this characteristic was perhaps only examined because it was the most outstanding one of a number of possible characteristics that might have been examined. A selection has, in fact, taken place somewhat analogous to the selection of the best of a series of sessions, but it is one in which one can assign no definite number to the range of possible characteristics from which the selection has been made. Only if the experimenter has specified beforehand what he is looking for, can he regard the P value obtained by standard methods as a reliable indication of how likely it is that the observed result might have turned up by chance. Otherwise he must regard any outstanding feature of his results as only an indication of a possible problem to be investigated in future research.

This is now accepted as a standard principle in experimental work in psychical research; it was not always so well understood. Whately Carington, for example, made an examination of some card-guessing experiments which had been published by Usher and Burt in 1910.* He pointed out that, although the complete successes were not significantly above mean chance expectation, one could apply a method for scoring partial successes which showed a somewhat significant positive deviation for which he estimated the odds against its chance occurrence as about 190 to 1. But this was not the observation which the experimenters intended to make; that had been made and proved insignificant. The estimate of how likely it was that this new way of treating the data would, by chance, lead to an apparently significant result could only be known if we knew how many other ways of treating the data might have been thought up by an ingenious critic. We cannot rely on the figure of 1 chance in 190. The fact that this method of scoring seemed to give better results could properly be used as a suggestion for a further experiment which was to be scored by this new method. Whately Carington, however, went much further than this, and said that he found this experiment 'extremely convincing'. Other experimenters have wisely refrained from following Whately Carington along this dangerous path.

We may notice in contrast the correct procedure in this matter adopted by Dr Soal in the investigation preliminary to his study of Shackleton.† He had studied a large number of experimental subjects and found that none of them seemed to have any power of getting the card right. It was only when, at the suggestion of Whately Carington, he re-examined his results to see whether any of his subjects were guessing the card ahead or the card behind the one turned up that he discovered that two of his subjects (one of whom was Mr Shackleton) were so scoring. For these subjects, the departures from expectation satisfied the ordinary criteria of significance.

If Soal had concluded from this observation that he had proved that these two subjects had telepathic powers which were displaced from the target card to one of the neighbouring cards, he would have been guilty of the fallacy discussed above. Some of his critics do, in fact, incorrectly suggest that this is what Soal did. In reality, his procedure was the correct one of starting a new series of experiments with Shackleton as subject, in which the aim was to discover whether he would continue to show the

* Whately Carington, W., *Telepathy*, 1945.
† Soal, S. G., and Bateman, F., *Modern Experiments in Telepathy*, London, 1954.

characteristic of scoring on one of the five cards centred round the card that was turned up as target. This follow-up experiment confirmed the hypothesis that Shackleton was showing such displaced scoring and that he was predominantly hitting the card next ahead of the target card. This led to the further experiment performed by Soal and Mrs Goldney on which they based their conclusion that Shackleton was showing 'pre-cognitive telepathy'.

If, on the other hand, the experimental parapsychologist allowed himself to base conclusions on peculiarities of his data that were noticed only after the conclusion of his experiment, he would be guilty of what we may call the 'crumpled paper fallacy'. If I take a smooth piece of paper and crumple it in my hands, it will, when unfolded, show an intricate pattern of creases. I might look at this pattern of creases and innocently marvel that the odds against this particular pattern having been produced are billions to one. I might even be able to pick out something meaningful in the pattern such as an arabic letter. It would obviously only make sense to conclude that there was some specific cause making just that pattern of creases and no other, if I had specified beforehand the pattern I expected and if just that pattern was what was afterwards produced. Even if I thought I could see an arabic letter in the pattern of creases, I could draw no conclusion from that observation; all that could be done with it would be to crumple another piece of paper and see whether the same letter appeared again.

To conclude that there is some specific cause for a peculiarity in one's observations that was noticed only after the completion of the experiment is to be guilty of the crumpled-paper fallacy. Parapsychologists have to be especially aware of the dangers of this fallacy. Unless the experimenter's expectations have been specified beforehand, the ordinary procedure of calculating significance will give no reliable guidance as to whether any real cause has been at work to produce the observed result.

# The internal control of Psi experiments

In Chapter IX, we discussed the type of ESP experiment which is based on a comparison between the results of an experimental series of guesses made under conditions in which it is supposed that ESP may be to some extent determining the subject's responses and a 'control' series in which conditions have been so arranged that what is used as response material could not have been affected by ESP. It was there pointed out that 'controlled' experiments of this type are not of essentially different kind from those of the more familiar experimental design in which the number of hits is compared with mean chance expectation. The results of the latter kind of experiment can also be treated by a method in which a comparison is made between scores which may be the result of ESP and scores which presumably are not. We can, for example, compare the frequency of call of 'cross' when 'cross' is target with the frequency of such calls when cross is not target, and similarly for all the other targets. One is then using the guesses made on each symbol when that symbol is not the target as a control series for comparison with the guesses when that symbol is target.

The evidence for ESP is then the fact that the percipient guesses each symbol more frequently when it is target than when it is not. If there were no significant difference between the relative frequency of guessing a symbol when that symbol was target and when it was not, there would be no evidence for ESP or for whatever paranormal capacity was being tested. The evidence is thus of the same kind as that obtained in an experiment with a control series; we may express this parallelism by saying that ESP experiments of the ordinary kind are 'internally controlled'.

Counting the number of guesses of each symbol when that symbol is or is not the target has little practical advantage over the more ordinary method of counting hits and comparing them with mean chance expectation. It is still necessary to make an estimate of significance, and this estimate gives much the same value by both methods. Displaying the results in a form which shows the internal control is a somewhat laborious operation for the experimenter although, no doubt, less time-consuming than the use of an external control. What is needed for the purpose of this display is a record of the number of times each of the 25 possible combinations of guess and target has occurred in the course of the experiment, instead of the usual record of the total number of guesses and the number of hits. This means that the results of an experiment must be displayed in the form of a 5 × 5 matrix, which is obviously more trouble to the experimenter than the ordinary record. An example of such a matrix recording is to be found in Table 3 which shows the results of one of the

*Table 3   Results of an ESP test shown by number of calls of each symbol with different targets*

| Calls | Targets | | | | | Total calls |
|---|---|---|---|---|---|---|
| | Circle | Square | Waves | Cross | Star | |
| Circle | 118 (+42·4) | 67 (−8·6) | 63 (−12·6) | 70 (−5·6) | 60 (−15·6) | 378 |
| Square | 62 (−7·8) | 101 (+31·2) | 75 (+5·2) | 54 (−15·8) | 57 (−12·8) | 349 |
| Waves | 57 (−16·2) | 74 (+0·8) | 109 (+35·8) | 61 (−12·2) | 65 (−8·2) | 366 |
| Cross | 73 (−8·4) | 62 (−19·4) | 60 (−21·4) | 127 (+45·6) | 85 (+3·6) | 407 |
| Star | 60 (−10) | 66 (−4) | 63 (−7) | 58 (−12) | 103 (+33) | 350 |
| Totals | 370 | 370 | 370 | 370 | 370 | 1,850 |

early tests of ESP reported in Appendix 5 of *Extra-sensory Perception after Sixty Years.** Each of the entries in this table shows the number of guesses of the symbol named at the end of the row when the symbol named at the top of the column was target. Thus the first row shows that the subject guessed 'circle' 118 times when circle was the target, 67 times when a square was the target, and so on. These were results obtained from 74 runs (1,850 guesses). Their general tendency may be best seen by comparing the actual number of guesses in each cell with the number we should expect on the assumption that the percipient was just as likely to guess 'circle' when the target was any other symbol as when it was circle, that is, on the assumption that there was no ESP or other cause tending to make guesses correspond with targets. In that case one would expect the 378 guesses of target to be spread approximately equally over the five targets, so that about 75·6 guesses were made on each. The numbers in parentheses in the table show the observed excess or deficiency in each cell as compared with

* By J. C. Pratt, J. B. Rhine, et al., New York, 1940.

this chance expectation. It will be seen that all the numbers in cells show-ing guesses on a symbol when that symbol was target show a large excess over the number to be expected if the nature of the target did not in-fluence the guess. On the other hand, the number of guesses of a symbol when that symbol was not target show a deficiency or a very small excess.

The value of a table like this is that it shows clearly that the evidence for ESP derived from such an experiment is not merely a matter of right guesses exceeding the number expected by chance, but is the result of a systematic tendency of guesses of any symbol to be more likely if that symbol is target than if it is not. The result is summarised in Table 4 which shows the total number of guesses of all symbols when that symbol was target and when it was not target, compared with the number expected of such guesses on the assumption that the nature of the target had no in-fluence on the guess. In calculating the latter quantity, it must of course be remembered that in a pack with five targets in equal numbers, there will be four times as many guesses made when any particular symbol is not target as when it is target.

*Table 4    Guesses on target symbol and on other symbols in data of Table 3*

| Guesses | On target | Off target |
| --- | --- | --- |
| Observed | 558 | 1,292 |
| Chance expectation | 370 | 1,480 |
| Deviation from expectation | +188 | −188 |

It will be seen from Table 4 that the subject of this experiment was influenced in his guessing by the target to an extent of about 50 per cent. If this set of results were evaluated in the ordinary way we should say that the number of hits was 558 and the number expected by chance would be one-fifth of the total number of guesses, i.e. ($\frac{1}{5} \times$ 1,850) which is 370, so the excess over mean chance expectation is 188. This is the same result as that already obtained by a more indirect method. The fact that it involves a lot of extra trouble and leads to the same end result perhaps explains why experimentalists have rarely put their results in the form of a 5 × 5 matrix.

Yet, although it does not lead to an essentially different end result, there are certain advantages in the display of experimental results in matrix form which it is hoped will lead to this method of showing results being more widely used by parapsychologists. It has two advantages. First, it shows what is involved in a positive result in a form more clear to those not mathematically minded than does a comparison between an observed total score and mean chance expectation. This, I suggest, is a reason for using this method of display for results of experiments that are intended as evidence for the reality of ESP. They have been very rarely displayed in this way; an exception is the experiment of Professor Lucien Warner which is described in Chapter X.

Secondly, this method of display may be used for experiments which serve the more ordinary function of finding out about the nature of ESP. It has the advantage over a mere record of the number of guesses and the number of hits that it is much more informative. It may contain information that the experimenter is not, at the time of experimenting, interested in. It should, however, be an aim of publication to present results in as informative a manner as possible since future workers may want to extract from our results something not foreseen by us.

A future investigator might, for example, be interested in such a question as whether hits were distributed equally over all targets or whether a particular percipient showed a preference for a particular target. In Table 3 it appears that the percipient succeeds in getting hits on all targets. There is some indication that he does better with circle and cross as targets, but a new experiment would be necessary to confirm whether this was a real preference or merely an accidental characteristic of the figures. Also, examination of this table does not indicate any strong tendency to guess systematically a particular wrong symbol for some other target symbol. There does seem to be some slight tendency for mutual substitution of 'square' and 'waves' but this may well be merely an accidental characteristic of the figures. No conclusion could be drawn from it though it may be regarded as suggestive for a possible future experimental enquiry.

The experimentalist naturally hopes that his results will be as widely understood as possible. He should also want them to be as informative as possible for other investigators. Since both these aims would seem to be best achieved by the presentation of experimental results in matrix form, it is to be hoped that this will be increasingly done in spite of the extra trouble it gives experimenters and the extra space taken up in journal reports.

# Variance as indicator of Psi

There is a good deal of evidence that ESP may act both in the direction of increasing scores above mean chance expectation and in the direction of 'psi-missing', depressing scores below mean chance expectation. If both negative and positive scoring occurred within the same set of results, the total result might not be significantly different from what would be expected by chance but the ESP process would have left its traces in the fact that the scores of runs might differ from each other more than would be expected by chance. The effect of ESP would then be shown, not by an increased (or decreased) total score but by an increased tendency for run scores to differ from one another. To test whether this is the case we need a measure of the extent to which run scores differ from one another, and a theory of how much they would be expected to differ from one another if the degree of their difference were determined by chance alone.

The commonly accepted measure of the degree to which a set of measurements differ amongst themselves is the 'variance' which is measured as the sum of the squares of the differences between each measurement and the mean of all the measurements, divided by one less than their total number. In mathematical symbolism, this may be expressed as $\Sigma(\text{x} - \text{M})^2/(\text{N} - 1)$, where x stands for each run score, M for their mean, and N for the total number of runs.

Those unfamiliar with mathematical symbolism may find it easier to understand a simple example. In an experiment showing no influence of psi either on the run average or on the run variance, the following scores were obtained in 10 successive runs: 4, 2, 7, 5, 4, 6, 9, 3, 6, 7. The average of these scores is 5·3 which differs from the mean chance expectation of 5 only by an amount such as (for that length of experiment) might be expected to occur by chance. The sum of squares of deviations from this mean is $1·3^2 + 3·3^2 + \ldots$ etc., which comes to a total of 40·1. This, divided by 9, gives 4·45 as the estimate of the variance.

One must also have a way of estimating what the variance would be expected to be if only chance were producing the differences between run scores. This estimate is made by the formula n.p.q. where n is the number of guesses in each run and p and q are the relative frequencies of hits and misses. In a chance-determined run with the standard ESP pack, n is 25 while p and q are $\frac{1}{5}$ and $\frac{4}{5}$ respectively, so the expected variance, if it were the case that chance alone is operative, would be $25.(\frac{1}{5}).(\frac{4}{5})$ which gives a value of 4·0.

In view of the smallness of the number of runs in the example given above the discrepancy between the value found and that expected by chance is not significant. The observed variance gives no more reason for supposing that any cause is at work making the scores differ amongst themselves, than does the observed mean of 5·3 give us for supposing that psi or any other cause is making the subjects tend to guess correctly. It would, therefore, be a foolish error to suppose that the differences between the run scores indicated that the experimental subject was sometimes succeeding in the ESP task and sometimes psi-missing; there is no reason for postulating any cause beyond chance for either the average score or for the differences between scores.

The case might, however, be different. Suppose that the subject was succeeding in the psi-task on some of his runs and was psi-missing on some of his runs, his mean might not differ significantly from mean chance expectation but his run scores would tend to differ amongst themselves more than would a chance series of scores. This increased tendency to difference would be reflected in an increased value of the run variance which could become significantly greater than its chance expected value of 4·0.

The comparison of the observed variance with its theoretically expected value gives the experimental parapsychologist an additional tool for enquiry but it is not one that has been widely applied for the detection of irregularly acting ESP. When it has been established that one set of subjects or of scores differs from mean chance expectation in a positive direction while another set differs from mean chance expectation in a negative direction, no new information is given by demonstrating that the variance of the combined scores of the two sets together is greater than its chance expected value. It might be a useful tool for the detection of the presence of combined positive and negative psi action in cases where there was no objective criterion for distinguishing between the runs which were under the two conditions; this form of problem does not, however, seem to have turned up in research practice.

The method of comparison between observed and chance expected values of the variance can be applied to other units than the run if the appropriate change is made in the value of n for the calculation of the theoretical value of the variance. If, for example, one wishes to study the variance of 5-guess units, the chance expected value of the variance will be $5.(\frac{1}{5}).(\frac{4}{5})$ which is 0·08. If the observed variance differs significantly from this, although the distribution of hits to misses has about the expected value of 1 : 4, one must look for some cause making the scores less (or more) alike than they would be expected to be without such a cause.

It must not be forgotten that the formula for the theoretical variance contains the quantity pq so the chance expected variance will depend on the distribution of hits. If the subject gets more than the expected number of five hits per run, the chance expected run variance will no longer be 4·0 but an amount greater than this until it reaches a maximum value of 6·25 when the subject is getting half his guesses right, slowly declining afterwards to zero when the subject is guessing right every time. In the same way if the subject is consistently missing so that he gets a smaller number right than the mean chance expectation of 5, the chance expected variance will be less than 4·0 and it will finally become zero when the subject is psi-missing with 100 per cent efficiency and getting none of his guesses right.

It follows from this that we cannot properly conclude that the run variance is greater or less than one would expect by chance merely because it is significantly greater or less than 4·0. To infer whether or not a cause is present, making run scores more (or less) different than they would be by chance, it is necessary to know at what rate the subject is scoring. Unfortunately this information is not always given in reports on the variance of ESP scores, so one is not certain whether an observed deviation from the chance expected value of 4·0 is an independent tendency of the variance to be unexpectedly large or small, or whether it is merely a secondary consequence of the subject showing ESP hitting or missing. It is only in the former case that the size of the variance is of research interest.

As was pointed out in Chapter XIII, however, there is considerable evidence that, in many cases, there is a significantly low value of the observed variance in ESP experiments which cannot be explained as merely a result of low scoring and seems to indicate the presence of a cause making scores resemble each other more closely than would be expected by chance alone. It seems that this is a genuine part of the pattern of psi-response, however odd it may seem.

# The problem of discrimination between precognition and PK

In the earliest experiments on psycho-kinesis, the experimental subjects chose which was to be the target face. This was open to an objection already discussed: that it led to a too frequent choice of fives and sixes which were also the faces favoured by dice bias. Another objection to this procedure is that, if the possibility of precognition is admitted, it seems possible that the subjects might not be influencing the fall of the dice but predicting which way the dice are going to fall next. In other words, the experiment fails to discriminate between PK and precognition.

The first of these difficulties is very easily got over by taking the choice of target away from the subject and introducing some method of selecting targets which ensures that each die face is target an equal number of times. The second difficulty cannot be so easily dealt with; even if the experimenter uses some random method to determine what are the targets, a sufficiently ingenious objector to the idea of PK might suggest that he chose that particular random method because he foresaw that it would lead to a target choice that would make the targets coincide with the dice falls which he also foresaw. In principle, this explanation of a PK result is possible, although in some experimental designs it may seem an improbable one. It will naturally be adopted by one who finds the movement of objects without contact an idea impossible to accept but who does not find it impossible to believe in a very considerable power of foreseeing the future.

There are, however, some who find that the idea of foreseeing the future is impossible of acceptance since it supposes the apparent absurdity of an event in the present being causally influenced by an event which has not yet taken place. These will explore the possibility that precognitive results may really be due to PK, that, let us say, the mechanical shuffling of a pack of cards that have been precognitively guessed may have produced an order corresponding to the order guessed, not by the percipient foreseeing the future order of the pack, but by the experimenter influencing the machine by PK to make it shuffle the cards into the already guessed order. Even if the pack of cards is also cut at a randomly determined point, one could suppose that the experimenter influenced by PK whatever mechanism he used to get the point of cut and so made it produce a cut at a point favourable to a high score.

The same problem of the discrimination between PK and precognition occurs in connection with spontaneous cases. If we find that the rain-producing spells of a medicine man are followed by rain, we may refuse to believe that his spells had any PK efficacy and suppose that he foresaw (by paranormal or normal means) that rain was coming before he started his magic. Similarly if we had a well-attested case of a witch putting a curse on a cow which subsequently ceased to give milk, we might explain it by supposing that she foresaw that the cow was about to go dry, so she was merely predicting and not exercising PK.

More commonly the opposite view has been put forward that cases of apparent prediction are really due to PK. That precognition is a manifest impossibility is the conviction of Dr Tanagras of the Athens Society for Psychical Research who would explain all ostensibly precognitive occurrences as results of paranormal influence of human minds on the course of events.* It is widely believed in Greece and other parts of Southern Europe that there is a power of human beings to influence events in the outside world by paranormal means (called by Tanagras, not PK, but 'psychoboulia'). This power is supposed to occur spontaneously and unconsciously in the presence of some individuals, causing injury to other people and also to animals and plants. Those to whom this capacity is attributed are said to have the 'evil eye'.

Acceptance of the possibility of psychoboulia and rejection of the possibility of precognition leads Dr Tanagras to explain cases of apparent precognition (whether of accidents or of earthquakes) as due either to psychoboulia (PK) by the person experiencing the ostensible precognition, or to his being influenced telepathically by some other person whose PK has caused the foreseen event. Such explanations may be somewhat difficult to accept. He records, for example, the case of a child living near Athens who saw a figure in white who threatened him with death by a motor-car. He went to live with his grandmother and remained indoors. One day, however, he went out to play in the road. A car was approaching and the child went on to the path and flattened himself against the wall, but the car mounted the path and the child was crushed against the wall. Tanagras explains this as unconscious psychoboulic action by the child on the brain of the driver of the car. Although some such explanation would be necessary if we admit the paranormality of the incident and the impossibility of precognition, it would be generally agreed that the precognitive explanation is easier to accept.

It is perhaps impossible to make an altogether convincing distinction between precognitive and psycho-kinetic spontaneous events, although one may say of a particular event that one explanation seems much more likely than the other. Can we make a more certain discrimination experimentally? As has already been pointed out, the same problem does arise in experiments on PK and precognition. There are, however, two directions

* Tanagras, A., *Le Destin et la Chance*, Athens.

in which experimental methods may be used in an attempt to solve the problem.

The first of these is a consideration of how much success each alternative could account for. If an apparent precognitive success in a card-guessing experiment were really due to the subject's (or experimenter's) PK action on the process of shuffling and cutting the cards, there would seem to be no limit on the amount of success that could be so obtained; there is no reason why PK should not produce perfect correspondence between the subject's prediction and subsequent card order. This will be exactly true if the experimenter uses a closed pack and the subject's guesses are equally distributed over the five targets; it is approximately true in any case unless the subject's guesses are very unequally distributed over the targets. We can, at any rate, say with confidence that if PK were operating in a precognitive experiment, it could in principle produce a rate of success greater than has ever been observed in such experiments.

This would not necessarily be the case in a PK experiment in which the successful result had been obtained by precognition of the way in which the dice were going to fall. Except in the case that only a single die is thrown at a time, the most perfect precognition could not give a score higher than the limit set by the degree of inequality in throws that will result from chance.

Let us suppose for example that a PK experiment is performed in which six dice are used in each throw. It will sometimes happen by chance alone that all dice fall with different faces uppermost. However perfect the precognition of the subject, his score must then necessarily be 1 which is the mean chance expectation. This event of all faces being different is, however, a very unlikely one. The most likely chance event will be that there will be one or more pairs of dice showing the same face; in that case precognition, if it is working at full efficiency, will give him a score of 2 right out of the six. Less commonly there will be three or more dice showing the same face, and precognition could give him a score of 3 or more. The average score given by precognition would be somewhere about 2½ which corresponds to a scoring rate of about 25 per cent over m.c.e. With a larger number of dice than six, the percentage scoring rate in a PK experiment that could be accounted for by precognition would be smaller. An absolute discrimination between PK and precognition could obviously be made if, in a PK experiment, the rate of score was higher than the limit that could be attained by perfect precognition. I do not know whether this condition has ever been fulfilled by a successful PK experiment.

Another direction which can be explored in the search for a means of discrimination between PK and precognition is that of modifying the design of experiments in such a way as to make one method of explanation much more difficult than the other even if we do not succeed in reaching the ideal of making one of the two ways of explanation impossible.

It was obviously easy to explain apparent PK success as due to pre-cognition in the first experiments in which subjects made a free choice of targets. It became more difficult when targets were selected by a random method (e.g. by the experimenter shuffling six cards with numbers from 1 to 6). Still a critic might object that it was possible that the experimenter foresaw the falls and knew by ESP the order of the shuffled cards and stopped shuffling when they were in such an order that they would give good correspondence with the falls already foreseen. This is a possible explana-tion but an improbable one since it would seem to demand an accuracy of precognition and of ESP on the part of the experimenter greater than any experimental observation would lead us to expect. The plausibility of the precognitive explanation is further reduced if, after shuffling, the pack is cut at a randomly determined point. Even if the pack were cut in a way which seems to be independent of human activity, as was done in pre-cognition experiments in the Duke Laboratory when the point of cut was determined by the difference between maximum and minimum tempera-tures reported in the Durham daily paper, it remains true that there was an act of choice by the experimenter when he chose this as his method of determining the point of cut. Still the critic might suggest that the experi-menter chose this way of cutting the cards because he foresaw that this would give good correspondence with the foreseen dice falls. Yet obviously the PK explanation of success in this experiment would be very much the more probable one since the alternative precognition explanation would require that precognition was working with an efficiency such as has never been observed in an experiment designed to measure precognition.

In the same way, we can complicate the design of a precognition experiment in such a way that explanation in terms of PK becomes very difficult because it would require an efficiency of PK greater than any that is justified by the findings of PK experiments. If we are, at present, unable to design an experiment in either PK or precognition which can only be explained in terms of one of these principles, we can use a design of experiment which will make success easily explainable by one of these principles and difficult of explanation by the other. Then if we get success, we can, with some slight doubt, regard that success as evidence of the particular psi-activity by which it is most easily explained. There is not, of course, any corresponding doubt about the fact that it must be one or other of these two modes of psi.

The question at issue is whether we seem to foresee the future because we produce it, or only seem to act on the outside world because we foresee its events, and whether these two paranormal activities of foreseeing and acting are two distinguishable modes of psi-activity. There seems to be no reason for supposing that it is, in principle, impossible to design an experi-ment which will make this discrimination, even if it is doubtful whether we have yet achieved such a design. If it were indeed impossible in principle to discriminate between them we should have to conclude that precognition and psycho-kinesis were identical although they seem to be different in any verbal account we can give of them. There does not seem to be good reason for supposing that this is the case.

# Index